CW01456722

THE NEW MIDDLE AGES

BONNIE WHEELER, *Series Editor*

The New Middle Ages presents transdisciplinary studies of medieval cultures. It includes both scholarly monographs and essay collections.

PUBLISHED BY PALGRAVE:

Women in the Medieval Islamic World:
Power, Patronage, and Piety
  edited by Gavin R. G. Hambly

The Ethics of Nature in the Middle Ages:
On Boccaccio's Poetaphysics
  by Gregory B. Stone

Presence and Presentation:
Women in the Chinese Literati Tradition
  by Sherry J. Mou

The Lost Love Letters of Heloise and Abelard:
Perceptions of Dialogue in Twelfth-Century
France
  by Constant J. Mews

Understanding Scholastic Thought with Foucault
  by Philipp W. Rosemann

For Her Good Estate:
The Life of Elizabeth de Burgh
  by Frances A. Underhill

Constructions of Widowhood and Virginity in
the Middle Ages
  edited by Cindy L. Carlson and
  Angela Jane Weisl

Motherhood and Mothering in
Anglo-Saxon England
  by Mary Dockray-Miller

Listening to Heloise:
The Voice of a Twelfth-Century Woman
  edited by Bonnie Wheeler

The Postcolonial Middle Ages
  edited by Jeffrey Jerome Cohen

Chaucer's Pardoner and Gender Theory
  by Robert S. Sturges

Crossing the Bridge: Comparative Essays
on Medieval European and Heian Japanese
Women Writers
  edited by Barbara Stevenson and
  Cynthia Ho

Engaging Words: The Culture of Reading
in the Later Middle Ages
  by Laurel Amtower

Robes and Honor: The Medieval World of
Investiture
  edited by Stewart Gordon

Representing Rape in Medieval and Early
Modern Literature
  edited by Elizabeth Robertson and
  Christine M. Rose

Same Sex Love and Desire Among Women
in the Middle Ages
  edited by Francesca Canadé Sautman and
  Pamela Sheingorn

Listen Daughter: The Speculum virginum and
the Formation of Religious Women in the
Middle Ages
  edited by Constant J. Mews

Science, the Singular, and the Question of
Theology
  by Richard A. Lee, Jr.

Gender in Debate from the Early Middle Ages
to the Renaissance
  edited by Thelma S. Fenster and
  Clare A. Lees

Malory's Morte Darthur:
Remaking Arthurian Tradition
  by Catherine Batt

The Vernacular Spirit: Essays on Medieval Religious Literature
edited by Renate Blumenfeld-Kosinski, Duncan Robertson, and Nancy Warren

Popular Piety and Art in the Late Middle Ages: Image Worship and Idolatry in England 1350–1500
by Kathleen Kamerick

Absent Narratives, Manuscript Textuality, and Literary Structure in Late Medieval England
by Elizabeth Scala

Creating Community with Food and Drink in Merovingian Gaul
by Bonnie Effros

Encountering Medieval Textiles and Dress
edited by Désirée G. Koslin and Janet Snyder

Eleanor of Aquitaine: Lord and Lady
edited by Bonnie Wheeler and John Carmi Parsons

Isabel La Católica, Queen of Castile
edited by David A. Boruchoff

HOMOEROTICISM AND CHIVALRY

DISCOURSES OF MALE SAME-SEX DESIRE IN THE FOURTEENTH CENTURY

Richard E. Zeikowitz

palgrave
macmillan

HOMOEROTICISM AND CHIVALRY
© Richard E. Zeikowitz, 2003.

All rights reserved. No part of this book may be used or reproduced in any manner whatsoever without written permission except in the case of brief quotations embodied in critical articles or reviews.

First published 2003 by
PALGRAVE MACMILLAN™
175 Fifth Avenue, New York, N.Y. 10010 and
Houndmills, Basingstoke, Hampshire, England RG21 6XS.
Companies and representatives throughout the world.

PALGRAVE MACMILLAN is the global academic imprint of the Palgrave Macmillan division of St. Martin's Press, LLC and of Palgrave Macmillan Ltd. Macmillan® is a registered trademark in the United States, United Kingdom and other countries. Palgrave is a registered trademark in the European Union and other countries.

ISBN 1-4039-6042-9 hardback

Cataloging-in-Publication data can be found at the Library of Congress.

A catalogue record for this book is available from the British Library.

Design by Newgen Imaging Systems (P) Ltd., Chennai, India.

First edition: May, 2003
10 9 8 7 6 5 4 3 2 1

Printed in the United States of America.

For my parents

ACKNOWLEDGMENTS

Many people have assisted me—both directly and indirectly—in the planning, research, and writing of this book. I have benefited enormously from the expertise of medievalists with whom I studied at the Graduate Center of the City University of New York and would like to thank Michael Sargent, Scott Westrem, and Gordon Whatley. I could not have performed the necessary historical research in a timely manner without the use of the invaluable resources of the New York Public Library and the possibility of working in the Wertheim Study. I thank the special collections department for extending this privilege to me.

This project could never have been undertaken without the trailblazing and ongoing work in queer medieval studies by Glenn Burger, Carolyn Dinshaw, Steven F. Kruger, and Karma Lochrie. I have been and continue to be inspired by their sound, innovative approaches to medieval texts. I am grateful to the anonymous reader for Palgrave whose attentive comments guided me in preparing what I believe is a more coherent and effective book. I thank Bonnie Wheeler as well as the production staff at Palgrave, Roee Raz, Ian Steinberg, and Mukesh V. S. I am indebted to the University of South Alabama, and, in particular, Sue Walker, chair of the English Department, for institutional support in the form of course reductions. Also, I could not have completed this project without the efficient services of the Interlibrary Loan department of the University Library. Finally, I would like to express my thanks to Steven Kruger, who has been so generous with his time and expertise. His attentive reading of drafts and his well-articulated feedback helped me enormously during various stages of this project.

CONTENTS

SERIES EDITOR'S FOREWORD

The New Middle Ages contributes to lively transdisciplinary conversations in medieval cultural studies through its scholarly monographs and essay collections. This series provides focused research in a contemporary idiom about specific but diverse practices, expressions, and ideologies in the Middle Ages. Richard E. Zeikowitz's *Homoeroticism and Chivalry: Discourses of Male Same-Sex Desire in the Fourteenth Century*, the thirty-fifth book in the series, is a provocative study of the literature, politics, and history of same-sex desire embedded in homosocial and heterosexual discourses. Did medieval persons and readers read undertows of same-sex desire in physically warm moments between friends, or is this interpretation a modern perversion of noble chivalric behavior? In admirably clear prose, Zeikowitz invites us to explore with him the many valences of affection and eroticism in the later Middle Ages. He keeps the cultural contexts and politics of these bodily (not necessarily sodomistical or genital) matters before us. His trajectory is clear: he intends to destabilize traditional readings that treat chivalric texts as if they (and the cultures that produced them) are centered on heteronormativity. Using a wide range of canonical texts, Zeikowitz analyzes both the corporeal and imaginative inflections of chivalric texts. At the same time, he never neglects the political tussle of the noble and knightly for whom expressions of same-sex desire were often ways of asserting or undermining power. The fear of seduction is matched by desire for intimacy. As Zeikowitz shows in his strong reading, this very visible tension sings keenly through the centuries.

Bonnie Wheeler
Southern Methodist University

CHAPTER 1

ARTICULATING PREMODERN MALE
HOMOEROTICISM

Three chivalric texts from the fourteenth century describe intimate interactions between knights. In his *Book of Chivalry*, Geoffroi de Charny describes the ritual bathing and dressing of novice knights who are about to be knighted. After the knights bathe and cleanse themselves of sins and lie down on a bed (presumably naked), "Puis doivent venir les chevaliers au lit pour vestir yceulz. . . . Puis les doivent vestir li chevalier de cotes vermeilles. . . . Et puis leur apportent les chevaliers chauces noires et les enchaucent" [Then the knights should come to the beds to dress those to be knighted. . . . Then the knights should robe them in red tunics. . . . Then the knights bring black hose and put them on those to be knighted].[1] In Geoffrey Chaucer's *Troilus and Criseyde*, Troilus, who is grateful to Pandarus for his help in wooing Criseyde, "with al th'affeccioun / Of frendes love that herte may devyse, / To Pandarus on knowes fil adown."[2] On the third night of the exchange of winnings in *Sir Gawain and the Green Knight*, Gawain "acoles. . .the knyght [Bertilak] and kysses hym thryes, / As saverly and sadly as he hem sette couthe."[3] In none of these three scenes does the narrator qualify or explain the intimate interaction between knights that he is describing. Apparently fourteenth-century readers would know how to read these scenes. But, do we? Because the narrators do not appear to be uncomfortable describing male–male intimacy, twenty-first-century readers who assume that late medieval chivalric society is heteronormative may conclude that these encounters are not erotically charged. One knight dressing the naked body of a novice knight would not look closely. Any kisses or affectionate exchanges between knights would be void of eroticism. They are just friends. While we cannot know for sure how fourteenth-century readers might have responded to these scenes, we can attempt to uncover late medieval cultural codes regarding homosocial intimacy. In doing so we might find that gazes, kisses, and affectionate words exchanged between knights had an erotic valence—and there was nothing "queer" about it.

In order to uncover expressions of same-sex desire in diverse texts of the Middle Ages, some medievalists have endeavored to "queer" these texts. "Queering" can be defined as attempts to uncover "rhetorical strategies that exclude same-sex relations, acts, and desires so that the world appears to be ordered along heterosexual lines."[4] Glenn Burger points out that queer theory is useful to "explore the structuration and instantiation of sexuality (and homophobia/anti-homophobia) rather than attempt to discover some prior and stable 'self' that will 'explain' sexual activity."[5] He goes on to explain that in "[e]mphasizing the performance of sexualities and identities," this theoretical approach "attempts to map a more dynamic, less assured account of the body in motion within prevailing discourses of power."[6] Glenn Burger and Steven Kruger describe a "[q]ueer study of the Middle Ages" as one which "promises the recovery of cultural meanings that are lost, obscured, or distorted in work that either ignores questions of sexuality or attends only to hegemonic or heteronormative understandings of it."[7] Karma Lochrie notes that queering aims "to unsettle the heterosexual paradigms of scholarship," which includes "produc[ing] . . . readings of medieval texts that trouble our assumptions about medieval culture and textual practices."[8] A queer approach can thus draw attention to normative expressions of same-sex desire in the Middle Ages and how heterosexuality is not necessarily a dominant impulse in particular sociocultural environments.

This book questions heteronormative assumptions regarding late medieval chivalric culture by offering an alternative paradigm. My project differs from some recent queer studies in that I am not seeking to articulate medieval "queer" desire—desire that was marginalized or absent from textual artifacts because it was "queer" at the time; rather, I am focusing on late medieval normative homoerotic desire, which is today considered "queer."[9] I queer fourteenth-century chivalric texts by delineating various expressions of male same-sex desire and possible homoerotic interactions, some only occurring in a reader's imagination. I explore erotically charged spectatorial acts between a novice knight and a model knight whom he desires to emulate, and emotionally charged chivalric bonds—same-sex unions that parallel modern understandings of heterosexual marriage. I examine mutually stimulating—or competing—forces of homosocial and heterosexual desire, demonstrating how in some late medieval chivalric romances, the modern hetero/homo binary is not clearly defined. And I illustrate how normative male same-sex desire in certain circumstances is tainted with sodomitical associations. Throughout this book, I use the term "heterosexual" (adj.) to describe relations, sexual or emotional, between persons of different genders, without implying that such persons are "heterosexuals" in the modern sense. I do not, however, employ the term "homosexual," but rather use "homosocial," "same-sex," "male–male," and, where appropriate, "sodomitical" for describing intimate relations (not necessarily sexual ones) between men. Like Burger, I understand a queer approach to be one that studies how bodies interact—literally, imaginatively, discursively—"within prevailing discourses of power," and I recognize both positive and negative discourses of male same-sex desire and the sociopolitical forces motivating those discourses.

Scholars working in the medieval and early modern periods have grappled with articulating male same-sex relations. Bruce Smith rightly points out: "To see the pattern [of homosexuality before the nineteenth century] we have to know, first of all, what to look for. To decipher the message we have to know the code."[10] Roberto González-Casanovas offers three distinct terms for studying medieval same-sex relations: "*Homosociality* refers to the preference in professional and recreational relations for members of the same-sex. . . . *Homophilia*. . .signifies a predilection for same-sex friendships based on close intimacy, which can extend over the full range of emotional attractions and sentimental expressions that lie outside genital interaction. . . . *Homoeroticism* develops homophilia further by stressing 'romantic love' within the same sex, which can include passionate expressions and courtship rituals that lead to physical intimacy with or without genital behavior."[11] While González-Casanovas nicely delineates varieties of same-sex relations that conform to neither "sodomy" nor "homosexual desire," are his categories mutually exclusive? Is homosociality necessarily void of emotional attractions characteristic of "homophilia" or of the physical intimacy (genital or nongenital) included under the heading "homoeroticism"? Recognizing the multiple forms same-sex behavior can take in chivalric contexts is an important step in identifying culturally specific codes of desire. But this should be only the first step in a process that does not end once a particular same-sex relation is fitted to its appropriate category; for further inquiry might reveal that a male–male bond blends elements of "homosociality," "homophilia," and/or "homoeroticism." The conclusion might thus not be easily labeled.

A project that aims to articulate premodern same-sex desire needs to uncover what Jonathan Goldberg describes as "sites of sexual possibilities, the syntax of desires not readily named."[12] My only qualification is that one need not limit the search to *sexual* possibilities. Recent scholarship often focuses on discourses of sexual relations rather than on expressions of subtler forms of same-sex desire—ones that do not suggest genital sex takes place. Bruce Holsinger points out that "[o]ur particular interest in sexual practices should not keep us from examining the wide variety of ways in which human bodies came together erotically when the goal or referent of such contact was not necessarily genital (or even orificial)."[13] In fact, the erotic interaction may take place within an individual's mind. Holsinger explores both the male reader and Dante—pilgrim and poet—as subjects of homoerotic desire in the *Divine Comedy*. In his discussion of the poet's identification with Ganymede in *Purgatorio* 9, he suggests how the reader becomes a participant in this homoerotic encounter: "Dante's Ganymedian *raptus*, though certainly a transumptive invitation to the reader, also invites us to consider the *unconsciousness* of reading it embeds, the collective memories and personal histories it cathects and through which it interpellates the reading subject."[14] In drawing attention to a homoerotics of reading—occurring consciously and unconsciously—Holsinger describes a type of interaction that has not received much attention in studies of male same-sex relations in chivalric contexts.[15] Although Holsinger does not focus on the mental process putatively taking place in the mind of the reader, his observation is a springboard for exploring how chivalric texts invite a knight/reader to produce homoerotically inflected fantasy images of a model knight.

Allen Frantzen notes that "[o]ne of the goals of queer theory is to demonstrate that same-sex relations are not incidental to the heterosexual world order."[16] In describing the inextricable link between the two, he offers the trope of a shadow cast on a field whereby the former represents same-sex relations and the latter the heterosexual system. He maintains that "same-sex relations are as closely attached to heterosexual relations as shadows are to their objects, and indeed that same-sex relations are indispensable to culture."[17] I interpret Frantzen's "shadow" to be not a subservient dependent of the dominant heterosexual system/"field" but rather a formidable presence that looms over the field. In fact, one may view the field and the shadow as competing forces. Frantzen's formulation, as I have defined it, is helpful in articulating the dynamic interdependency that exists between heterosexual and homosocial relations in some late medieval chivalric romances. For instance, in *Sir Gawain* and *Troilus and Criseyde*, the same-sex "shadow" overtakes the heterosexual "field." I do not mean to suggest that same-sex relations are presented here as menacing or threatening to heterosexual relations; instead, by privileging the homosocial bond, these texts, in effect, reduce the prominent visibility of the heterosexual relation.

A queer approach to premodern texts often involves identifying sites of potential homoerotic desire. Referring to the triangular relation among Gawain, the lady, and Bertilak in *Sir Gawain*, Carolyn Dinshaw argues that "the poem both produces the possibility of homosexual relations *and* renders them unintelligible. The narrative, that is, produces the possibility of homosexual relations only to—in order to—preclude it, in order to establish heterosexuality as not just the only sexual legitimacy but a principle of intelligibility itself."[18] She points out, however, that despite its heteronormative impulse, the poem depicts "two men kissing feelingly, solemnly, seriously."[19] Sheila Fisher takes a similar position, observing that after raising the possibility of homosexuality, the poem "swerves in order to forefront not the homosexual, but rather the homosocial."[20] Like Dinshaw, she views the potential homosexual relation between Gawain and Bertilak as an indication of the "intensity" of the chivalric bond. While not disagreeing with the above readings, David Boyd also recognizes the text's homophobic agenda: "by setting up a potentially queer situation and then rejecting it, *Sir Gawain* ultimately frees up both heterosexual activity and homosocial relations from perversity by relegating sodomy and homosexual desire to the realm of a transgressive Other."[21] All three interpretations illustrate a new, "queer" direction in medieval scholarship—one that articulates possibilities of desire suggested but not explicitly treated in a text. Yet a recognition of potential same-sex desire—whether realized or not—leads to many important questions that have not yet been thoroughly explored: Could a text's homophobia be a reaction to the *real* possibility of same-sex desire among knights? And might this desire be not transgressive but rather normative within chivalric society? Also, are homosocial and "homosexual" desire always mutually exclusive? What nuances of "homosexual" desire exist in chivalric discourse? While not necessarily indicative of further genital sexual activity, kisses exchanged "feelingly, solemnly, seriously" between knights might very well be erotically charged.[22]

Recent studies have also focused on politically motivated anxieties about male–male intimacy. Alan Bray observes a "curious symmetry between the sodomite and the masculine friend" in Elizabethan England.[23] Bray points to an idealized discourse of male friendship that celebrated physical displays of affection. He also draws attention to a negative discourse that arises when a particular relationship transgresses social hierarchies and is thus perceived as "dangerous."[24] Robert Matz summarizes Bray's argument: "The highly praised alliance of friendship was frequently eroticized, yet what kept (or did not keep) the celebrated closeness of friendship from appearing to be the sin of sodomy was not the degree of physical contact, but the appropriateness of the relationship."[25] Studies that document what Barbara Weissberger aptly terms "discursive sodomy" are not concerned with proving whether or not sexual acts actually occurred but rather focus on the language that casts male–male intimacy in a negative light.[26] For instance, Gregory Hutcheson examines sexually inflected narratives of the relationship between Juan II, King of Castile (1405–54) and his court favorite, Alvaro de Luna, that position the king as a victim of the evil machinations of his friend. While sodomy is never named, it exists as a subtext.[27] Chronicles of the relationship between Juan II and Alvaro de Luna have much in common with those historical narratives that negatively depict the intimate friendship of Edward II and Piers Gaveston as well as that of Richard II and Robert de Vere. Yet the discursive sodomy evident in these texts has not been closely studied.[28]

While there has been significant interest in examining the political motivation behind discourses that negatively depict male same-sex relations, less attention has been given to investigating how those discourses that celebrate and affirm male homosocial intimacy are, likewise, politically motivated. Bray alludes to the "mutual interest" generating Elizabethan male friendships but does not explore how idealized depictions of normative emotional—and physical—intimacy between social equals might serve the economic and political interests of the aristocracy. However, Richard Corum, in his engaging reading of Shakespeare's *Henry V*, sets out "to analyze specific aspects of Henry's reactionary homosocialization and homonationalization of himself and England as these are illuminated in the play."[29] Although Corum does not leave room for homoeroticism in the "homosocial Christian paradise," which, he maintains, the play celebrates,[30] he recognizes political motives behind textual affirmations of male–male bonding. Corum's study is thus an excellent springboard for exploring links between Christianity and homosocial intimacy in some late medieval chivalric texts.

★ ★ ★ ★ ★

It is imperative that queer studies of the Middle Ages examine a wide range of texts in order to understand better a particular sociocultural environment. Frantzen maintains that "[i]t is necessary to analyze historical conditions and unknown or undervalued sources. . . . It is more important to understand medieval attitudes as clearly as possible than it is to maneuver those attitudes into alignment with our own."[31] Frantzen is taking issue with what he sees as political bias in some queer scholarship, where an anti-homophobic agenda might compromise the historical accuracy of the findings. One of the difficulties in determining medieval attitudes toward same-sex desire is that much of the "evidence" is not explicitly documented. Unstated attitudes need to be gleaned from texts that ostensibly take no position on homosocial intimacy. In addition, desire between men who are not recognizably "homosexual" can be expressed in many forms. What is needed is a queer historical methodology that is open to articulating a wide range of homoerotically inflected relations in a particular cultural environment.

In his landmark study of same-sex relations, John Boswell makes the contentious claim that gay people, whom he defines as "persons who are conscious of erotic inclination toward their own gender as a distinguishing characteristic," existed in the Middle Ages.[32] He defends his preference for using the term "gay" over "homosexual" in that the latter term stresses sexuality while " '[g]ay' allows the reader to draw his own conclusions about the relative importance of love, affection, devotion, romance, eroticism, or overt sexuality in the lives of the persons so designated."[33] Thus, "gay," according to Boswell, describes persons engaging in a variety of same-sex interactions—not all of which need be genital. Boswell's articulation of the multifarious ways people of the same sex might interact with one another is an important insight and one that has not received as much attention as his essentialist terminology. Boswell recognizes that sexualities can be culturally specific; yet he also maintains that "it might happen that different societies would construct similar ones."[34] Although Boswell resists the label "essentialist," which others have used to describe his historical approach, many would agree with Dinshaw that "a specific gay essence grounds both community and history [in Boswell's work]; and that essence looks very post-Stonewall."[35] A key question driving the essentialist/ constructionist debate is whether people in the premodern era recognized sexual identities.

"Constructionists" are strongly influenced by Michel Foucault's now famous distinction: "As defined by the ancient civil or canonical codes, sodomy was a category of forbidden acts; their perpetrator was nothing more than the juridical subject of them. The nineteenth-century homosexual became a personage, a past, a case history, and a childhood. . . . It was consubstantial with him, less as a habitual sin than as a singular nature. . . . The sodomite had been a temporary aberration; the homosexual was now a species."[36] David Halperin has recently reinterpreted Foucault's (and his own) position on premodern sexuality. He points out that Foucault's "schematic opposition between sodomy and homosexuality is first and foremost a discursive analysis, not a social history, let alone an exhaustive one." He goes on to explain that "[b]y documenting the existence of both a discursive and a temporal gap between two dissimilar styles of defining, and disqualifying, male same-sex sexual expression, Foucault highlights the historical and political specificity of sexuality, both as a cultural concept and as a tactical device. . . ."[37] Halperin maintains that in distinguishing between premodern sodomites and modern homosexuals, Foucault did not intend to close off historical investigation of premodern sexual identity formation.[38] Foucault's intentions notwithstanding, Dinshaw notes that in some cases Foucault's "dictum has been used to authorize reductive and ignorant views of sex in the Middle Ages."[39] She argues that Foucault's pronouncement cannot be applied to all the societies of the Middle Ages because "it is clear from a number of different kinds of premodern sources. . .that men who engaged in acts of male–male sex were thought to be visibly marked, known at least to others if not to themselves, grouped with others of the same kind, and defined by sexual desire."[40] In drawing attention to those who observe— and, possibly, define—others' sexual behavior, Dinshaw leaves open the possibility that the observer and the observed might not agree on the defining label. In fact, the observed might not have engaged in sexual acts at all. One might simply affix a stigmatizing label—an *apparent* sexual identity—to one's political opponent.[41] Like Foucault, Dinshaw considers sexual acts to be the chief distinguishing marker of sexual identity or category.

Robert Padgug offers a definition of sexuality that is particularly useful for studying premodern same-sex relations. He explains that "[t]he content of sexuality is ultimately provided by human social relations. . . . [Sexuality] consists of activity and interactions—active social relations—not simply 'acts,' as if sexuality were the enumeration and typology of an individual's orgasms." He goes on to point out that "[t]he particular interrelations and activities which exist at any moment in a specific society create sexual and other categories which, ultimately, determine a broad range of modes of behavior available to individuals who are born within that society."[42] In applying Padgug's observations to the study of late medieval sexuality, one would not focus exclusively on acts of genital sex but rather on a broad range of erotically informed social behavior. By examining various means by which some men express their attraction to other men, it becomes difficult, if not impossible, to find an identity or label that fits all of these men. While scholarship seeking to establish whether or not one can accurately speak of premodern sexual identities is extremely important, attention should also be given to articulating multiple forms of same-sex desire expressed in premodern texts—for the sole purpose of making these expressions visible. But how does one excavate premodern codes of homoeroticism? How does one read the past?

Part of the recent debate by historians on methods of recovering the past centers on the question of whether the past exists outside of textual artifacts. Perhaps the most contentious claim made by New Historicists is that historians have no access to a material history outside the texts within which that history is preserved. Louis A. Montrose suggests that we cannot discover a "full and authentic past, a lived material existence, unmediated by the surviving textual traces of the society in question—traces whose survival we cannot assume to be merely contingent but must rather presume to be at least partially consequent upon complex and subtle social processes of preservation and effacement."[43] Although Montrose does not simply reduce history to textuality, he nevertheless situates material existence in a position that is dependent on and, thus, subservient to, textual artifacts. While most historians would probably not disagree that historical texts do not contain *all* the facts about *all* the people living at a specific time, some strongly protest the notion that history is nothing but text. Elizabeth Fox-Genovese insists that "history must also be recognized as what did happen in the past—of the social relations and. . .'events,' of which our records offer only imperfect clues."[44] And referring to the tendency of some historians to focus on how history is written rather than the events being written about, she argues that "[h]istory cannot simply be reduced—or elevated—to a collection, theory, and practice of reading texts."[45] According to Fox-Genovese, historians do not merely read and analyze written recordings of the past but also seek to "reconstruct the conditions of consciousness and action, with conditions understood as systems of social relations, including relations between women and men, between rich and poor, between the powerful and the powerless."[46]

Medievalists have also questioned the notion that history is just another form of textuality. According to Lee Patterson, "[t]o adopt an interpretive method that assumes that history is not merely known through but constituted by language is to act as if there are no acts other than speech acts."[47] He accepts the idea of the "historically real" and, while not denying that history is primarily accessible to us in a textual form, urges us to "seek to accommodate, in however inevitably partial a fashion, something of the palpability and unavoidability of historical action."[48] Gabrielle Spiegel proposes a method of textual analysis that does not exclude the material realities of human subjects of the past. Reminding us that "texts represent situated uses of language," she notes that "[s]uch sites of linguistic usage, as lived events, are essentially local in origin and therefore possess a determinate social logic of much greater density and particularity than can be extracted from totalizing constructs like 'language' and 'society.' "[49] She attributes to a text social agency, noting how "texts both mirror *and* generate social realities, are constituted by *and* constitute the social and discursive formations which they may sustain, resist, contest, or seek to transform."[50] Spiegel suggests that a literary text, for example, might "mirror" contemporary social values and/or political concerns yet also produce a unique "discursive formation" that will affect the social sphere it enters and, in turn, influence future texts. She also acknowledges non-textualized sociohistorical subjects—authors who write the texts and, at least implicitly, people who live in the "social realities" that these texts generate.

Paul Strohm regards both literary and nonliterary texts of the fourteenth century as fictional yet also valuable historical artifacts because "[t]hey offer crucial testimony. . .on contemporary perception, ideology, belief, and—above all—on the imaginative structures within which fourteenth-century participants acted and assumed that their actions would be understood."[51] He also aptly notes that "fictive elements teem within historical narratives, trial depositions and indictments, coroner's rolls, and other officially sanctioned accounts."[52] While acknowledging that "[t]exts do, indeed, regulate our access to the past," Strohm, like Patterson and Spiegel, also emphasizes "the contingency of texts, their reliance on a material reality beyond their own bounds."[53] A new historical approach, therefore, should, as David Aers states,

"attempt to relocate...[the text] in the web of discourses and social practices within which it was made and which determined its horizons."[54]

Consistent with the views expressed by the medievalists above, I offer
here a historically informed study of discourses of male same-sex desire in
a wide range of fourteenth-century chivalric texts. The historical "facts" I
endeavor to uncover are attitudes, dramatized behavior, imagined effects,
and social mores. Although the evidence I draw on is all textual, I do not
deny the material, referential world of the texts I examine. Part of my study
is thus conjectural, suggesting that homoeroticism informs the mental
images "real" authors and readers create of model knights or the dramatizations of male–male relations in chivalric texts. Historical inquiry is, in part,
an imaginative activity—not in the sense of making something up, but
rather imagining *possibilities* from evidence contained in a text. The "discursive formations" of male–male desire expressed in or suggested by these texts
are products of a historically specific social reality. Without direct access
to actual late medieval knights/readers, we can, nevertheless, identify how
a text generates, for instance, a homoerotically charged economy of
male–male spectatorship. In addition, I examine chronicles and trial records,
which though "historical" are also—as Strohm notes—"fictional" in that
they are not objective reports; and these historical narratives vividly illustrate
politically motivated negative discourses of same-sex behavior.

Louise Fradenburg and Carla Freccero draw an important conclusion
regarding historical inquiry: "The historian does not so much retrace the
past as magnify our power to see it; history is not pure repetition, because
its very pursuit of sameness (in the form of accurate representation) requires
a technology of transformation. As such, history is riddled by the paradoxes
of identification: by the impossible pleasures and obligations of imitating the
past."[55] Thus, they justly question "those historicist practices that repudiate
the roles of fantasy and pleasure in the production of historiography."[56]
Following Fradenburg and Freccero, I recognize the impossibility of replicating perfectly the referential world of fourteenth-century chivalric texts
but take pleasure in making a close, interpretative approximation. And
engaging in this process of historical inquiry, I will attempt to "magnify our
power" to discern the workings of male–male desire suggested in these texts.
A key element of recent historical approaches is an acknowledgment of the
subjectivity of the historian/critic. As Montrose states: "our analyses and our
understandings necessarily proceed from our own historically, socially and
institutionally shaped vantage points."[57] Marilyn Butler observes that in
order to practice a "genuinely historical criticism," it is necessary "to declare
our interests, whether personal, national, or professional."[58] I therefore do
not claim to be offering objective historical readings; my replication of a
particular late medieval social environment is, by necessity, informed by my

culturally shaped vantage point. I have an agenda: namely, to "dethrone" interpretations informed by heteronormativity, which have dominated our reading of chivalric texts.

Like Eve Sedgwick, I seek "[t]o draw the 'homosocial' back into the orbit of 'desire,' of the potentially erotic."[59] I am not concerned with delineating specific sexual identities but rather, as Burger aptly puts it, bodies in motion, homoerotically charged moments suggested or dramatized in fourteenth-century chivalric texts. I agree with Holsinger that one can speak of *"homoerotic subject positions"* that are "historically contingent, fleeting, unstable, produced at certain moments, by certain texts, and through specific cultural practices."[60] Yet these historically contingent subject positions are nevertheless interpreted—mediated—through our senses, and we cannot hope to replicate expressions of desire in the past without connecting them with present understandings of desire.[61] While I follow a "constructionist" position, viewing socially contextualized subjects engaging in "acts" of eroticized looking, imagining, emotional intimacy, kissing, and embracing, I also assume that a subject expresses "individual" desire—desire that is both essential to human subjects and anchored in a particular cultural environment. I thus follow Gregory Bredbeck and risk speaking of "homoeroticism *as* homoeroticism" while acknowledging "that all the discourses that variously inscribe this phenomenon are necessarily historically bounded and contingent."[62]

I draw on psychoanalytical theories regarding the processes of identification/ desire and fantasy—particularly those advanced by Freud and his feminist/ queer interpreters—to articulate the potential homoeroticism that informs chivalric society as it is presented in some representative texts. By using modern theories to understand medieval texts, I am not claiming that people living at that time would have used similar formulations; the fact, however, that psychological processes were not conceptualized, or were conceptualized in different terms, does not necessarily mean that they did not occur. In offering us a language for articulating human interactions depicted in medieval texts, psychoanalytically inflected theories help bridge the gap between past and present, and, at the same time, help maintain the historical otherness of the medieval work. I agree that "[t]he challenge is to look at the Middle Ages without presentist assumptions yet without forfeiting the tools of contemporary theories of sexuality and, at the same time, to remain attentive to how thinking differently about medieval sexuality may change the way we think about sexuality in the present."[63]

My project explores both positive and negative discourses of male same-sex desire in chivalric contexts. Valerie Traub points to the role of difference in homoeroticism: "Erotic arousal is always imbricated with power differences— it functions by means of exchanges, withholdings, struggles, negotiations."[64]

Power disparity between men will have a positive or negative erotic valence depending on the context. A novice knight enthusiastically studying an exemplary man-of-arms or the narrator/Arthur's knights mesmerized by the Green Knight's formidable body are "aroused" by difference; but this difference is stigmatized in situations where a king, who should arouse the erotic attention of his male subjects/favorites because he is more powerful is instead viewed as passive and vulnerable. I focus my investigation on the fourteenth century because it generated (or circulated) a variety of texts that not only affirm but also denigrate male same-sex desire in chivalric contexts. That these discourses are coeval highlights the link between political motives and expressions of homoeroticism. All the major primary texts of my survey offer a sustained engagement with male–male desire in a chivalric context—an engagement that dramatizes, suggests, or interprets actual or imagined homoeroticism. The texts themselves are diverse—treatises, chronicle narratives, romances, trial testimonies—as are the discourses they illustrate. Any survey is selective to some extent and I make no claim that all, or even most, fourteenth-century chivalric texts express discourses of homoeroticism; yet, as we shall see, some significant texts clearly do.[65]

Part 1 focuses on discourses of normative homoerotically charged desire—discourses that affirm, celebrate, or privilege male–male intimacy. As Frantzen observes, "[n]onsexual intramale acts, including embraces and kisses, took place within an institution of male friendship, defined by the bonds between a lord and his retainer, that the culture authorized and indeed valorized. . . . And so long as sexual intercourse is not involved, the acts cannot be considered deviant. But neither are they meaningless, or without erotic significance."[66] I do not assume that a culture that "authorized" and "valorized" male–male intimacy did not have some underlying motive for doing so. I thus not only articulate various textual expressions of normative homoeroticism but also explore possible sociopolitical agendas behind these discourses. Part 2 investigates negative depictions of male same-sex behavior in key fourteenth-century historical narratives. I am less concerned with uncovering evidence indicating whether or not the allegations were true than with highlighting the language used to denigrate homosocial desire. In each of the studied cases, I argue that attacks made against male–male intimacy do not represent a rejection of male same-sex intimacy per se but rather the vilification of certain relations deemed by some to be politically dangerous and/or economically disadvantageous. My project endeavors to articulate the tension—and the inextricable link—between two contrasting types of discourses occurring in the fourteenth century.

Part 1 begins with an introductory chapter that surveys political motives for promoting male homosocial intimacy between knights or between a knight and his lord. I look at what Maurice Keen refers to as the "crisis in chivalry" in the late Middle Ages—the inconsistency between actual knightly conduct and chivalric ideals. I examine how Geoffroi de Charny's and Ramon Lull's chivalric treatises attempt to correct this inconsistency by defining positive and negative uses of violence. I then draw attention to Edward III's politically motivated promotion of Arthurian idealism in his formation of the Order of the Garter. Chivalric orders developing in both France and England in the fourteenth century were based on close personal ties, and I suggest that these ties could include eroticized interactions between knights.

Chapter 2 studies ideas regarding male–male intimate relations expressed in Aristotle's *Nicomachean Ethics* and Cicero's *De amicitia*, and the reformulation of these ideas in Aelred's *De spiritali amicitia* and Reason's discourse on friendship in the *Roman de la Rose*. I point to how love and intimacy between friends is central to each of these treatises. Cicero and Aelred, in particular, view perfect friendship as a lifelong union, each friend considering the other a second self. I go on to illustrate how these concepts are usefully employed in chivalric discourse. I conclude chapter 2 with an examination of male same-sex unions in two chivalric romances, *Amys and Amylion* and the *Prose Lancelot*. These texts dramatize—and *homoeroticize*—key ideas contained within the treatises on ideal friendship, such as loyalty, selfless behavior, and brotherly love.

Drawing on Eve Sedgwick's observation that heterosexual and homoerotic desires do not compete in heteronormative societies, chapter 3 explores what happens in those chivalric romances where heterosexual relations do not enjoy a privileged status. In the first section, I examine how male–male desire competes with heterosexual desire in *Troilus and Criseyde* and in *Amys and Amylion*. These desires compete in the sense that both texts tacitly make a comparison between two expressions of desire and foreground one. In the first three books of Chaucer's text, Troilus and Pandarus's relationship is privileged over each one's familial relationships and, most prominently, the heterosexual love story; in *Amys and Amylion*, the bond uniting the two knights is given prominence over each knight's marriage. In the second section, I use René Girard's concept of triangular desire to map out a series of configurations that delineate the desire(s) circulating during key moments in *Troilus and Criseyde, Sir Gawain and the Green Knight*, and Chaucer's "Knight's Tale." I explore how each of these texts reveals a fluidity—a lack of clearly marked boundaries—between homoerotic and heterosexual desires.

Chapters 4 and 5 analyze male–male spectatorial acts suggested or dramatized in chivalric texts. Building on chivalric texts' implicit invitation to male readers who are novice knights (or merely enthusiastic about chivalry)

to imagine exemplary knights, chapter 4 explores the potential homoeroticism of this putative act. I study Augustine's concept of the imagination and
his articulation of how one conjures images of persons and scenes that are
being described. Then, drawing on psychoanalytically inflected film theory,
as well as Laplanche and Pontalis's understanding of fantasy, I point to the
interlinking forces of identification and scopophilia that inform the fantasy
images some male readers might form. While I limit my investigation
to male readers I do not deny the possibility that female readers could
likewise engage in this erotically charged imaginative process. Finally,
adapting Freud's essay, "A Child Is Being Beaten," to a chivalric context,
I examine sadomasochistic identifications some male readers might form
with fighting knights in the *Stanzaic Morte Arthur*. Chapter 5 continues to
explore homoerotic spectatorship in chivalric contexts; however, I now
articulate the visual dynamics of a knight looking closely at another knight
using his corporeal sight rather than his imaginative faculty. Beginning with
a theorizing of the viewer, I examine medieval theories of vision, specifically the idea that neither the observed nor the observer occupies an exclusively active or passive position. With this in mind, I study several visual acts
in *Troilus and Criseyde* and *Sir Gawain* that dramatize the erotic effects an
observed person has on the observer. I also focus on the role the observer
plays in eroticizing the visual act. Chapter 5 concludes with an examination
of how the Green Knight stimulates—mesmerizes, intrigues—Arthur's
knights, which draws attention to the potentially homoerotic exhibitionism
in chivalric society.

Part 2 opens with a brief survey of how accusations of sodomy were
used in the Middle Ages to attack a group deemed threatening or a political opponent. Chapters 6 and 7 explore politically motivated sodomitical
discourses, that is, discourses that cast a direct or indirect shadow of sodomy
over particular male–male relations because the perpetrators are viewed as
dangerous or serve as convenient victims in a political campaign. Chapter 6
examines three historical narratives that illustrate this stigmatizing discourse. Testimony from the trials of the Knights Templar, who were accused
of engaging in illicit male same-sex contact, generates a discourse of apparently one-sided interactions between an active/initiator and passive/victim.
Chroniclers of the reign of Edward II, aligning themselves with powerful
nobles, vilify Edward's intimate relationship with Piers Gaveston, depicting
Edward as a victim of the evil machinations of his favorite. Likewise, chroniclers stigmatize Richard II's personal bonds with Robert de Vere and
others by describing sodomitically inflected scenarios that position Richard
being "seduced" by perverse men. I demonstrate that in both Edward's and
Richard's cases male–male intimacy itself is not being attacked, but rather
those homosocial associations that threatened the interests of the nobles.

Drawing on characteristics that defined the sodomitical discourses in chapter 6, particularly the perceived power disparity in the relationships between each king and his respective intimate companions, chapter 7 studies how *Troilus and Criseyde* taints Troilus and Pandarus's friendship with hints of sodomy. I examine how Chaucer's text depicts Pandarus and Troilus as, respectively, manipulating adviser and passive advisee—roles that suggest the highly criticized relationship between Richard II and his court favorites (as well as that between Edward II and Gaveston)—and, like the chronicles, it renders this normative male–male bond in a sodomitical discourse. I delineate the process by which Pandarus successfully seduces Troilus into revealing the details of his secret love. Once established as Troilus's trusted counselor, Pandarus wields a form of sexual power over him. I demonstrate that, unlike the chronicles, Chaucer's text illustrates how the seduced disengages himself from his seducer. I conclude that despite its sodomitical discourse, *Troilus and Criseyde*, like the historical narratives, also affirms normative male homoeroticism.

PART ONE

AFFIRMATIONS OF MALE SAME-SEX DESIRE

INTRODUCTION

PROMOTING HOMOSOCIAL INTIMACY

Richard Kaeuper observes that "in the [later] Middle Ages one of the greatest threats to the peace of the realm came from the day-to-day conduct of the knightly classes whose tendency to violent self-help was often proudly proclaimed and recognized as a right, rather than condemned as a crime. . . . In fact, these lords and gentlemen who were especially in France possessors of extensive rights of justice, and who even in England exercised wide authority either in their own name or as agents of the king, were all too frequently themselves plunderers, bandits, arsonists, slayers."[1] According to Maurice Keen, there was a "crisis of chivalry" in the fourteenth century—an inconsistency between actual knightly conduct and chivalric ideals.[2] Before exploring how (and why) chivalric texts promote homosocial intimacy, I want to examine contemporary writers' response to this "crisis" and politically motivated appropriations of chivalry.

In his *Letter to Richard II*, Philippe de Mézières allegorically depicts the corruption and violence committed by men-at-arms as a garden of war:"in the said steams were many leeches, large and small, which sucked the blood of those who lived in the garden. . .so much so that many of these leeches burst asunder. . .in this parable the leeches represent the commanders and their men at arms, who suck the blood of the poor, that is to say the substance of their livelihood, by ransom, pillages, taxes, and oppression without measure."[3] Geoffroi de Charny likewise points to the misbehavior of contemporary knights but also reminds knights of their priorities:

> pluseurs sont qui regardent a prendre prisons et autre gaing; et quant il les ont pris et autres biens, il ont plus grant volenté et desir de sauver leurs prisons ou leur gaaing que de secourir et aidier de mettre la journee a bonne fin. Et bien puet avenir que par tele maniere peut l'en perdre la journee. Et l'en doit bien doubter le gaing qui fait perdre honneur, corps et avoir.

> [there are a number of men who pay more attention to taking prisoners and other profit, and when they have seized them and other winnings, they are

more anxious to safeguard their captives and their booty than to help to bring the battle to a good conclusion. And it may well be that a battle can be lost in this way. And one ought instead to be wary of the booty which results in the loss of honor, life, and possessions.]⁴

Charny's text illustrates the twofold agenda of some chivalric texts: condemning *un*chivalric actions and promoting ideal chivalric behavior. Chivalric writers did not condemn all violent acts—for military prowess was an integral part of chivalry; instead they encouraged knights to channel chivalric energy into preserving order in the society. Kaeuper remarks that "the balancing act [between condemning and praising chivalry] requires celebration of chivalry as the grand guide to civilized life, while simultaneously pressing with some degree of urgency for the changes that could make chivalry truly that force in the world."⁵ Ramon Lull nicely illustrates this twofold aim in that he condemns knights who burn and pillage towns and castles, considering such acts to be against the order of chivalry, yet he maintains that "Thoffyce of a knyght is also to enserche for theues / robbours and other wykked folke / For to make them to be punysshed / For in lyke wyse as the axe is made for to hewe and destroye the euylle trees / in lyke wyse is thoffyce of a knyght establysshyd for to punysshe the trespacers and delynquau[n]ts."⁶ Lull's language implies that knights are permitted—and encouraged—to commit violent acts against disorderly elements in society.

Keen observes that "[t]he late medieval answer to the problem of the disorders and crimes of martial men. . .lay not in the abandonment of chivalrous values, but in a re-appeal to the traditional value of loyal and faithful service."⁷ A knight was to serve his lord, his king, or the common interest of all people. According to Lull, "Thoffyce of a knyght is to mayntene and deffende / his lord worldly or terryen / for a kyng ne no hyhe baron hath no power to mayntene rygtwysnes in his men without ayde & helpe / Thenne yf ony man do ageynst the comma[n]dement of his kyng or prynce / it behoueth that the knyghtes ayde their lord."⁸ Since one tenet of ideal chivalric conduct was loyalty to one's superior, it is not surprising that some fourteenth-century kings, particularly Edward III, found chivalry to be politically expedient.

Kaeuper notes that "[k]ings could easily praise and adopt as their own the chivalric virtues of loyalty, generosity, prowess, largesse. . .[but] [k]ings would increasingly have second thoughts about this glorification of lordly freedom of action and knightly independence. . .[and] shared with churchmen the desire to channel the potentially destructive energy of knights in directions they approved."⁹ Edward III's idea for channeling potentially disorderly knights was to reestablish the Arthurian idea of the Round Table. D'Arcy Boulton explains that Edward was evidently inspired by the protagonist in a contemporary French romance, *Perceforest*, who establishes an Arthurian-like society. Edward is reported to have selected three hundred knights, and his society was to be "a perpetual association of lay knights attached permanently to the royal court of England."[10] Edward thus hoped that his successors would maintain an association that he presumably thought would be beneficial to the monarchy. Juliet Barker points out that although Edward's order of the Round Table was very much influenced by Arthurian romance, the three hundred knights selected for membership—which equals the number of knights in the *franc palais* of *Perceforest*—"retained their identity and did not attempt to play the part of Arthurian heroes."[11] Although Edward's project is cloaked in Arthurian idealism, it should also be viewed as a clever political maneuver. Boulton aptly observes that "the 300 knights who were to be admitted to the 'revived' society would have been highly gratified to be thus made the successors of Arthur's heroic knights, and that such a society—including nearly a third of the militarily active knights in England, and a majority of the earls and major barons—would have served at the very least to smooth the relations between Edward and the more important members of the English knightly class."[12] We can therefore assume that Edward's motivation was not to repeat or relive the legendary past but rather to use the past for his own political purpose; namely, to forge loyal bonds with potentially disorderly knights and other aristocrats whose actions were apt to be propelled by self interest.

It is not clear why Edward abandoned his plans for establishing the society of the Round Table but a few years later, in 1349, he founded the Order of the Garter. Juliet Vale supports the general view taken by historians that "the foundation of the Order of the Garter. . .[was] a unifying act little short of political genius," but situates Edward's action within the broad scope of his political policy during the 1340s. Vale maintains that in founding the Order, Edward "crystallized a co-operative relationship [between the monarchy and the knights] that had been gradually developing over several years."[13] Since Edward hoped the Order would strengthen his ties with important noblemen, he had to be politically savvy in choosing which men were to be included. Vale points out that "[t]he great danger with an order of limited number was that those excluded—above all, the highest nobility—would feel resentful and alienated from the king, deprived of their traditional advisory role close to him." She concludes that "Edward was careful to include anyone who might otherwise be a potential focus for discontent."[14] One must not forget that the Order of the Garter while, indeed, an elite club of aristocrats was also a chivalric society of men who were expected to fight in real battles in support of king and nation. Historians are unanimous in recognizing Edward's political acuity in exploiting the contemporary passion for chivalry. Drawing a line from Edward's attempts to "restore" the Round Table and culminating in the foundation of the Order of the Garter, Boulton remarks that Edward was "concerned from the start with cementing his relations with the knights of his kingdom, whose enthusiasm for chivalry was hardly less than his own, and with celebrating their martial prowess and their achievements in the first campaigns of the war with France."[15]

Although there were not many major crusading enterprises in the fourteenth century, Keen points out that English knights participated in campaigns taking place in Alexandria in 1365 and Tunis in 1390. He also draws attention to Henry of Grosmont and William Montagu, who both played a prominent role in Alfonso XI's crusade of 1343–44 in Algeciras.[16] He reminds us that chivalry "was at once Christian and martial and aristocratic."[17] Centuries after the first crusades, chivalry continued to be infused with Christian elements. Kaeuper explains that model knights, such as Geoffroi de Charny, "largely appropriated religion; they absorbed such ideas as were broadly compatible with the virtual worship of prowess and with the high sense of their own divinely approved status and mission. . . . [I]n one of its essential dimensions chivalry rested on the very fusion of prowess and piety; it functioned as the male, aristocratic form of lay piety. . . . The worship of the demigod prowess—with all the ideas and practices of the quasi-religion of honour—was merged with medieval Christianity."[18] Kaeuper describes the inextricable link between religious devotion and chivalry illustrated in Charny's treatise as "knightly lay piety."[19] The political undertones of a Christianized chivalry is evident in Lull's treatise: "the wycked knyght that aydeth not his erthely lord and naturel countrey / ageynst another prynce / is a knyght withoute offyce / And is lyke vnto faith withoute werkes and lyke vnto mysbyleue / which is ayenst the feyth."[20]

These examples illustrate politically motivated appropriations of chivalry. But how did the founding of chivalric orders, Lull's and Charny's call for a renewal of chivalric ideals, and "knightly lay piety" promote or encourage intimacy between knights? While not necessarily suggesting an erotic interaction, the ritual dressing of a novice knight just prior to the knighting ceremony illustrates an intimate encounter between men—one of whom presumably naked at the beginning.[21] Charny describes the sequence of steps, infusing them with Christian symbolism:

> Puis doivent venir les chevaliers au lit pour vestir yceulz et les doivent vestir de neufs draps, linges et toutes choses neuves qui y appartiennent. . . . Puis les doivent vestir li chevalier de cotes vermeilles en segnefiant que il sont tenus d'espendre leur sanc pour la foy de Nostre Seigneur defendre et maintenir et les droiz de Sainte Eglise et toutes autres droitures dessus dites que chevalier soit tenu de faire. Et puis leur apportent les chevaliers chauces noires et les enchaucent. . . . Et puis leur apportent les chevaliers une courroie toute

blanche et l'en seignent et mettent entour de lui en seignefiance que il soient environné en tout entour leurs corps de chasteté et de netteté de corps.

[Then the knights should come to the beds to dress those to be knighted; the stuff in which they dress them, the linen and all that goes with it should be new. . . . Then the knights should robe them in red tunics, signifying that they are pledged to shed their blood to defend and maintain the faith of Our Lord and the rights of the Holy Church and all the other just rights set out above which it is the knight's duty to protect. Then the knights bring black hose and put them on those to be knighted. . . .Then the knights bring them white belts with which they gird them, signifying that they should surround their bodies with chastity and purity of the flesh.][22]

The homosocial encounter here is not between a knight and an attendant but rather between two knights—two men-at-arms who embrace the ideal tenets of Christianized chivalry. One knight dresses another knight in (under)linen, tunic, hose, and belt. While each step in the ritual dressing is given a Christian, or, at least, pious meaning, we should not ignore the fact that a man is placing items of clothing upon the naked body of another man. A knight dressing another knight in a white belt symbolizing chastity does not preclude present or future erotically charged interactions between knights. Is it not possible that the dresser feels brotherly affection toward the novice knight as he touches his body? Might the novice knight also feel affection and gratitude toward the experienced knight as he is being dressed? We need not rule out these possibilities simply because Charny gives us no indication regarding what each knight is thinking or feeling during the dressing sequence. Even without the slightest trace of eroticism, the Christianized chivalry of the traditional bath and dressing ritual promotes a form of homosocial intimacy.

Although in monarchical orders, such as Edward III's Order of the Garter or King John of France's Order of the Star, knights were first and foremost bonded to the sovereign—a bond that the kings utilized politically—there was also evidently a feeling of fraternal union among the knights. Boulton observes that in Edward's order, members were given the title "companions," which "had the advantage of emphasizing the fraternal relationship that was ideally to exist among the knights."[23] Likewise, the knights of the Star "were to swear to aid all their fellow knights . . . in the fashion of brothers-in-arms."[24] Keen notes that in addition to the monarchical orders, there were a number of confraternities of "lesser knights" in the fourteenth century.[25] While one had to be of noble birth to join, Keen points out that "the orders were. . .remarkably unhierarchical, internally. Within their ranks, the companions stood upon a par with one another, regardless of differences of wealth and title."[26] Keen recognizes that these orders promoted homosocial intimacy: "The loyalty which their statutes stressed over and again was not the corporate loyalty of nationalism, but the intimate personal loyalty of the fighting vassal or retainer to this lord, and of the companion-in-arms to his fellow."[27] While these orders were not necessarily founded for the purpose of promoting male–male intimacy, the success of their campaigns was, in part, dependent on "intimate personal loyalty" between men. Keen describes chapters of an order as "solemn family councils in which the affairs of the companions were reviewed not individually, but as they affected the whole society. The dishonour of one was the dishonour of the whole order."[28] Thus, a knight might be less inclined to commit an illegal or immoral act because of his commitment to his fellow knights and the order in general. Personal loyalties are indeed suffused with emotions and feelings of affection, as the following oath taken in 1414 by the knights of John of Bourbon's order demonstrates: "Item, we all swear and promise to be on terms of good and loyal affection, and during the terms of this our common enterprise to observe the same bond of loyalty and confraternity as brothers and companions ought to observe towards one another."[29] This oath implies that "loyal affection" is a normative component of knightly associations. And the success of the "common enterprise" hinged to some extent on the strength of emotionally charged bonds between fellow knights.

Keen recognizes that a "psychological force" operating in personal relations between brothers-in-arms, similar to that which occurred in close ties between a lord and his vassals, exerted an influence on a knight's behavior. He goes on to explain that in both sets of relations, "there was the same close, intimate connection, which gave those entering it a sense of partnership and of sharing with one another's reflected glory."[30] The emotional support a knight feels he has from his brother knights may propel him to perform better; also, because he has a sense of fraternal union, a knight might refrain from engaging in conduct that would tarnish the reputation of the order. Keen finds that in the absence of a legal contract like that which bound a lord and retainer, knightly orders promoted an "intimate connection" among brothers-in-arms, modeled on "the natural relationship of the family."[31] Keen's analogy with the family does not diminish the emotional intensity of these bonds; for he clearly points to the significant role homosocial intimacy plays in ideal knightly conduct, the stability of a chivalric order, and the success of a particular campaign.

Chivalric treatises also illustrate how ideal chivalric conduct promotes male–male intimacy. Lull repeatedly stresses the obligations of a knight to his lord and to chivalry as a whole. He addresses the novice knight: "yf thou be a knyght / thow receyuest honour and the seruytude that must be hadde vnto the frendes of chyualrye." He warns him that "treason pryde / ne none other vyce corrupte not the othe that the knyght hath made to his lord & to chyualrye."[32] The knight is not only bound to honor and serve his lord but also the "friends of chivalry," which situates him within a brotherhood of knights all upholding the same ideals.[33] At the ordination ceremony the officiating knight kisses the squire who is about to be made a knight.[34] While the kiss is ceremonial it illustrates a normative expression of male–male affection; the kiss is emotionally charged, as is the ritual bathing and dressing prior to the ordination, because presumably the squire has a strong desire to become a knight and the officiating knight is desirous to welcome the novice knight into the brotherhood of chivalry.

Charny focuses on the loyalty knights feel for their lord: "la foy et loyauté qu'ilz doivent a leur seigneur ne peut estre miex monstree que de li servir et aidier loyaument a tel besoing come de fait des guerres qui est si pesant come de mettre corps, honneur et chevance tout en aventure" [the faith and loyalty which they owe to their lord cannot be better demonstrated than by serving him and assisting him loyally in such urgent need as that of war which is so grave as to put person, land and resources all at risk].[35] The knight's "loyal affection" to his lord is thus periodically affirmed through actions that protect the interests of the lord. And the lord's affection and respect for his knights increase as a result: "uns grans sires. . .il en aime miex et prise plus les bons pour la cognoissance qu'il a des biens qu'il a veuz qu'il ont faiz" [a great nobleman. . .loves and values men of worth all the more for the knowledge he has of the great deeds he has seen them perform].[36] Charny also draws attention to the mutual love knights and lord feel for one another: "li grans sires. . .les [bons] aime et les honnore et prise et leur fait proffit, et le doubtent, aiment, honorent et present pour le bien qu'ilz voient et cognoissent qui est en li avecques les amours, honours et proufiz qu'il leur fait" [the great lord. . .loves, honors, and values them (i.e. the good warriors) and rewards them, and they respect him, love, honor, and esteem him for the great valor they see in him in addition to the love, honor, and reward that he has bestowed on them].[37] Male homosocial intimacy propels ideal chivalric conduct (knights perform commendable acts out of feelings of "loyal affection" for their lord) and ideal chivalric conduct strengthens male homosocial intimacy (knights and lord love and honor one another more as a result of good deeds done). These passages also demonstrate how ideal homosociality is tied to the socioeconomic interests of both knights and lord.

According to Kaeuper, although most of the fighting men in fourteenth-century England were not knights, chivalric ideals were still very popular and embraced by those who were not technically "knights." He finds that "chivalry served as a source of inspiration even beyond the ranks of lords and active, strenuous knights; it touched all men-at-arms."[38] We can assume that at least some men-at-arms—whether they were nobleman or not—felt they were members of a chivalric brotherhood and tried to live up to the ideals celebrated in Lull's and Charny's texts. The founding of chivalric orders and a concomitant affirmation of ideal chivalric conduct in the fourteenth century were, to some extent, motivated by social, economic, and political factors. Although certain forms of male–male intimacy were celebrated prior to this period, we see how in the fourteenth century chivalric homosociality was appropriated and, wittingly or not, promoted by kings, lords, knights, and the Church. Having outlined some of the sociopolitical contexts within which chivalric treatises and romances were written, I now explore in-depth how these texts produce discourses that affirm and directly or indirectly promote male–male desire.

CHAPTER 2

CHIVALRIC BONDS AND THE IDEALS
OF FRIENDSHIP

Classical Treatises on Friendship

Two important classical treatises on friendship are Books VIII and XI
from Aristotle's *Nicomachean Ethics* and Cicero's *De amicitia*. Some of
the ideas regarding male–male intimate relations expressed in these texts
are reformulated by medieval clerics and dramatized in chivalric romances
such as *Amys and Amylion* and the *Prose Lancelot*. According to Aristotle,
there are three types of friendship, which are distinguished by whether the
object of love is based on utility, pleasure, or good. The first two, he maintains, are not ideal because they cannot last: "these sorts of friendships are
easily dissolved, when the friends do not remain similar [to what they
were]; for if someone is no longer pleasant or useful, the other stops loving
him."[1] It is only the last one that can lead to true, long-lasting friendship,
for "these people's friendship lasts as long as they are good; and virtue is
enduring."[2] The three types are, however, not mutually exclusive. Ideal
friendship based on moral goodness encompasses the other less-perfect
types and raises them to a perfect whole: "good people are both unconditionally good and advantageous for each other. They are pleasant in the
same ways too, since good people are pleasant both unconditionally and for
each other."[3] As H. H. Joachim aptly summarizes: "The main characteristic
of ideal friendship is its inclusiveness: each friend loves the other because
that other is what he is, i.e. the whole character or personality of each friend
is comprehended in the union."[4]

The understanding that ideal friendship can occur only between virtuous
men is central to Cicero's theory as presented in his *De amicitia*. He clearly
states: "nisi in bonis amicitiam esse non posse" [friendship cannot exist
except between good men].[5] He goes on to define the qualities of good men
as "Qui ita se gerunt, ita vivunt, ut eorum probetur fides integritas aequitas

liberalitas, nec sit in eis ulla cupiditas libido audacia, sintque magna Constantia" [Those who so act and so live as to give proof of loyalty and uprightness, of fairness and generosity; who are free from all passion, caprice, and insolence, and have great strength of character].[6] Cicero's description of "good" men matches the qualities of men-of-worth outlined in chivalric treatises. We should not understand Cicero's dismissal of "passion" as a statement against the suitability of intense attachment or love between friends since he finds that "Est enim amicitia nihil aliud nisi omnium divinarum humanararumque rerum cum benevolentia et caritate consensio" [friendship is nothing else than an accord in all things, human and divine, conjoined with mutual goodwill and affection].[7] In fact, according to Cicero, love is very much a part of friendship.

Despite the ideal nature of each author's concept of friendship and the fact that few could actually live up to these conditions, both treatises were intended as guides for forming friendships between "real" people—friendships that were based on love and affection. Aristotle claims that when good people form close associations, "loving and friendship are found most of all and at their best."[8] According to Aristotle, goodwill is not enough for true friendship, "for when they have goodwill people only wish goods to the other, and will not cooperate with him in any action, or go to any trouble for him."[9] However, mutual goodwill can be channeled into ideal friendship after friends develop greater love and intimacy for each other. After a period of time, when friends "grow accustomed to each other," goodwill becomes true friendship, "for, as the proverb says, they cannot know each other before they have shared the traditional [peck of] salt, and they cannot accept each other or be friends until each appears loveable to the other and gains the other's confidence."[10]

Friends who have achieved mutual trust and find each other "loveable" might also feel attracted to each other. Although Aristotle is not necessarily advocating sexual relations between friends, he does in fact draw a parallel between close friendship and erotic relations, both of which he says can involve only a few people: "indeed, it. . .seems impossible to be an extremely close friend to many people. For the same reason it also seems impossible to be passionately in love with many people, since passionate erotic love tends to be an excess of friendship, and one has this for one person; hence also one has extremely close friendship for a few people."[11] Carolinne White concludes, "Such an attitude is indicative of how intense a friendship his ideal friendship was considered to be."[12] Moreover, in describing erotic love as merely "an excess of friendship," Aristotle is not denying passion a place in friendship, but rather limiting passion in ideal friendships to that which is *not* excessive. He draws another parallel between erotic love and complete friendship: "for [complete friendship, like erotic passion,] is like an excess, and an excess is naturally directed at a single individual."[13] What kind of excess does he mean? I suggest that this excess refers to all the qualities that make up complete/ideal friendship: namely, mutual goodwill, usefulness, and pleasure, which are all grounded in love and intimacy. While it falls short of erotic passion perhaps, Aristotle's concept of ideal friendship posits two friends steeped in mutual warmth and affection.

Cicero considers love to be the foundation upon which true friendship is built. He draws the following etymology: "Amor enim, ex quo amicitia nominata est" [it is love (*amor*), from which the word "friendship" (*amicitia*) is derived].[14] He finds that: "a natura...potius quam indigentia orta amicitia, applicatione magis animi cum quondam sensu amandi, quam cogitatione quantum illa res utilitatis esset habitura" [friendship springs rather from nature than from need, and from an inclination of the soul joined with a feeling of love rather than from calculation of how much profit the friendship is likely to afford].[15] Friendship, thus, from its inception, is inextricably linked to feelings of love. Cicero goes on to describe how love develops between friends: "similis sensus exstitit amoris, si aliquem nacti sumus, cuius cum moribus et natura congruamus" [that kindred impulse of love, which arises when once we have met someone whose habits and character are congenial with our own].[16] In keeping with his definition of true friendship being possible only between virtuous people, he observes that "Nihil est enim virtute amabilius, nihil quod magis alliciat ad diligendum, quippe cum propter virtutem et probitatem etiam eos, quos numquam vidimus, quodam modo diligamus" [There is nothing more lovable than virtue, nothing that more allures us to affection, since on account of their virtue and uprightness we feel a sort of affection even for those whom we have never seen].[17] What is particularly interesting here is that Cicero identifies the alluring attraction of a virtuous person. The originating point for developing a true friendship with someone is thus desire—not necessarily erotic desire, but a longing that leads to affectionate relations. Therefore, Cicero does not consider friendship to be an emotionless bond between virtuous persons but rather an association within which love and mutual admiration grow.

Before I look at what each treatise says about friendship being a union of two individuals, I want to explore what is in essence a variation on the theme that a true friend is a second self. Both authors expound on the intimacy that exists between close friends. According to Aristotle, "[t]he excellent person is related to his friend in the same way as he is related to himself, since a friend is another himself."[18] Thomas Aquinas expands on this: "Et dicit quod virtuosus se habet ad amicum sicut ad se ipsum, quia amicus secundum affectum amici est quasi alius ipse, quia scilicet homo afficitur ad amicum sicut ad se ipsum" [Aristotle notes that a virtuous man is disposed to his friend as to himself because a friend is—so to speak—another self by affection, that is, a person feels for a friend what he feels for himself].[19] This idea is also expressed by Cicero, who asks "Quid dulcius quam habere quicum omnia audeas sic loqui ut tecum?" [What is sweeter than to have someone with whom you may dare discuss anything as if you were communing with yourself?].[20] He goes on to point out: "Verum etiam amicum qui intuetur, tamquam exemplar aliquod intuetur sui" [Again, he who looks upon a true friend, looks, as it were, upon a sort of image of himself].[21] And most relevant for understanding the intimacy inherent to chivalric bonds is Cicero's observation in De officiis that "in quibus enim eadem studia sunt, eaedem voluntates, in iis fit ut aeque quisque altero delectetur ac se ipso" [when two people have the same ideals and the same tastes, it is a natural consequence that each loves the other as himself].[22]

In both Aristotle's and Cicero's view the unions are permanent and informed by intense affection. Aristotle draws a parallel between erotic lovers and true friends, noting that, like lovers who enjoy most to see their beloved, "what friends find most choice worthy is living together."[23] Irwin points out that Aristotle is not implying that friends need to live in the same house, but rather share the same activities and thus spend much of their time together.[24] In his restatement of Aristotle's observation that true friendship is a "partnership" that is best carried out by friends living together, Thomas Aquinas points out that this union is indeed pleasurable because friends share in those activities that they enjoy most—activities that "constitute their whole life."[25] Regarding the permanence of this union, Joachim observes that since ideal friendship incorporates the whole being of both partners—and both are completely moral in character—"the union is therefore stable and unlikely to change."[26]

Cicero consistently describes ideal friendship in terms that connote a long-lasting relationship between two people: "solitaria non posset virtus ad ea quae summa sunt pervenire, coniuncta et consociata cum altera perveniret" [virtue cannot attain her highest aims unattended, but only in union and fellowship with another].[27] He goes on to consider that "Quae si quos inter societas...eorum est habendus ad summum naturae bonum optimus beatissimusque comitatus" [Such a partnership as this...should be considered the best and happiest comradeship along the road to nature's highest good].[28] In De officiis, he distinguishes intimate friendship from ordinary bonds of friendship, praising the former: "Sed omnium societatum nulla praestantior est, nulla firmior, quam cum viri boni moribus similes sunt familiaritate coniuncti" [But of all the bonds of fellowship, there is none more noble, none more powerful than when good men of congenial character are joined in intimate friendship].[29] He brings together here the two dominant features of ideal friendship: intimacy and permanency. Permanence is implied because ideal friendship is based on the union of two virtuous men, and nowhere does Cicero warn that good men could "lose" their virtue. The union Cicero envisions is also based on mutual love and affection, and thus he is describing a sort of same-sex marriage.

For Aristotle and Cicero, in a perfect friendship both partners lead a virtuous life and are intimate with each other—each one viewing the other as a second self. Such friends share the same values and interests, spending much time together, and develop an emotionally informed permanent union. These ideas also had currency in the Middle Ages, finding expression in treatises and discourses on ideal friendship, and filtered into chivalric culture.[30]

Medieval Concepts of Ideal Friendship

Aelred of Rievaulx's *De spiritali amicitia* draws heavily on Cicero's *De amicitia* and thus suggests that classical ideas about perfect friendship were "in the air" in the European Middle Ages. In fact, the early chivalric romances, in which relationships between knights (and/or a knight and his lord) play a prominent role, were written around the same time that Aelred was composing his treatise.[31] Although Aelred's text was not well known in the later Middle Ages, Douglass Roby notes that "[b]y the end of the fourteenth century there were at least four short versions of the *Spiritual Friendship* in existence."[32] Aelred's text is interesting in that it marks an attempt to align classical pagan ideas of friendship with Christian spirituality. For Aelred, there are three types of friendship: carnal, worldly, and spiritual. True friendship can be only of the spiritual type and should be desired: "non utilitatis cuiusque mundialis intuitu, non qualibet extra nascente causa, sed ex propriae naturae dignitate, et humani pectoris sensu desideratur; ita ut *fructus eius* praemiumque non sit aliud quam ipsa" [not for consideration of any worldly advantage or for any extrinsic cause, but for the dignity of its own nature and the feelings of the human heart, so that its fruition and reward is nothing other than itself].[33] Like Aristotle and Cicero, Aelred stresses that only "good" people sharing similar values and interests can form true friendship: "Amicitia itaque spiritalis inter bonos, uitae, morum, studiorumque similitudine parturitur" [And so spiritual friendship among the just is born of a similarity in life, morals, and pursuits].[34]

Aelred offers an etymology of "friend" similar to that put forth by Cicero: "Ab amore, ut mihi uidetur, amicus dicitur; ab amico amicitia" [Now I think the word *amicus* (friend) comes from the word *amor* (love), and *amicitia* (friendship) from *amicus*].[35] And, like Cicero, Aelred maintains that friendship depends on love: "Fons et origo amicitiae amor est, nam amor sine amicitia esse potest, amicitia sine amore numquam" [The fountain and source of friendship is love. There can be love without friendship, but friendship without love is impossible].[36] Yet Aelred gives more attention

than Cicero to the role of love in friendship. He identifies four characteristics of friendship—all of which are related to love in a broad sense:

> Ad amicitiam quatuor specialiter pertinere uidentur: dilectio et affectio, secu-
> ritas et iucunditas. Ad dilectionem spectat, cum beneuolentia beneficiorum
> exhibitio; ad affectionem, interior quaedam procedens delectatio; ad securi-
> tatem, sine timore uel suspicione omnium secretorum et consiliorum reuelatio;
> ad iucunditatem, de omnibus quae contingunt, siue laeta sint, siue tristia; de
> omnibus quae cogitantur.
>
> [Four elements in particular seem to pertain to friendship: namely, love and
> affection, security and happiness. Love implies the rendering of services with
> benevolence, affection, an inward pleasure that manifests itself exteriorly; secu-
> rity, a revelation of all counsels and confidences without fear and suspicion;
> happiness, a pleasing and friendly sharing of all events which occur, whether
> joyful or sad, of all thoughts.][37]

These four elements of friendship find expression in the chivalric romances,
Amys and Amylion and the *Prose Lancelot*. Although all four elements are not
given equal emphasis in each romance—security and happiness are predominant in the former and love and affection in the latter—each text
demonstrates how an ideal chivalric bond between two knights is informed
by mutual love and affection as well as concern for each other's security and
well-being.

Aelred's classifies three types of kisses, "osculum corporale, osculum spiri-
tale, osculum intellectuale" [a corporeal kiss, a spiritual kiss, and an intellectual kiss], and describes those occasions when exchanging a "corporeal kiss"
with a friend is acceptable: "in signum reconciliationis, quando fiunt amici,
qui prius inimici fuerant ad inuicem. . .in signum dilectionis, sicut inter spon-
sum et sponsam fieri permittitur; uel sicut ab amicis, post diuturnam absen-
tiam et porrigitur et suscipitur" [as a sign of reconciliation, when they become
friends who were previously at enmity with one another. . .as a symbol of
love, such as is permitted between bride and bridegroom or as is extended
to and received from friends after a long absence].[38] Aelred's explanation is
valuable for uncovering medieval mores regarding socially acceptable displays
of affection, and in considering a kiss to be "a symbol of love" exchanged
between a bride and groom or between two reunited friends, he juxtaposes
heterosexual unions alongside male homosocial ones.[39]

Aelred quotes Cicero, exclaiming "At quae felicitas, quae securitas, quae
iucunditas habere *cum quo aeque audeas loqui ut tibi*" [But what happiness,
what security, what joy to have someone to whom you dare to speak
on terms of equality as to another self].[40] But he goes on to lift Cicero's
words to a higher plane, so to speak, offering a vision of intimacy where
one could reveal one's spiritual progress as well as one's innermost secrets.

Like Aristotle and Cicero, Aelred finds that true friendship involves a relationship of such extreme intimacy that one's friend is essentially an extension of oneself. All three treatises are not describing narcissism but rather the ultimate closeness two friends can achieve. And love is the driving force. This is aptly expressed by Aelred: "Nisi igitur et tu hunc ipsum in alium transferas affectum, gratis amicum diligens...uera sapiat amicitia non poteris. Tunc enim erit ipse quem diligis tamquam alter tu, si tuam tui in ipsum transfuderis caritatem" [Unless, therefore, you transfer (t)his same affection to the other, loving him gratuitously...you cannot savor what true friendship is. For then truly he whom you love will be another self, if you have transformed your love of self to him].[41]

For Aelred ideal spiritual friendship is achieved when the souls of each friend join together in a permanent union. He quotes Ambrose: "*amicus tui consors sit animi, cuius spiritui tuum coniungas et applices, et ita misceas ut unum fieri uelis ex duobus*" [your friend is the companion of your soul, to whose spirit you join and attach yours, and so associate yourself that you wish to become one instead of two].[42] In stressing the permanence of the bond, Aelred echoes Cicero: "Cum enim amicitia de duobus unum fecerit, sicut id quod unum est non potest diuidi, sic et amicitia a se non poterit separari" [For when friendship has made of two one, just as that which is one cannot be divided, so also friendship cannot be separated from itself].[43] Aelred's union is not only on a spiritual level but also on a temporal one: "ille ita tuus, et tu illius sis, tam in corporalibus quam in spiritalibus" [he is yours, and you are his, in body as well as in spirit].[44] That Aelred had in mind some sort of marriage between friends is observed by Brian McGuire, who notes that except for denying sexual relations a place in his scheme, Aelred presents ideas of union that conform to those later realized in concepts of heterosexual marriage. However, I do not agree with McGuire that "Aelred was perhaps ahead of his time when he imagined such a bond not only between a man and a woman but also between two people of the same sex";[45] for some chivalric romances illustrate precisely the union of friends that Aelred had in mind.

Another medieval appropriation of Cicero's *De amicitia* is Reason's discourse on friendship in Jean de Meun's portion of the *Roman de la Rose*. I draw the following excerpts from the fourteenth-century Middle English translation. Reason's opening remarks focus on two key components of the classical concept of ideal friendship, love and permanence: "Love of freendshipp also ther is, / Which makith no man don amys, / Of wille knytt bitwixe two, / That wole not breke for wele ne woo."[46] This rather concise discourse on friendship deals with several topics that are central to chivalric relations. Reason notes "that ech helpe other at her neede, / And wisely hele bothe word and dede; / Trewe of menyng, devoide of slouthe, / For witt is nought without trouthe" (5213–16). A knight must be prepared to aid his brother knight in any situation that may arise and, moreover, "trouthe" must cement their relationship. Alan Gaylord rightly observes that "the classical virtue of fidelity is reaffirmed with a word ['trouthe'] which was one of the cornerstones in the edifice of medieval chivalry, extending from feudal loyalty to the blood-brotherhood of warriors."[47] Sharing all of one's thoughts with a friend is touched on by both Cicero and Aelred, and this intimacy is also referred to by Reason: "the ton dar all his thought / Seyn to his freend, and spare nought, / As to hymsilf, without dredyng / To be discovered by wreying" (5217–20). Reason also maintains that a "Man shulde maken his request / Unto his freend, that is honest" (5287–88), but notes two situations when one may rightly call on a friend to do a dishonest need: "If men his freend to deth wolde drive, / Lat hym be bisy to save his lyve; / Also if men wolen hym assayle, / Of his wurshipp to make hym faile, / And hyndren hym of his renoun, / Lat hym, with full entencioun, / His dever don in ech degre / That his freend ne shamed be" (5293–300). De Meun was evidently highly selective in choosing passages from Cicero's lengthy text (Reason's discourse on friendship is just over one hundred lines).[48] In the quoted passage, de Meun presents a concept of loyalty that is illustrated in some chivalric romances; for instance, as we shall see, in *Amys and Amylion*, one knight performs a dishonest deed—and endangers his own life—for the benefit of his brother knight.

Reason also elaborates on the intimacy that exists between friends: "Yit shal a trewe freend do more / To helpe his felowe of his sore, / And socoure hym, whanne he hath neede, / In all that he may don in deede, / And gladder [be] that he hym plesith, / Than his felowe that he esith" (5267–72). This selfless sharing and easing of a friend's sorrow is one manifestation of the key classical concept that a friend is another self. Although most clearly stated by Aristotle, all the treatises I have examined assume that an ideal friendship exists between just two persons. Likewise, Reason points out that "tweyne of noumbre is bet than thre / In every counsell and secre" (5259–60). The idea that two friends are joined in a permanent union based on mutual love, so vividly expressed by Aelred, is also presented here: "If bothe the hertis Love hath fered (inflamed), / Joy and woo they shull depart, / And take evenly ech his part. / Half his anoy he shal have ay, / And comfort [him] what that he may; / And of his blisse parte shal he, / If love wel departed be" (5278–84).

The treatises on ideal friendship stress that friends should be joined together in a permanent union, sharing the same interests, and demonstrating unswerving loyalty to one another. These same ideas inform Lull's and Charny's understanding of proper ties between knights. Lull states that "yf thou be a knyght / thow receyuest honour and the seruytude that must be hadde vnto the frendes of chyualrye."[49] In joining an order of knighthood, a novice knight enters into a long-standing relationship with his fellow knights, upholding the same values. The love between friends, stressed in the discourses on friendship, is also mentioned by Charny who tells knights: "Amez et servez vos amis" [love and serve your friends].[50]

The chivalric treatises, however, concentrate on the relationship between a knight and his lord. The ceremony initiating this bond, whereby the knight vows to defend the interests and well-being of his lord, points to a union commensurate with that envisioned by Aelred. Lull recommends that the lord kiss the novice knight followed by an exchange of gifts: "The knyght [the lord] ought to kysse the squyer [the novice knight]. . . & the lord that maketh a newe knyght / ought to yeue to the newe knyght also a present or yefte / And also the newe knyght ought to yeue to hym and to other that same day."[51] The treatises on ideal friendship all propose an inclusive, intimate relationship between two men. Reason stresses the importance of defending one's friend against an adversary. These two aspects of friendship—inclusiveness and loyalty—inform Lull's understanding of a knight's relationship to his lord: "the knyght ought to apparaylle hym / & presente his body to fore his lord / whan he is in peryl hurte or taken."[52] Likewise, Charny assumes that a knight and lord are linked in this type of intimate bond: "la foy et loyauté qu'ilz [gens d'armes] doivent a leur seigneur ne peut estre miex monstree que de li servir et aidier loyaument a tel besoing come de fait des guerres" [the faith and loyalty which they (men-at-arms) owe to their lord cannot be better demonstrated than by serving him and assisting him loyally in such urgent need as that of war].[53]

While Lull's and Charny's texts do not offer details about particular personal relationships, some chivalric romances vividly illustrate close ties between men. Maurice Keen rightly points out that literary references are valuable sources of information about "brothers-in-arms," and argues that "[i]t is . . . unwise to assume that anything which writers of medieval romance took seriously was a matter of indifference in practice, simply because official records, whose survival is notoriously chancy, do not underline its importance."[54] In order to get a better sense of an intimate bond—a union—between knights informed by the ideals of perfect friendship, and the homoeroticism such a bond suggests, one needs to turn to dramatizations of two chivalric relationships.

Male Same-Sex Unions in *Amys and Amylion* and the *Prose Lancelot*

The story of the friendship between Amys and Amylion was popular in the Middle Ages. Besides the early fourteenth-century English text that I am examining there were Latin, French, and Anglo-Norman versions.[55] William Calin suggests a didacticism regarding male friendship operates within *Amys and Amylion*: "the friendship [between the two knights]...is capable of imitation; it is contagious. Amiloun's nephew Amaurant serves him with as much devotion and sacrifice as Amiloun had served Amis."[56] While Calin justly points to the text's focus on a homosocial bond in a cultural milieu more often defined by courtly heterosexual relations, he apparently dismisses the same-sex passion underlying the story.[57] *Amys and Amylion* not only illustrates many of the ideals set forth in the classical and medieval treatises on friendship but also depicts the *emotional intensity* of a bond between two knights.

Even as children, Amys and Amylion were "Both curteys, hende and guode," thus qualifying them for perfect friendship in the classical tradition.[58] The true love that the children feel for each other is reaffirmed when they reach adult age. Amylion, in reminding Amys of their earlier pledge of "truth," restates it: "Brother, we are trowth-plyght, / Both in word and dede. / Ffro this dai forward ever moo, / Nother faile other, for well ne woo, / To helpe other at nede. / Brother, be now trew to me, / And y schall be as trew to the, / As wys God me spede!" (24, 5–12).[59] Like the ideal unions described in the treatises on friendship, Amys and Amylion's "truth" is to last "ever moo." In addition, they are committed to aiding each other when needed, and will stand by each other in good times as well as bad ones. Amylion's words are spoken on the occasion of his departure from Amys. He is "ferly woo" to leave his dear companion, one who was always in his thoughts (20, 1–3). And Amys, "for thought and kare, / For mornyng and sekyng sare, / Allmost swonned" (21, 4–6). Since the two knights are like two halves of one soul, very similar in appearance and character, each feels incomplete without the other. This romance takes the classical idea that a friend is a second self and puts it to a test: Will one half survive without the physical proximity of the other half? And, more significant, will the bond itself survive physical separation?

Despite the fact that Amys and Amylion are virtually identical and thus Amylion can pretend to be Amys in the fight against the steward, the two men are nonetheless two individuals. Amylion warns Amys of the "fals steward" and urges his friend to be on his guard (25, 11). Amys evidently does not have the same intuitive skills as Amylion because he does in fact fall prey to the steward's scheme. Observing the uncanny similarity—yet individuality—of the "brothers" opens the possibilities for studying the eroticism or passion underlying the relationship between two men who are not related by birth.

After they have separated, when Amys is challenged by the treacherous steward, Amylion, "In his bedde lay anyght, / A dreme he mette anon. / Him thought he saw sire Amys with syght" (83, 2–4). Amylion's reaction confirms that the image of Amys that appears to him is quite vivid; it is as if Amys were somehow inside of him. He knows: "Ffor certes…with som wrong, / My brother ys in perell strong" (84, 7–8). He then rushes up immediately to go to the aid of his friend. The two are so intimately bonded to one another that not only does Amylion know when Amys is in danger, but there is nothing one friend will not do for the other. Amylion freely agrees to take Amys's place in the fight with the steward. What more clearly illustrates the classically derived chivalric ideal of a knight defending the body of his brother knight than Amylion risking his life to protect Amys? In addition, we see here an example of the inclusiveness of true bonds of friendship in that one knight agrees to do a dishonest act to save his friend's life. Amys and Amylion also evidently trust each other: Amys reveals his innermost troubles to Amylion knowing that Amylion will keep the information secret; and Amys sleeps in a chaste manner with Amylion's wife. While the text does not dwell on physical expressions of the love that binds the two friends, there are hints of what I would refer to as "passionate affection." For instance, when the two friends meet by chance as Amylion, responding to his dream heads for Amys's residence, they instantly dismount "And kyste togeder both two" (87, 9). That this is not a passionless kiss of peace but rather an emotional reunion between two friends in love with each other is evident from Amylion's concern over his friend's "sory chere," and Amys's breathless pouring out his troubles to Amylion, sparing no intimate detail.

Perhaps the most powerful depiction of the extraordinary love between Amys and Amylion occurs toward the end of the romance, when Amys takes in his sickly friend. Considering the behavior of Amylion's wife— banishing him from his own table and reducing him to a beggar—Amys's compassion is remarkable indeed.[60] As a further attestation to the bond between the friends, Amys, without hesitation, slays his children according to the directions he receives in a dream and anoints Amylion with their blood.[61] Although the text does not offer explicit details of the scene, the two friends are alone as Amys bathes Amylion's naked body in blood and then dresses him. The scene is eroticized in that Amys is not performing this act as a professional physician but rather as someone who evidently loves his "patient" more than his own children. Yet, because the children miraculously come to life again, the poem does not set male–male intimacy against Christian procreation, thus suggesting that the relationship between Amys and Amylion is not condemned but rather sanctioned by God. This same-sex union is not broken even when they die. They are laid in one grave and we are told that they enjoy eternal bliss together.

Although the love affair between Lancelot and Guinevere holds a prominent position in Arthurian romance, in the French *Prose Lancelot* a great deal of attention is also given to another amorous relationship—the one between

Lancelot and Galehot. In fact, as Reginald Hyatte aptly observes, "The *Prose Lancelot* provides the title character with a compliment to Queen Guinevere's love in the perfect...chivalric friendship of *compagnonnage* [with Galehot] which shares many extreme affective characteristics with romance representations of erotic love."[62] While this male–male friendship is perhaps offered as a parallel to heterosexual *fine amor*, I do not agree with Hyatte that the bond between Galehot and Lancelot does not conform to some of the key principles of the Aristotelian–Ciceronian code of perfect friendship. Hyatte maintains that Galehot's "benevolence, beneficence, disinterestedness, sacrifices, and affection for Lancelot are *extreme*, and, therefore, they transgress the ethical limits of the classical code of *amicitia*."[63] Both Aristotle and Cicero (as well as Aelred) acknowledge that love is the force that binds friends—and love can generate "extreme" actions. Non-fictional examples of same-sex relationships, such as Augustine's youthful friendship with another young man, as reported in his *Confessions*, or Gregory of Nazianzus's relationship with Basil (who later became Arch-bishop of Caesarea), reveal excessive behavior or feelings on the part of one or both friends.[64] While not illustrating ideal restraint, these relationships conform to the basic principles of perfect friendship as outlined by Aristo-tle and Cicero. Unlike the love affair between Lancelot and Guinevere, the union between Lancelot and Galehot is presented as one destined to be per-manent. In addition, the two male characters demonstrate mutual love and intimacy—two key components of true friendship in the classical tradition. However, my intention is not to insist on how perfectly this particular male–male union conforms to ideal friendship but rather to explore how the *Prose Lancelot* reveals the passion and potential eroticism that underlie the classical and medieval discourses of same-sex friendship.

That Galehot initiates and sets the tone of his relationship with Lancelot cannot be denied. In fact, Gretchen Mieszkowski refers to Galehot as "one of the great homoerotic portraits of medieval literature," and observes that his "role in the Prose *Lancelot* is virtually entirely as a lover."[65] The night before he offers his friendship to Lancelot, Galehot closely observes his future friend as he sleeps: "la nuit dormi li cheualiers moult durement & toute nuit se plaignoit en son dormant & galahos looit bien car il ne dormoit gaires ains pensa toute nuit a retenir le cheualier" [That night...(Lancelot) slept heavily, and ever he made moan in his sleep, and Galehot, that scarce slept, heard him well and thought all the night through on how he might keep him].[66] The next morning, Galehot reveals his feelings for Lancelot: "sachies que vous porres bien auoir compaignie de plus riche homme que ie ne sui. Mais vous ne laures iamais a homme qui tant vous aint" [wit ye well that ye can have the company of a more powerful man than I, but ye will never have that of a man that loveth you so well].[67]

While Lancelot does not respond in kind, he does accept Galehot's offer of friendship. Galehot's love for Lancelot is the determining factor in this budding relationship because, if one assumes Galehot is honest in admitting that he is not exceptionally powerful, then the only thing he is qualified to offer, and which Lancelot apparently feels is worthwhile accepting, is his professed love. The treatises on friendship suggest that an ideal bond develops gradually over time. The *Prose Lancelot* illustrates one way this process may occur, how a friendship evolves from one characterized by one-sided love—or attraction—to a more ideal union in which both partners love each other with equal intensity.

That Lancelot and Galehot's relationship is to be "monogamous" is evident from Galehot's request to Lancelot, and Lancelot's subsequent agreement, not to give his "company" to another. The narrator informs us that a "covenant" between Lancelot and Galehot has taken place, and as further indication that they are united in a formal bond, Galehot asks Lancelot to wear his arms "por commenchement de compaignie" [for the beginning of our fellowship].[68] Lancelot also refers to their "covenant." When Galehot is about to follow Lancelot's wishes and pretend to take Arthur (after Lancelot, in Galehot's armor, defeats Arthur's men), Lancelot reminds Galehot of the solemn union between them: "couent me tenes" [keep your covenant with me].[69] The inclusiveness of their relationship is apparent here; Galehot's bond to Lancelot is stronger than any tie he might have to another knight. Although Lancelot does not illustrate the same selflessness toward Galehot as Galehot does to him, he does clearly love and appreciate his friend:

> Et quant li boins cheualiers en uoit aler galahot & faire si grant meschief pour lui si quide bien & dist que nus si boins amis ne si veritable compaignon not il onques mais si en a si grant pitie que *il en souspire del cuer aual & pleure des iex de la teste sous le hiaume* & dist entre ses dens biax sire diex qui porra ce deseruir.

> [When the good knight (Lancelot) saw Galehot go to do himself such great mischief for his sake, he thought and said that never had he had so good a friend and so true a comrade, and he felt so great pity for him that *he sighed from the depths of his heart and wept beneath his helmet* and he said between his teeth, "Fair Lord God, who can recompense this?"][70]

Central to classical and medieval concepts of ideal friendship is that a friend is like a second self. Thus, one wishes to please a friend in the same manner that one wishes to please oneself. This is illustrated in the relationship between Galehot and Lancelot, but unlike the treatises, which stress the importance of the doer, here the focus is on how performing deeds for a friend offers pleasure to *both* friends. Galehot, occupying the role of "doer," obviously enjoys fulfilling his friend's wishes and Lancelot clearly finds pleasure in being the recipient of Galehot's good gestures (not least of which is his liaison with Guinevere, which Galehot arranges). But Lancelot is also emotionally attached to Galehot and not merely taking advantage of Galehot's love, as is demonstrated in the quoted passage; and likewise he is a "doer" in that he permits Galehot to perform deeds that he knows will bring pleasure to Galehot as well as to himself. Although a male–male relationship characterized by selflessness / mutual self-pleasure exists perhaps in fiction only rather than in "real" chivalric society, the concept that a knight would (and should) perform deeds that will bring pleasure to his lord (or fellow knights)—and that such acts will also bring pleasure to the doer—is suggested in both Lull's and Charny's treatises.

In contrast to the informal arrangement between Guinevere and Lancelot—she is, after all, married to Arthur—the union linking Galehot and Lancelot is presented as a form of same-sex marriage. Galehot asks Guinevere, his "rival," for permission to have Lancelot's company forever. She grants it formally, "ie vous doing cest cheualier a tous iors" [I give you this knight forever], but with this stipulation: "sauf ce que ie i aie eu auant" [save that I have him afore ye].[71] Implied in Guinevere's remark is her acknowledgment of the parallel nature of the two relationships. Galehot and Lancelot's union is, in a sense, "consummated" when Galehot later goes to Lancelot "& se couchent ambedoi en j lit & parolent toute nuit de ce dont lor cuer sont moult a aise" [and they rested that night in one bed, and they talked all the night long of that whereof their hearts had full great ease].[72] While the text offers no *explicit* evidence of physical contact taking place between the two men, the scene is erotically charged in that the friends are committed to each other and have on several occasions professed their mutual love. We are told that their all-night "talk" brings their hearts "full great ease." That the narrator makes the point of indicating that they rest in one bed—a fact that might have been omitted if this were the usual sleeping arrangement for friends—suggests that this is an occasion of eroticized male bonding. In addition, although the text does not elaborate on the living arrangement of the two friends, it appears that for a while at least they spend much of their time together, an arrangement that both Aristotle and Cicero recommend. Granted, the treatises on friendship do not suggest that friends share one bed, and they do not endorse sexual relations between men; however, the intimacy generated by friends remaining in one another's physical presence, which Aristotle and Cicero clearly endorse, can certainly be realized in such a sleeping arrangement.

The intense love that Galehot and Lancelot have for each other is further illustrated in a dialogue initiated by Galehot, who believes that they are about to be separated: "Que ferai iou qui tout ai mis en vous mon cuer et mon cors" [what shall I do that have given me wholly, body and soul, to loving you?].[73] And Lancelot acknowledges his love for

Galehot: "Certes. . .iou vous doi plus amer que tous lez hommes del monde. Et si fai iou" [I ought to love you more than all other men in the world. And so I do].[74] Galehot reveals his dependency on Lancelot, telling Arthur: "Ne si mait diex iou ne sa[u]roie viure sans lui si me tolries ma vie" [so help me God, I could not live without him, and how would ye take my life from me?].[75] This idea that two friends are so closely entwined with each other that neither can live without the other is directly related to the classical concept that true friends share one soul. A measure of the intimacy between two friends is that one visualizes a future crisis that affects them both. Galehot reveals his premonition to Lancelot: "me fu il auis que iou auoie ij cuers en mon ventre et estoient si pareil ca paines pooit len connoistre lun de lautre. Et iou nesgardai leure que iou oi perdu lun" [me seemed that I saw two hearts in my body, and they were so alike that one might scarce be known from the other. And even as I looked, I lost one].[76] Galehot's dream proves to be accurate and the two friends are forced to separate.

Galehot's self-inflicted death is caused by a form of lovesickness suffered by someone who loses his "other half." The root of Galehot's "sickness" is not the unrequited desire for an aloof beloved, as is the situation of the lover in courtly romances, but rather his refusal to live without the sharer of his soul. Galehot does not plunge into despair simply because Lancelot is not with him—quite the contrary. We are told that "Galehot sen comfortast sil ne quidast que il fust mors certainement" [he (Galehot) would have been consoled, if he had not thought that Lancelot was assuredly dead].[77] Although Galehot's death demonstrates the negative repercussions when a close relationship becomes invested with too much emotion, it also offers a positive illustration of an intimate and affectionate same-sex union.

The story of Galehot and Lancelot's friendship does not end with Galehot's death. While Galehot is alive Lancelot does not express his feelings for his companion in a manner that equals Galehot's effusive outpourings. However, that Lancelot does indeed love Galehot in "body and soul" is brilliantly revealed in the grief he expresses at Galehot's grave:

> Et quant il voit chou si chiet a terre tour pasmes et iut grant piece sans dire mot. . . . Et quant il est reuenus de pasmisons si dist ha diex quel doel et quel damage & quel anui. Lors fiert lun poing sor lautre et esgratine son visage si quil en fait le sanc saillir. Si se prent par ses cheueus et se fiert del poing grans cops en mi le vis et pleure si durement que il ni a celui qui nen ait pitie.

> [When he saw this (i.e. the inscription), he fell to the earth in a swoon, and he lay long time without saying a word. . . . And when he was come out of his swoon, he cried on high and said, "Alas, what sorrow and what loss!" Thereupon he beat one fist upon the other, and he tore his hair and gave himself great buffets with his fists on his brow and on his breasts, and he wept so sore that there was none there but had pity on him.][78]

Mieszkowski notes that "Lancelot's response to Galehot's death is one of the episodes most thoroughly reconceived by the cyclic version."[79] One can speculate whether in adding this scene, the author was striving to privilege the male–male bond over the heterosexual relations each knight had experienced. Lancelot even contemplates suicide, thus demonstrating the idea that in true friendship one cannot bear to live without his other half. What prevents him from taking this action is the message he receives from the Lady of the Lake informing him of her plan to have Galehot buried in his own tomb. Thus, like partners in any other blessed union, Galehot and Lancelot will be united eternally.

The loving bond between Galehot and Lancelot is not really that extraordinary when one considers classical and medieval discourses of intimate male friendship. Intense love and loyalty between friends, and a desire to perform any action to aid one's other half, are stressed in these discourses. What is remarkable, however, is that the *Prose Lancelot* offers such a vivid dramatization of a same-sex amorous relationship in a genre that generally reserves excessive displays of love for partners who are of the opposite sex. Nevertheless, a modern heteronormatively informed reading of the *Prose Lancelot* would undoubtedly not focus on Lancelot and Galehot's union. On the other hand, medieval readers, whose view of same-sex friendship was presumably more informed by classical ideas of true love between men, might very well have noted and responded to this dramatization of male–male intimacy.[80]

Although Aelred lived far removed from the secular world of chivalric romances, his moving depiction of same-sex friendship in the *De speculo caritatis* offers a context for understanding the affection, intimacy, and union between knights illustrated in *Amys and Amylion* and the *Prose Lancelot*:

> Porro non modicum uitae huius solatium est, habere quem tibi affectu quodam intimo ac sacratissimi amoris unire possis amplexu...qui tibi collacrymetur in anxiis, collaetetur in prosperis, tecum quaerat in dubiis...ac quiescente mundi strepitu in somno pacis, in amplexu caritatis, in osculo unitatis, interfluente Spiritus sancti dulcedine, solus cum solo repauses: immo ita te ei adiungas et applices, et animum animo misceas, ut de pluribus unum fiat.

> [It is in fact a great consolation in this life to have someone to whom you can be united in the intimate embrace of the most sacred love...who weeps with you in sorrow, rejoices with you in joy, and wonders with you in doubt...with whom you can rest, just the two of you, in the sleep of peace away from the noise of the world, in the embrace of love, in the kiss of unity, with the sweetness of the Holy Spirit flowing over you; to whom you so join and unite yourself that you mix soul with soul, and two become one.][81]

Galehot and Lancelot, as well as Amys and Amylion, support each other in times of need, share their sorrows or joys, and at the end of their lives are united eternally, resting together "in the sleep of peace away from the noise of the world."

None of the discourses of male–male bonds I have examined in this chapter recommend, portray, or even suggest genital sexual conduct between men. But all of the texts imply that an emotive force drives ideal friendships. And the men who are bonded together in unions characterized by loyalty, inclusiveness, love, and soul-sharing, may very well be strongly attracted to one another. This possibility of same-sex attraction—and homoeroticism—needs to be acknowledged when interpreting homosocial behavior both expressed and suggested in chivalric texts.

CHAPTER 3

COMPETING DESIRES

Philip Culbertson makes the following observation regarding intimacy between heterosexual men in the late twentieth century: "Because men have been taught to be uncomfortable with male friendship, men mask their fear by making sure their heterosexual status is clearly proven in public, by reaffirming marriage as more important than friendship."[1] This modern concept of male heterosexual friendship, which overlooks or minimizes the intensity of same-sex relations, often informs readings of chivalric texts. Vern Bullough notes that in the later Middle Ages, young knights often developed close relations with one another: "[u]sually, the young noble youth was incorporated into a group of friends who were taught to love one another as brothers. . .and whose every waking moment was spent in each other's company."[2] He goes on to point out that these young men often stayed together for many years until at around the age of thirty they were supposed to marry. But since eligible women were not always available, Bullough maintains that some men continued their close friendships and "it is quite possible that they turned to each other for friendship, encouragement, and even sexual relief."[3] While recognizing the importance of male bonds in chivalric society, Bullough also implies that knights chose one another as intimate companions out of necessity rather than preference. As we shall see, this is not always the situation in literature.

Addressing the dynamics of homoerotic and heterosexual desires in Shakespeare's sonnets, Eve Sedgwick maintains that "within the world sketched in these sonnets, there is not an equal opposition or a choice posited between two such institutions as homosexuality (under whatever name) and heterosexuality." She observes that "[t]he Sonnets present a male–male love that, like the love of the Greeks, is set firmly within a structure of institutionalized social relations that are carried out via women: marriage, name, family, loyalty to progenitors and to posterity, all depend on the youth's making a particular use of women that is not, in the abstract, seen as opposing, denying, or detracting from his bond to the speaker."[4] Thus, in this sociocultural framework, the two sets of relations do not compete with each other. But what happens in those chivalric romances where heterosexual relations are not firmly institutionalized, where marriage and procreation are either not the goal or not emphasized?

Privileging "frendes love"

In *Troilus and Criseyde* and *Amys and Amylion*, male–male desire competes with heterosexual desire—competing in the sense that both texts tacitly make a comparison between these two expressions of desire and foreground one. Chaucer's text, which I examine first, privileges Troilus and Pandarus's friendship over the relationships between Pandarus and Criseyde, Troilus and Deiphebus, and, most significant, Troilus and Criseyde. Moreover, in the first three books the developing relationship between Troilus and Criseyde effects an even greater intimacy between Troilus and Pandarus.

That Pandarus treats his niece with far less love and respect than he does Troilus is apparent in book 2 when he attempts to persuade Criseyde to accept Troilus as her lover. He refers to his friend, who he claims will die if Criseyde does not acknowledge his plight, as "my lord so deere, / That trewe man, that noble gentil knyght."[5] He then warns Criseyde that if by her neglect Troilus should die, she would be guilty of a deed so cruel for which her beauty could never make amends (2.337–38; 341–42). He goes even further, denying her the right to live if she proves herself so "routheles" (2.346): "If therwithal in yow ther be no routhe, / Than is it harm ye lyven, by my trouthe" (2.349–50). He continues to verbally torture her by drawing attention to the unstoppable deterioration of her beauty: "Thenk ek how elde wasteth every houre / In eche of yow a partie of beautee; / And therfore er that age the devoure, / Go love; for old, ther wol no wight of the" (2.393–96). In contrast to his compassionate depiction of Troilus, who he claims heroically "hasteth hym with al his fulle myght / For to ben slayn" (2.334–35), Pandarus taunts his youthful niece with a horrifying picture of slow physical degeneration. He also indicates his lack of respect for her by switching from the more polite "yow," which he usually uses when addressing her, to the familiar "the." Rather than effecting a positive familiarity, it actually reinforces the abusiveness of his remarks by lowering her social status from an eligible, beautiful woman who has lost only "a partie of beautee" to one whom no man—particularly a worthy man—would want because she is old and unattractive.[6]

Pandarus's earlier coercion of Troilus serves to stop the flow of tears; here, however, the unrelenting pressure he applies on his niece triggers tears. Almost immediately after these comments, Criseyde "began to breste a-wepe anoon, / And seyde, 'Allas, for wo! Why nere I deed?' " (2.408–09). Pandarus sets Troilus's needs above those of his niece; he does not consider the possibility that Criseyde's acquiescence might jeopardize her already delicate position in Troy. Criseyde alludes to this possibility in her gentle reprimand: "Allas, what sholden straunge to me doon, / Whan he that for my beste frende I wende / Ret me to love, and sholde it me defende?" (2.411–13). Although she expects Pandarus to have her interests at heart and considers him her "beste frende," the feelings are evidently not mutual, for Pandarus's heartfelt concern is directed toward Troilus only. Later, when Pandarus forces her to respond to Troilus's letter she openly accuses him of placing more importance on Troilus's "lust" than on her safety (2.1133–34). Rather than empathizing with Criseyde's fears, Pandarus accuses her once again of "wickedly" bringing about the deaths of Troilus and himself (2.441). Pandarus repeatedly links his fate with Troilus's and Criseyde does not question the veracity of her uncle's claim. In fact, she weighs her personal concerns against Pandarus's fate, considering that her "estat lith in a jupartie" and, at the same time, her uncle's "lif is in balaunce" (2.465–66). By placing Pandarus's situation before her own and not dismissing his fears as a hyperbole of courtly convention, she tacitly recognizes the intense bond between Troilus and Pandarus. In this interaction, the same-sex relationship is privileged not only over the familial one but also over the developing heterosexual one. Although Troilus's love for Criseyde is ostensibly the motivation for Pandarus's coercion of Criseyde, he does not focus on the pleasure she— and Troilus, for that matter—might derive from the relationship; rather, his major concern is to alleviate Troilus's suffering. Thus, a male–male bond, not a heterosexual love affair, dominates this interaction.

The scene at Deiphebus's house illustrates that Troilus and Pandarus's friendship is also privileged over same-sex familial ties. Deiphebus and Helen not only believe that Pandarus is genuinely concerned that "To brynge in prees...myghte don hym [Troilus] harm, / Or hym disesen" (2.1649–50), but also accept his role as caretaker of Troilus—a role that Deiphebus occupies before Pandarus arrives (2.1541–45). In allowing Pandarus to take control of Troilus's well-being in his own home, Deiphebus, Troilus's blood brother who claims to love Troilus above everyone else (2.1410–11), in effect acknowledges that the bond between Troilus and Pandarus is more intimate than that between Troilus and himself.

I want to focus, however, on how Troilus and Criseyde's budding relationship heightens the homoeroticism between Troilus and Pandarus, and how the text seems to foreground the latter. This becomes evident toward the end of book 1: "Whan Troilus hadde herd Pandare assented / To ben his help in lovyng of Cryseyde, / Weex of his wo, as who seith, untormented, / But hotter weex his love, and thus he seyde, / With sobre chere, although his herte pleyde: / 'Now blisful Venus helpe, er that I sterve, / Of the, Pandare, I mowe som thank deserve' " (1.1009–15). Pandarus's promised "*help* in lovyng of Cryseyde" and not Criseyde herself stimulates the "hotter" growth of his love. In addition, rather than asking Venus for her aid in winning Criseyde, he calls on her to assist him in performing a good deed for Pandarus. While one could argue that Troilus has no need of Venus's help in procuring Criseyde because Pandarus fulfills that role, it is remarkable that Troilus not only fails to evoke Criseyde in his request but also turns his "playful" heart and gaze to Pandarus. Although winning Criseyde's love is indeed Troilus's goal, in this passage Troilus's love is directed toward Pandarus.

In the dialogue that follows, Troilus refers to Criseyde but displays increasing affection for his friend: "Tho Troilus gan doun on knees to falle, / And Pandare in his armes hente faste" (1.1044–45). Where would Troilus's mouth be in this position? This erotic moment is situated within a chivalric framework. Troilus's thoughts are not on Criseyde, nor are they focused directly on Pandarus, but rather on military activity that both friends will presumably take part in together. Apparently still kneeling with his arms around Pandarus, he says: "Now, fy on the Grekes alle! / . . .God shal helpe us atte laste; / . . . / And God toforn, lo, som of hem shal smerte" (1.1046–47; 1049). While Criseyde is the catalyst for this expression of male–male intimacy, she is in effect excluded from the world of homosocial affection.

Although Troilus, with Pandarus's help, is poised to become Criseyde's lover, the following words he addresses to Pandarus reveal that quite a different type of bond is being solidified: "thow wis, thow woost, thow maist, thow art al! / Mi lif, my deth, hol in thyn hond I leye" (1.1052–53). Elaine Tuttle Hansen observes that "[t]he homoerotic cast to this scene is intensified not so much when Troilus embraces Pandarus as when he speaks words to Pandarus that are elsewhere directed to the lady, laying his life in Pandarus's hands and seeking his mercy."[7] This scene also tacitly makes a comparison. After expressing his complete submission to Pandarus in courtly language, Troilus goes on to ask Pandarus to recommend him "To hire that to the deth" commands him (1.1056–57). Two parallel relationships are being forged; but the text is not focusing on them equally. In this pivotal scene for the developing heterosexual love story, Criseyde is only an oblique reference whereas Troilus repeatedly addresses Pandarus by name (1.1015; 1030; 1051), thus implying that the friends are facing each other. Moreover, if Troilus is still on his knees with his arms wrapped around Pandarus, which given the fact that the quoted passages directly follow one another is not an unreasonable assumption, then Troilus's words ring very much like a form of marriage proposal—one that combines elements of a vassal's lifelong pledge of loyalty to his lord with that of a courtly lover's submission to his lady.

After Troilus returns home from his triumphant ride through Troy in book 2, he immediately sends for Pandarus to find out if Criseyde has agreed to accept him as her lover. The initial exchange between the two friends in the privacy of Troilus's bedchamber is, I would suggest, sexually charged. Not only is Troilus so excited to see Pandarus that he sends two or three messengers to find him (2.936–37) but also Pandarus is evidently excited to see Troilus. Pandarus "com lepyng in atones" and finding Troilus in bed, teases him mercilessly: "Who hath ben wel ibete / To-day with swerdes and with slynge-stones, / But Troilus, that hath caught hym an hete? /...Lord, so ye swete!" (2.939; 940–43). Pandarus exhibits a sort of sadomasochistic pleasure, observing Troilus in his "beaten" state and punishing him by withholding the news that he so desperately wants to hear. Pandarus's remarks about Troilus's "hete" and sweating suggest that he actually enjoys watching his friend suffer the heat of passion. Pandarus's playful control over Troilus is further illustrated in the mock-formal tone of the last line. Troilus, helplessly dependent on the whims of his friend, defers to him completely: "Do we as the leste" (2.945). Pandarus prolongs Troilus's tension until after dinner when they are in the, presumably dark, seclusion of Troilus's bedchamber. And still he lets Troilus, who "thoughte his herte bledde / For wo, til that he herde som tydynge" (2.950–51), burn in anticipation. The two friends are apparently both in bed and while not necessarily in the same bed they are in such close proximity that Troilus's fidgeting would disturb Pandarus; for he tells Troilus: "Ly stylle and lat me slepe" (2.953).[8] Although Pandarus finally informs him that his "nedes spedde be" (2.954), the text prolongs the tension in that Troilus's reaction to this long-awaited news is deferred for another nineteen lines. Moreover, Troilus's "release" is cloaked in the imagery of springtime awakening: "But right as floures, thorugh the cold of nyght / Iclosed, stoupen on hire stalke lowe, / Redressen hem ayein the sonne bright, / And spreden on hire kynde cours by rowe, / Right so gan tho his eighen up to throwe, / This Troilus, and seyde, 'O Venus deere, / Thi myght, thi grace, yheried be it here'" (2.967–73). While flowers drooping in the cold night seem a more appropriate expression of Troilus's earlier sorrows than of his present heated state, the image of reawakened flowers standing up straight in the warm sunlight suggests not only the literal action of Troilus casting his eyes up to Venus but also the implied rising of his sexual organ.[9] And in this heightened sexual state, Troilus addresses not Criseyde but Pandarus to whom "he held up bothe his hondes, / And seyde, 'Lord, al thyn be that I have'" (2.974–75). While I am not suggesting that Troilus is making a sexual offer to Pandarus, this formal gesture of union occurs within the warm aftermath of Troilus's recent release of tension. He is exuberant, claiming his "herte, / It spredeth so for joie it wol tosterte" (2.979–80). The union is, in a sense, "consummated" in that Troilus and Pandarus spend the entire night together.[10]

Early in book 3, in language strikingly similar to the above pledge he makes to Pandarus, Troilus offers himself completely to Criseyde: "I have / . . . / Ben youres al, God so my soule save, / And shal til that I, woful wight, be grave" (3.100; 102–03). This next step in the developing heterosexual relationship stimulates yet another intimate encounter between Troilus and Pandarus. Immediately after the scene at Deiphebus's house where the lovers speak for the first time and pledge their hearts to each other, "Pandarus, as faste as he may dryve, / To Troilus tho com, as lyne right; / And on a paillet al that glade nyght / By Troilus he lay, with mery chere, / To tale; and wel was hem they were yfeere" (3.227–31). Pandarus does not visit his friend merely to fulfill an obligation. Like the earlier occasion where Pandarus tantalizes Troilus with his news, Pandarus here, too, apparently enjoys Troilus's company—particularly when Troilus's heart is joyful—lying beside him "with mery chere." Noticeably absent from this picture of homosocial intimacy is Criseyde. Although Troilus's recent encounter with Criseyde is ostensibly the reason for Pandarus's visit, the two friends spend a "glade nyght" on adjacent beds (or the same bed?), taking pleasure in *each other's* company.[11]

During this night, Pandarus pledges that he will always be "trewe" to Troilus (3.333), thus balancing the union initiated earlier by Troilus. In addition, Pandarus's assurance that he will make the necessary arrangements for the affair to progress has a powerful physical effect on Troilus—an effect that once again is presented in sexually charged language: "But right so as thise holtes and thise hayis, / That han in wynter dede ben and dreye, / Revesten hem in grene whan that May is, / Whan every lusty liketh best to pleye; / Right in that selve wise, soth to seye, / Wax sodeynliche his herte ful of joie (3.351–56). In the wake of this *sudden* reaction, eroticized because it is situated in the time of year when "every lusty liketh best to pleye," Troilus directs his gaze to Pandarus, whom he promises never to betray. He goes on to swear lifelong devotion to Pandarus: "I wol the serve / Right as thi sclave, whider so thow wende, / For evere more, unto my lyves ende" (3.390–92). Here again the union between Troilus and Pandarus is highlighted immediately following a significant event in the developing relationship between Troilus and Criseyde. A second "consummation" of their bond occurs as the two friends "held hym ech of other wel apayed, / That al the world ne myghte it bet amende" (3.421–22). Moreover, since the two friends get dressed in the morning, they evidently experience this perfect happiness not only in close proximity but also not fully clothed (3.423). And thus two nights of male-male intimacy take place before the heterosexual consummation scene of book 3.

While heterosexual love is ostensibly the dominant subject of book 3—for the book opens with an elaborate invocation to Venus—Troilus's relationship with Pandarus figures prominently in the early and latter portions of the book, serving as sort of homosocial "bookends" for the heterosexual love story. After Troilus returns home from his night of love with Criseyde, he eagerly desires Pandarus's company, sending word for him "to com in al the haste he may" (3.1586). And as on earlier occasions, Troilus expresses his heartfelt gratitude to his friend: "This Troilus, with al th'affeccioun / Of frendes love that herte may devyse, / To Pandarus on knows fil adown" (3.1590–92). It is telling to compare Boccaccio's presentation of this same scene: "Troilo. . . / . . .con disio gli si gittò al collo / . . . / E nella fronte con amor baciollo" [Troilus. . .threw himself upon his (Pandarus's) neck with eagerness. . .and kissed him lovingly on the forehead].[12] Whereas Boccaccio merely describes one friend's exuberant display of affection to the other, Chaucer situates Troilus's response in the context of male–male love. Although Troilus is less physically demonstrative than Troilo, Chaucer offers a more erotically charged scene. Troilus is on his knees as he expresses "al th'affeccioun. . .[o]f frendes love," and while there is no indication that he is embracing Pandarus as he did on an earlier occasion (1.1044–45), the two men are evidently in close proximity with Troilus's gaze directed at Pandarus. He attempts to inform his "alderbeste" friend how much he appreciates him: "though I myght a thousand tymes selle / Upon a day my lif in thi servise, / It myghte naught a moote in that suffise" (3.1601–03). Such "frendes love" cannot be adequately expressed even in the extravagant language of courtly love. The text again links the two relationships: Troilus declares he belongs to Criseyde until he dies (3.1607) followed almost immediately with a pledge to Pandarus that he will be obliged to him for all of his life (3.1612).

Thus, two types of love—"frendes love" and Venerian love—are dramatized in the first three books. Chaucer's text, wittingly or not, privileges the homosocial one. The developing heterosexual relationship creates occasions where Troilus's desire for Criseyde is in effect channeled toward Pandarus. Troilus may be moving closer to consummation with Criseyde but in the meantime he periodically expresses love and affection to his friend. These homoerotically charged encounters are progressive, and by the end of book 3 the two friends have declared their lifelong devotion to each other. The reverse is not true. Although the courtly love story would not advance without Troilus and Pandarus's friendship, the male–male bond does not heighten the heterosexual consummation when it finally occurs in the middle of book 3.

★ ★ ★ ★ ★

Similarly, in *Amys and Amylion* male–male desire competes with heterosexual desire, but here the bond uniting the two main characters proves stronger than marriage. When Amylion must leave Amys in order to take possession of his property, he reminds him of their bond: "Brother, we are trowth-plyght, / Both in word and dede. / Ffro this dai forward ever moo" (24, 5–7). He takes two identical gold cups and gives one to Amys as a "tokne" of their parting (26, 2–12). These cups serve as a sort of wedding ring linking the two together. (Years later when Amylion is suffering from leprosy Amys's recognition of the gold cup leads to the friends' reunion.) It is evident even at this early stage in the story which relationship the text privileges. The sorrow Amys and Amylion experience at their imminent separation, culminating with a farewell kiss "without lesing" [falsehood], occupies seven full stanzas, while the narrator describes in just three lines Amylion's meeting and marriage to an unnamed woman (27, 10–12).

The developing relationship between Amys and Belesaunt, which is given more attention than Amylion's marriage, lacks the emotional intensity and mutual devotion of Amys and Amylion's friendship. Belesaunt is attracted to Amys because he has "the fayrest body" and is "of most honour" (38, 5–6). Given his suitability and her noble status one would expect a typical courtly love story. However, Amys's response to Belesaunt's amorous advances is ambivalent at best. He gives in only after she threatens him: "But thou graunte me my thought, / My love schall be well dere ybought / With peynes hard and strong" (51, 4–6). Before replying to her request that he pledge her his "truth," he thinks to himself: "Yt ys better to graunt here asking / Then thus my lyfe to spylle" (53, 2–3). Unlike a jubilant courtly lover who effusively swears service to his lady, Amys merely says: "as y am trewe knyght, / I schall graunt the thi wyll" (53, 11–12). The narrator does not elaborate on their exchange of oaths but simply states that "plyght here trowthes both twoo" (54, 8). What a contrast with the heartfelt words spoken between Amys and Amylion as they pledged their "truth" to each other!

Amys's rebuff of the steward's offer of friendship highlights the inclusiveness of Amys and Amylion's bond.[13] Amys reaffirms his loyalty and devotion to Amylion: "Ffor onys y plight trouth to that hend, / Where in lond that y wend, / Y schall be to him trewe" (31, 4–6). Amys's belief that he can have only one intimate bond in his life is commensurate with the concept of ideal friendship. The text distinguishes Amys and Amylion's bond not only from other types of male–male relationships but also from heterosexual marriage; in fact, it eroticizes this privileged same-sex bond. Amys expresses his fidelity to Amylion in language typically used by courtly lovers, swearing that he "schall never, be nyght ne day, / Chonge him [Amylion] for no newe" (31, 11–12). In refusing to "chonge" Amylion for someone new, Amys is ruling out the possibility of developing a bond—with a man or woman—that is as intimate as the union he enjoys with Amylion.

Amys's future marriage to Belesaunt is thus not grounded on the same principles of permanence or intensity of devotion as Amys and Amylion's bond.

The text also invites a comparison between Amys and Amylion's union and Amylion's marriage. Although Amylion's wife is aware that her husband has a "brother" about whose safety he is concerned, after Amylion seeks Amys and exchanges places with him, she does not realize that the man sharing her bed is not her husband. Although the two men look very much alike, they are not identical in all ways. Amys is not as good a fighter as Amylion is (otherwise he would not have needed him to take his place in the fight against the steward) and is more naïve—a naivety that Amylion recognizes. For before leaving Amys, he warns him about the potential danger posed by the steward. Apparently Amylion's wife does not know her husband as intimately as Amys does. Her failure to realize that the man with whom she is sharing a bed is not her husband—and the narrator's lack of commentary or surprise at her failure to realize this—suggests a cultural norm in which marriage and ideal homosocial unions operate on different levels of intimacy.

There is a complex, antagonistic interrelation between homosocial and heterosexual desires in *Amys and Amylion*. In contrast to *Troilus and Criseyde*, where growing heterosexual intimacy strengthens a homosocial bond, here a same-sex bond is strengthened as a result of an attack on a heterosexual relationship. When the steward betrays Amys to the Duke, accusing him of having sexual relations with Belesaunt, Amys seeks help from Amylion. The bond between the two friends is thus reinforced at a time when they are both involved in heterosexual relationships. The attack on Amys and Belesaunt's developing love affair fuels male–male intimacy because Amylion risks his life in order to save Amys's and years later when Amys makes a great sacrifice to save Amylion's life, he recalls Amylion's earlier act of fidelity. *Amys and Amylion* also illustrates another form of competition between same-sex and heterosexual desires, whereby the former effects a deterioration of the latter. Amylion's marriage suffers as a result of Amylion's coming to the aid of Amys. Amylion's wife is furious to learn what her husband has done: "[she] ofte mysseid here lorde that nyght, / With spise [contempt] betwene hem two" (122, 2–3). Interestingly, she focuses not on his indiscretion in allowing Amys to take his place in bed but rather on the good deed he performs for his friend's benefit. The narrator, obviously on Amylion's side, comments on the wife's cruelty: "So wikked and schrewed was his wiffe, / Sche brake his herte withoute knyffe, / With wordes hard and kene" (127, 1–3). She later considers his leprosy punishment for this wrongful act.

Finally, *Amys and Amylion* illustrates how the disintegration of a marriage brings about a new homosocial bond and intensifies an existing one. When Amylion's wife exiles the leprous Amylion to a lodge half a mile from the gate, he takes with him only the gold cup. Thus, as Amylion's marriage falls apart, the text draws attention to the homosocial union that still survives. Before Amylion is reunited with Amys, he develops a close relationship with his nephew, Oueys. In striking contrast to the behavior of Amylion's wife, Oueys dedicates himself to Amylion's well-being for three years. Oueys pledges "That he never wold wonde / To serve his lorde, a fote and honde, / While he alyve were" (132, 10–12). This new male–male bond, built upon the ruins of a heterosexual relationship, also leads to greater intimacy between Amys and Amylion. Amys's squire is struck by Ouey's devotion to the gravely ill Amylion, notices the gold cup, and brings both observations to his lord's attention. Amys eventually recognizes Amylion and, in contrast to Amylion's wife's behavior, takes his friend home and cures him by sacrificing his own children. Amys evidently privileges his bond with Amylion over his marriage to Belesaunt—and his relationship to his children—because he does not consult his wife before slaying their children. He tells her afterwards, and instead of rewarding his wife for understanding his desire for committing such a deed, he ultimately leaves her in order to spend his remaining days with Amylion. We are not actually told that Amys leaves his wife; the marriage simply disappears from the text. This romance ends happily for Amys and Amylion's relationship but offers little support for heterosexual unions. The text describes two failed marriages and concludes with an affirmation of the resilience and permanence of male–male desire: Amys and Amylion "Togeder lad thei here lyfe," and when they died, "in on grave thei were leyde" (200, 11; 201, 8).

Troilus and Criseyde and *Amys and Amylion* foreground homosocial intimacy most likely because the cultural milieu within which they arose also did. The male friendships in these texts illustrate some key characteristics of ideal chivalric bonds: namely, fidelity, love, devotion, and permanence (or, at least, an intended permanence). Although both fall short of the perfect friendship extolled in the treatises—Pandarus and Troilus do not engage in mutual acts of selflessness;[14] Amys and Amylion are not always honest—these same-sex relations are presented as serious, emotionally charged bonds. Late medieval chivalric society emphasized and, in fact, depended on strong bonds between men. And like fictional friendships, the "real" ones undoubtedly were not perfect. *Amys and Amylion* and *Troilus and Criseyde* not only affirm male–male intimacy but also suggest that in chivalric societies where heterosexual desire competes with homosocial desire, the latter might be preferred or, at least, not undervalued.

Triangular Configurations of Desire

Examining key moments in three chivalric romances reveals a fluidity—a lack of clearly marked boundaries—between (male) homoerotic and heterosexual desires. René Girard's theory of triangular desire provides a useful methodological tool for studying this dynamics. Girard notes that in Cervantes's *Don Quixote* the title character seeks to imitate Amadis of Gaul, a perfect knight errant. According to Girard, Don Quixote does not choose his own object of desire but rather "pursues objects which are determined for him...by the model of all chivalry." He calls this model figure the "*mediator* of desire."[15] Although the model does not determine the desire of the subject in the texts I am examining, Girard's concept is applicable. The triangular relation outlined by Girard can be represented as follows:

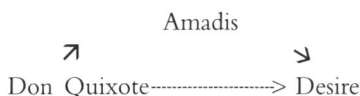

Amadis

Don Quixote----------------> Desire

According to Girard, since Don Quixote is far removed from the legendary Amadis, this is an example of "external mediation," where both subjects do not share the same desire despite the fact that Don Quixote's desire is mediated through his model (Amadis). However, in the case of "internal mediation," the desiring subject and his mediator inhabit the same socio-cultural world thus raising the possibility of "competing desires"; in other words, the subject and his mediator could both desire the same object.[16] Girard goes on to suggest that the mediator could therefore be an obstacle for the subject in that "the impulse toward the object [of desire] is ultimately an impulse toward the mediator; in internal mediation this impulse is checked by the mediator himself since he desires, or perhaps possesses, the object."[17] Although Girard identifies the conflicting feelings of reverence and malice that the subject holds toward his model/mediator as "hatred," I suggest that it could equally be viewed as "love." The two emotions are not necessarily mutually exclusive.[18] Moreover, Girard's observation that in tri-angular desire the desiring subject's movement toward the object of desire involves a simultaneous movement toward the mediator raises the possibil-ity of an erotic attraction between a male subject and his male mediator.

In his study of erotic triangles in Chaucer's "Miller's Tale," Martin Blum observes that "[t]he intricacies of the various bonds existing between both men [John and Nicholas; Nicholas and Absolon] and the woman betray the locations on the erotic triangle not as fixed, but rather as inherently dynamic and unstable demarcations of the interplay between notions of gender, desire, power, and identification, themselves highly contested *loci* in the economy of erotic exchanges."[19] Like Blum, I use the erotic triangle as "a register of instability" to examine how "each new development of the narrative upsets its already precariously unstable balance of gender and desire";[20] however, in my examination of triangular relationships in three chivalric romances, I focus on the unstable dynamics not between masculinity or femininity and desire—how a male character does not always occupy a "masculine" active position—but rather between heterosexual and homoerotic desires. The sequence of events in each narrative, with an accompanying shift in the gender of the mediator/rival in the triangle, illustrates that these two forms of desire are neither stable nor completely independent from each other.

The rivalry between subject and mediator that Girard articulates can be viewed in an oedipal framework. In his discussion of identification among group members, Mikkel Borch-Jacobsen points out that when group members identify with one another "although the identificatory bonds are not in themselves libidinal, the fact remains that they *depend* on the libidinal object bond: just as the little Oedipus identifies with his father *because* he wants to possess the mother, so the members of the group identify among themselves *because* they love the leader."[21] In *Troilus and Criseyde*, Troilus and Pandarus are, in a sense, rivals for King Priam's love. They are both "brotherly" knights serving to protect Troy. Although this rivalry is not acted out in the poem, an oedipal relationship is implied in the chivalric subtext; Pandarus is apparently very close to the royal family—he is a good friend of Deiphebus's (2.1408–14) and even spends a day with Priam without Troilus (5.281–84). According to Freud, feelings of hatred between brotherly rivals can be repressed and transformed into "homosexual love."[22] The implicit rivalry between Troilus and Pandarus for Priam's love informs their bond and thus also the rivalry that is played out during the consummation scene. Freud's and Borch-Jacobsen's observations of the fluidity between brotherly identification or rivalry and homoeroticism offer a psychoanalytical framework for studying the circulation of desire among Troilus, Pandarus, and Criseyde.

For the sake of continuity and because Pandarus initiates and takes an active part in the events leading up to the consummation scene, I examine homoerotic impulses within the triangular movement of desire among Troilus, Criseyde, and Pandarus by focusing on Pandarus as subject of desire. Troilus is—but not in every moment of the scene—the model/mediator/rival through whom Pandarus must pass in order to obtain his object of desire: Troilus's successful consummation with Criseyde. The roles of model and mediator are inextricably linked in a chivalric context; for in identifying with a worthy knight the subject of desire hopes to attain something better (status, pleasure, respect, etc.) than what he already has. Likewise, the roles are linked in Chaucer's text: Troilus serves as a model knight–lover for Pandarus, demonstrating or defining the obtainment of sexual satisfaction that has eluded Pandarus; and, at the same time, he serves as a conduit for

Pandarus's desire, leading him to vicarious sexual pleasure. In the moments I examine, this second function predominates. Girard defines "Proustian homosexuality" as "a gradual transferring to the mediator of an erotic value which in 'normal' Don Juanism remains attached to the object itself." He goes on to explain that this transfer can occur in "the acute stages of internal mediation, characterized by a noticeably increased preponderance of the mediator and a gradual obliteration of the object."[23] A similar "transferring" occurs in Chaucer's text; for at times it appears that Pandarus's mediator/rival is his object of desire. Referring to Girard's concept, Sedgwick notes that the rivals need not both be males, for "*any* relation of rivalry is structured by the same play of emulation and identification."[24] As we shall see, at certain moments, Criseyde, not Troilus, occupies the role of mediator/rival. The series of triangular configurations that delineate Pandarus's relationship to his object of desire as the scene plays out illustrates that homoerotic and heterosexual desires in this cultural context are neither mutually exclusive nor easily distinguishable from each other.

Just before the consummation scene, Pandarus assures Troilus that his desire will be satisfied: "it shal be right as thow wolt desire; / So thryve I, this nyght shal I make it weel" (3.709–10). Pandarus *knows* exactly what Troilus desires because he identifies with Troilus as a courtly lover/knight. Pandarus's emotional—and erotic—investment in the scene is suggested in his impatience with Troilus: "Thow wrecched mouses herte, / Artow agast so that she wol the bite?" (3.736–37). He then leads Troilus into Criseyde's room, holding him "by the lappe" (3.742). The relationship among the three protagonists at this stage can be represented in the following triangle:

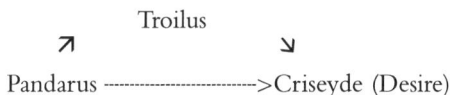

Troilus

↗ ↘

Pandarus ----------------------------->Criseyde (Desire)

Following the Girardian model, Pandarus, in the position of desiring subject, can reach his object of desire, who is not Criseyde herself but rather Troilus's consummation with Criseyde, through his model/mediator (Troilus). Whoever occupies the endpoint in the triangular flow of Pandarus's desire has an eroticized valence. By identifying with his model/ mediator, Troilus, Pandarus vicariously experiences what Troilus does. However, in Girardian terms, Troilus is also a rival, checking Pandarus's impulse toward their shared desired object (Criseyde/consummation). Heterosexual desire (Pandarus's movement toward sharing Troilus's pleasure at the endpoint of the triangle) and homoerotic desire (Pandarus's transferring of his desire to his mediator/rival as a result of internal mediation or the rival's hindrance) compete because they may occur simultaneously.

The diagram is, however, not completely accurate. I agree with Sedg-wick that it is important to consider how gender affects the symmetry of a particular triangular configuration. She observes that "both Girard and Freud (or at least the Freud of this interpretive tradition) treat the erotic triangle as symmetrical—in the sense that its structure would be relatively unaffected by the power difference that would be introduced by a change in the gender of one of the participants."[25] The homosocial bond linking Pandarus to Troilus is not comparable to the heterosexual desire linking Troilus to Criseyde. As I demonstrated earlier, in the scenes leading up to the consummation, the text privileges the homosocial relationship. The following more precisely expresses the relationship among the three protagonists at this point:

Troilus

↗   ↘

Pandarus --------------------------------->Criseyde (Desire)

While the circulation of desire remains the same, this configuration more accurately expresses the relative distances separating Pandarus, Troilus, and Criseyde within the sociocultural framework of the poem. Because the subject and his mediator/rival are in closer proximity than either one is from his object of desire suggests a heightened eroticism/tension between the subject and his mediator/rival.

Before Troilus actually enters the scene, Pandarus, in his attempt to persuade Criseyde to see Troilus immediately, accuses her of not caring about Troilus: "If that ye suffre hym al nyght in this wo, / God help me so, ye hadde hym nevere lief" (3.863–64). She defends herself by revers-ing his accusation: "Hadde I hym nevere lief? by God, I weene / Ye hadde nevere thyng so lief" (3.869–70). Although it is unclear what "thyng" she is accusing him of not holding dear, Pandarus interprets her remark as engaging him in a sort of competition regarding each one's concern for Troilus. He responds that since she has made an "ensaumple" of him, if he is in fact guilty of wishing to see Troilus suffer all night, he renounces any further joy in life (3.872–75). He then attempts to shame her into demonstrating that she likewise would never wish to make Troilus suffer (3.876–82). Since Pandarus needs to convince his niece to receive Troilus at that moment in order to bring about their consummation, Criseyde is here in a sense a mediator for Pandarus's desire. In prodding Criseyde to assume an active role in the proceedings, Pandarus reveals his dependency on her. The actions Criseyde shortly performs on Troilus, in effect, bring Pandarus closer to his desired object—the consummation. The circulation of desire from Pandarus's point of view can thus be represented as follows:

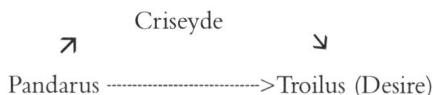

Criseyde

↗   ↘

Pandarus ---------------------------->Troilus (Desire)

In her position as mediator, Criseyde is also an object of identification for Pandarus. In the dialogue just quoted Pandarus draws a parallel with Criseyde regarding their respective relations with Troilus. In addition, he reveals that he has an image of how one who is Troilus's "love" should behave. He situates himself in Criseyde's position by taking the hypothetical role of a lady accused by her jealous lover: "if a fool were in a jalous rage, / I nolde setten at his sorwe a myte, / But feffe hym with a fewe wordes white" (3.899–901). Although his example highlights how "this thyng stant al in another kynde" (3.903), he effects an identification with Criseyde as the accused lady. He also identifies with her as Troilus's beloved, describing Troilus as one who is "so gentil and so tendre of herte" (3.904)—a view *she* should have. In constructing these images for his "model," Pandarus takes more initiative than that of the desiring subject in Girard's description. While not a model knightly lover for Pandarus—as Troilus is when occupying this position—Criseyde is a model figure with whom he identifies at least temporarily; and she is a mediator for the attainment of his desired goal. Following Freud and Girard, we can draw the following scenarios from this triangular configuration: Pandarus's identification with Criseyde could cause him to "assume" her desire for Troilus; or as Pandarus's rival for Troilus/ Desire—and thus an obstruction—his desire could become transferred to her. Each scenario illustrates how undefined the boundary is between homoerotic and heterosexual desires. In the former instance, heterosexual identification could slip into homoerotic desire; in the latter situation, the rivalry that might result in heterosexual desire is based on a preliminary same-sex attraction.[26]

Immediately after Troilus swoons, Pandarus rushes to the bed and takes control of the situation: "he into bed hym [Troilus] caste, / And seyde, 'O thef, is this a mannes herte?' / And of he rente al to his bare sherte" (3.1097–99). By literally throwing Troilus into bed and stripping him to his bare shirt, Pandarus appears ready to rape Troilus. At this moment, Troilus serves as both mediator and endpoint of Pandarus's desire. In Girardian terms, this is an illustration of "Proustian homosexuality," whereby the mediator becomes erotically cathected. Two points of the triangle thus collapse together and only the two men are interacting. But Pandarus immediately brings Criseyde into the scene: "Nece but ye help *us* now, / Allas, youre owen Troilus is lorn" (3.1100–01; emphasis added). Pandarus and Criseyde both attempt to revive Troilus: "Therwith his pous and paumes of his hondes / They gan to frote, and wete his temples tweyne" (3.1114–15). Troilus, who is lying in bed wearing nothing but his "bare sherte," is acted upon equally by both. This moment can be represented as two parallel, unobstructed streams of desire—one homoerotic, the other heterosexual. Reviving Troilus is the immediate goal for Pandarus as well as for Criseyde; and both the action itself and the endpoint are erotically informed. But this interaction may also be delineated in two parallel triangular configurations. Although I have been examining the scene from Pandarus's point of view exclusively, in order to understand better the competing desires at work here it is necessary to also consider Criseyde as subject of desire. Both Criseyde and Pandarus are here actively pursuing the same object of desire: namely, Troilus's regaining of consciousness. Because they depend on each other's actions, they are mediators for each other's desire, best illustrated in two triangles:

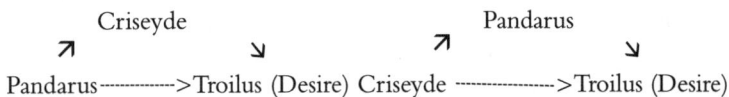

Criseyde   Pandarus

↗   ↘   ↗   ↘

Pandarus----------->Troilus (Desire) Criseyde -------------->Troilus (Desire)

They are also rivals, "competing" with each other for the same desired object. This interaction illustrates four synchronic movements of desire: the potential transferring of a (hetero)erotic value to the mediator/rival (from Pandarus to Criseyde and, likewise, from Criseyde to Pandarus) as well as two impulses—one heterosexual, one homoerotic—from the mediator to the object.

The dynamics soon alter and Pandarus and Criseyde are no longer equally acting on Troilus. Criseyde "ofte hym [Troilus] kiste; and shortly for to seyne, / Hym to revoken she did al hire peyne; / And at the laste, he gan his breth to drawe" (3.1117–19). The text here privileges Criseyde as subject of desire, for it is her actions that are most effective in reviving Troilus. However, since Pandarus is the director of the entire scene, we return to his point of view. Criseyde is still the mediator of Pandarus's desire. By bringing Troilus back to life, she is enabling him to reach his desired goal (the consummation).[27] Following Girard's concept, the mediator is also a model for the subject of desire. Pandarus identifies with Criseyde not as a model knight–lover but simply as a model lover actively pursuing their shared goal. The scene is homoerotically charged. Standing very close to Criseyde as she kisses Troilus, Pandarus is vicariously—through his model/mediator—performing these actions as well.[28] Criseyde continues to occupy this position during the initial moments after Troilus awakens, facilitating the consummation: "therwithal hire arm over hym [Troilus] she leyde, / And al

foryaf, and ofte tyme hym keste" (3.1128–29). And after dismissing Troilus's
(false) accusation that she was unfaithful, she jokingly threatens to beat him:
"Wol ye the childissh jalous contrefete? / Now were it worthi that ye were
ybete" (3.1168–69). Her threat has a sexualized valence despite being
cloaked in the image of beating a naughty child because Troilus is lying
undressed in her bed as she utters it. Poised to act—possibly sexually—upon
Troilus, Criseyde is clearly at this moment Pandarus's model/mediator.[29]

After Criseyde assumes a more passive role, asking Troilus to forgive her
(3.1182–83), Troilus takes the initiative: "This Troilus, with blisse of that
supprised, / . . . / . . .and sodeynly avysed, / He hire in armes faste to hym
hente" (3.1184; 1186–87). The circulation of desire changes accordingly to:

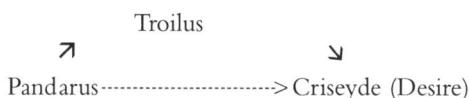

Troilus

↗   ↘

Pandarus ··············docin·········--> Criseyde (Desire)

From Pandarus's position, Troilus takes a major step toward effecting the
consummation; and thus Pandarus's vicarious pleasure is closer to being
realized. Pandarus is in a sense linked with Troilus's actions. In the very next
line, "Pandarus with a ful good entente / Leyde hym to slepe" (3.1188–89).
His work completed, Pandarus can leave the bedroom scene; his
model/mediator is finally positioned to reap the rewards—rewards that he,
too, will somehow enjoy.[30] The return of the circulation of desire to this
configuration at the end of a series of interactions among the three protagonists suggests that Pandarus's homoerotically charged desire is the
motivating force for the entire scene. For in this configuration, with Troilus
as model/mediator/rival for Pandarus, three homoerotic scenarios are possible: Pandarus's identification with his model knight–lover may slip into
desire for him; or as a result of internal mediation, he may transfer an erotic
value to his mediator (Girard's concept of "Proustian homosexuality"); or
his rivalry with his model/mediator for the same desired object/goal may
effect a (homo)eroticization. Yet, the previous shifts in the gender of the
model/mediator/rival demonstrate that in triangular configurations neither
homoerotic nor heterosexual desire flows directly from subject to object.

★ ★ ★ ★ ★

The competing dynamics between homoerotic and heterosexual desires are
quite differently expressed in *Sir Gawain and the Green Knight* and Chaucer's
"Knight's Tale." My examination of triangulated desire in *Sir Gawain* focuses
on Gawain, Bertilak, and the lady in Fitt 3. Claude Lévi-Strauss's description
of kinship systems is useful for articulating the interrelationships among

these three characters. Gayle Rubin, in "The Traffic in Women," explains that Lévi-Strauss "sees the essence of kinship systems to lie in an exchange of women between men," resulting, in the case of marriage, of kinship being established between two men. Thus, "[t]he exchange partners have become affines, and their descendents will be related by blood" while the woman is merely "a conduit of a relationship [between men] rather than a partner to it."[31] *Sir Gawain* offers an odd dramatization of Lévi-Strauss's theory in that the exchange partners are Bertilak and the lady, and Gawain is the exchanged gift. The actual marriage between Bertilak and the lady is not emphasized in the text; what is important, however, is their partnership, and it is through Gawain that their partnership is maintained. Rubin goes one step further than Lévi-Strauss and maintains that "the social organization of sex rests upon gender, obligatory heterosexuality, and the constraint of female sexuality."[32] *Sir Gawain* disrupts all three principles of the social organization of sex in that it posits a married couple as equal exchange partners, a biological male as the "exchanged goods," and implies homosexuality—or, at least homoerotic desire—in the transposition of the kiss.

Bertilak and Gawain pledge a solemn oath to exchange the day's winnings with each other. Thus, at the end of the first day, Bertilak gives Gawain the game he caught and Gawain in turn "hasppes his [Bertilak's] fayre hals his armes wythinne, / and kysses hym as comlyly as he couthe awyse."[33] Particularly striking is that Gawain repeats the body language of the lady kissing him: "Ho comes nerre with that, and caches hym in armes, / Loutes luflych adoun and the leude kysses" (1305–06). This parallel holds true on the second and third days as well. Drawing on Foucault's argument that in Western cultures since the eighteenth century the increased discourse on sex has produced something like an *ars erotica* with its accompanying pleasure, Geraldine Heng asks: "if speaking about sex brings a quotient of pleasure very like or coeval with sexual pleasure, might not the speaking itself instance a type of sexual practice?" Heng answers yes and suggests that if speech does not merely substitute for sex but rather *is* sex itself, then in *Sir Gawain* sex does in fact take place between Gawain and the lady.[34] What does this imply about the kisses Gawain gives Bertilak? If we agree with Heng that a form of sex transpires between Gawain and the lady—the kisses she gives him being the culmination of their sexually informed "luf-talkyng"—and assuming that Gawain is true to his oath, then the kisses he gives Bertilak are sexually charged as well. David Boyd rightly points out that "the hugs and kisses he receives from the Lady and later gives to Bertilak each night are not the original kisses but rather his own which mimick [*sic*], replace, and substitute for them."[35] And there is a notable progression in intensity. On the third day, Gawain "acoles. . .the knyght and kysses hym thryes, / As saverly and sadly as he hem sette couthe" [with as much relish and vigour as he could muster] (1936–37).[36]

The circulation of desire among the three characters can be represented in three different triangles. Since Bertilak admits in Fitt 4 that he has orchestrated the temptation scenes, we can reread the exchange of kisses in Fitt 3 with this knowledge. The following configuration delineates the circulation of desire in the three bedroom scenes:

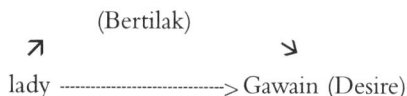

$$\begin{array}{ccc} & \text{(Bertilak)} & \\ \nearrow & & \searrow \\ \text{lady} \dashrightarrow & \longrightarrow & \text{Gawain (Desire)} \end{array}$$

The lady occupies the subject position pursuing her object of desire, Gawain. Bertilak serves as the mediator of the lady's desire. I place him in parentheses because, unlike the mediator in *Troilus and Criseyde*, he is not physically present in the bedroom scenes. Yet, as orchestrator of the scheme, he facilitates his wife's pursuit of Gawain. Following Girard's concept, Bertilak is also his wife's rival. Being absent, he is unable to hinder the circulation, and thus the lady's desire cannot "get stuck" on her mediator. However, because Bertilak desires that his wife tempt Gawain—and, as I will demonstrate shortly, he enjoys the result of her actions—his desire and that of his wife compete with each other; they are both directed toward the same object. The circulation of desire here is therefore not exclusively heterosexual. Despite the fact that the bedroom scenes take place between a male and female only, Bertilak's mediation—and his own desire—adds a homoerotic dimension that is inextricably linked to the heterosexual "luftalkyng."[37]

The scenes where Gawain bestows kisses on Bertilak can be illustrated in the following triangle:

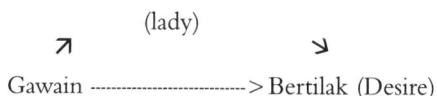

$$\begin{array}{ccc} & \text{(lady)} & \\ \nearrow & & \searrow \\ \text{Gawain} \dashrightarrow & \longrightarrow & \text{Bertilak (Desire)} \end{array}$$

Gawain is here in the subject position because he in a sense pursues Bertilak, who is at these moments his desired object. For on each occasion, Gawain approaches Bertilak to give him the kisses. The public forum for Gawain's acts illustrate the cultural normativity of one knight expressing affection for another. Since the narrative leads us to believe that Gawain fully lives up to his oath to offer Bertilak whatever he wins during the day, the kisses he gives him are equal to those he receives from the lady. By dismissing the eroticism of the male–male kisses, one also dismisses the sexual valence of the lady's kisses. Nonetheless, the scene is not exclusively homoerotic. The lady's role as absent mediator must not be overlooked. If she had not kissed Gawain he would have had no winnings to pass on to Bertilak.

The fact that Gawain is passing on to Bertilak the essence of the kisses he received from the lady renders these kisses *both* heterosexually *and* homo-erotically charged. Unlike the previous configuration, the subject and mediator are not competing for the same object; rather, Gawain's homo-erotic act is mediated by and inextricably linked to the previous hetero-sexual interaction.

Finally, I offer the following triangle to represent the entire series of inter-actions among Bertilak, Gawain, and the lady, from Bertilak's point of view:

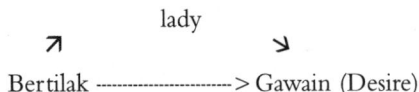

$$\text{lady}$$
$$\nearrow \qquad\qquad \searrow$$
$$\text{Bertilak} \text{---------} > \text{Gawain (Desire)}$$

As the mastermind behind the lady's attempted seduction of Gawain, Bertilak is clearly the subject of desire. He does not pursue Gawain directly; he in effect attempts to seduce him through the actions of his wife. While I am not suggesting that the text offers any indication that Bertilak desires Gawain sexually, Gawain is Bertilak's object of desire in the sense that he desires that Gawain be subjected to his wife's seductive maneuvers; and Bertilak derives an erotically charged pleasure in the outcome. At the end of each exchange of winnings, Bertilak and Gawain bond with each other. For instance, after the first exchange, "Thay laghed and made hem blythe" and later that evening "thay *lovelych* leghten leve at the last" (1398; 1410; emphasis added). The lady brilliantly illustrates the role of mediator; she even performs Bertilak's seduction for him! This triangular configuration delineates the interlinking forces of Bertilak's homoerotic desire that informs his test of Gawain's "truth" and the lady's heterosexual desire, which carries out that test.[38]

Chaucer's "Knight's Tale" also illustrates the inextricable connections between eroticized homosociality and heterosexual desire in a chivalric romance. Girard's concept of "internal mediation," whereby the desiring subject and his mediator/model may be rivals for the same object, is keenly observed here. Palamon and Arcite are mediators/models for each other. They are mediators in that each one stimulates the other's desire for Emelye. After Palamon is struck by the sight of Emelye in the garden and tells Arcite about it, Arcite looks and is likewise struck. Each knight's desire spirals as a result of the other's insistence that he is more justified in loving Emelye. Palamon and Arcite are also in a sense models for each other. They are chivalric brothers who are "Ysworn ful depe" to help each other in every situation until death should part them.[39] Each knight therefore expects the other one to live up to the chivalric ideal of "truth." Although they both fall short of this ideal, each one is potentially a model knight. Because the tale is built on a foundation of chivalric brotherhood, there is a possibility—increasingly remote as the tale continues—that one of the knights will give in and support his "brother's" pursuit of Emelye. The following triangular configurations illustrate the circulation of desire at this stage of the tale:

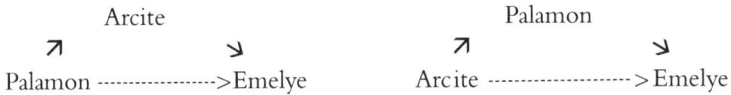

<pre>
        Arcite   Palamon
    ↗   ↘   ↗   ↘
Palamon ·············>Emelye   Arcite ··············· > Emelye
</pre>

The slight asymmetry of each triangle reflects the sociocultural privileging of (ideal) bonds between knights over that between a knight and his beloved lady. Each subject's movement toward his object of desire leads him first toward his mediator/model who, more clearly than in *Troilus and Criseyde* and *Sir Gawain*, is a rival. The fight scene in the second section of the tale suggests the eroticized valence of their rivalry. Each subject's "passing through" his loved/hated rival involves intense physical contact with him: "As wilde bores gonne they to smyte, / That frothen whit as foom for ire wood. / Up to the ancle foghte they in hir blood" (I.1658–60). The knights' frenzied attempts to eliminate each other are driven by their shared object of desire; but she is absent from the scene. According to Girard, in extreme situations of internal mediation—as this is since both knights are social equals and, moreover, related to each other—a transfer of desire from the object to the mediator/rival may occur. At this moment, Arcite and Palamon become erotically cathected objects for each other. The "obliteration" of the desired object, Emelye, is only temporary, however. Emelye's appearance—and the first direct interaction among Palamon, Arcite, and Emelye—reaffirms that heterosexual desire informs the rivalry. The desire circulating from subject to object in each triangle is thus neither exclusively heterosexual nor homoerotic but rather a confluence of the two.

Theseus then steps in and complicates the triangular configuration. He forgets his initial anger at the two knights for fighting illegally and identifies with them since he himself once suffered the pain of love. He even wishes to forge a bond of friendship with them: "And ye shul bothe anon unto me swere / That nevere mo ye shal my contree dere, / Ne make werre upon me nyght ne day, / But been my freendes in all that ye may" (1.1821–24). With the promise of Palamon and Arcite's friendship, Theseus sets the terms for settling their rivalry. In declaring that he will give Emelye to the knight who wins the tournament (1.1860), Theseus positions himself directly within the triangular configuration. Two versions of this scenario can be represented as follows:

$$\text{Arcite} \qquad\qquad \text{Palamon}$$
$$\nearrow \qquad \searrow \qquad\qquad \nearrow \qquad \searrow$$

Palamon ----------> Theseus→Emelye   Arcite ------------> Theseus→Emelye

As in the previous configurations, Palamon and Arcite are mediators/rivals for each other. Each knight must move through/eliminate the other in order to reach his object of desire. These two scenarios are to be resolved in the eroticized venue of the tournament. In her discussion of the "Love Day" tournament of 1458—a temporary truce in the War of the Roses—Patricia Ingham observes that when an event such as this "mingles, however awkwardly, the serious business of stagecraft, strategy, and violence with the delights of chivalric spectacle, it places violent power in relation to delight and desire."[40] She suggests that not only the spectators but also the knights carrying out violent acts experience "delight and desire."[41] In the spectacular tournament Theseus organizes, Arcite and Palamon repeatedly attack each other: "Ful ofte a day han thise Thebanes two / Togydre ymet, and wroght his felawe wo; / Unhorsed hath ech oother of hem tweye" (I.2623–25). The narrator offers the images of an angry tiger whose cub was stolen and a lion mad with hunger to describe the passionate intensity with which each knight attacks his rival (I.2630–33). That neither one gives up suggests that both knights find pleasure in fighting this protracted struggle to the end. Moreover, Palamon and Arcite are driven by their competing desires for Emelye. She is, however, only obtained through Theseus. Palamon and Arcite's heterosexual desire passes through two homoeroticized stages: In order for Palamon to reach his ultimate desired object he must first negotiate the love/hate of his mediator/rival, Arcite, and then satisfy the conditions set down by Theseus. The same is true for Arcite. Theseus is thus positioned as the *immediate* object of desire for each knight. Even after the tournament is over, the winner's continued "courtship" of Theseus is implicitly imperative for eventually obtaining Emelye. This scenario, like all of the triangular configurations I have examined, reveals a dynamics of desire not easily contained within exclusively same-sex or heterosexist spheres.

Amys and Amylion, "The Knight's Tale," *Sir Gawain,* and *Troilus and Criseyde* illustrate not only the inextricable link—or competition—between eroticized homosociality and heterosexual desire but also the normative impulse of male–male intimacy. The scenarios I have outlined where heterosexual desire is somehow infused with homoeroticism alert us to the limited usefulness of modern categories of desire. These texts dramatize nuances of attraction—between characters both of the same sex and of the opposite sex. All four romances also present cultural milieus where heterosexuality is not necessarily the dominant form of desire.

CHAPTER 4

HOMOEROTIC IDENTIFICATIONS

In chivalric texts, whether chronicles, treatises, or romances, the narrator frequently describes an exemplary knight, implicitly inviting the reader/listener to imagine him.[1] These texts motivate male readers who are novice knights—or who are merely enthusiastic spectators of knightly endeavors—to identify with model figures.[2] Thus, inextricably linked to the discourse in chivalric texts celebrating the ideal qualities and successful exploits of perfectly built knights is one that engages the reader to identify with an imagined exemplary knight. Moreover, since chivalric texts often describe model knights in action, readers are prompted to imagine scenarios in which they in effect participate. Medieval theories of the imagination suggest that the mental images constructed and viewed by the mind's eye can be quite vivid and potentially erotic.

Reading and Imagination

Thomas Aquinas, commenting on Aristotle's concept of memory in *De anima*, draws attention to the vividness of mental images and the ease with which they are brought forth: "Images can arise in us at will, for it is in our power to make things appear, as it were, before our eyes—golden mountains, for instance, or anything else we please, as people do when they recall past experiences and form them at will into imaginary pictures."[3] He also suggests that such mental imagining is a pleasurable activity willfully undertaken. According to Carolyn Collette, "[m]edieval theology and psychology both maintained that the mind could control what the eyes see and what the inner sight visualizes in the form of images and intentions recalled from memory."[4] She also points out that "[t]heories of medieval faculty psychology, stressing the creative nature of *phantasy*, simultaneously stressed the need to control that creative power, to make it subservient to reason."[5] This anxiety suggests that creative imaginings could be emotionally—or, even, erotically—charged. Aristotle maintains that the imagined, remembered object is independent of the original one: "One must...conceive the image in us to be something in its own right and to be of another thing. In so far, then, as it is something in its own right, it is an object of contemplation or an image. But in so far as it is of another thing, it is a sort of copy and a reminder."[6] The mental image thus has a life of its own and it might reflect the emotional state of the viewer at the time of recollection.

In *De trinitate*, Augustine explains how he visualizes places both seen and not seen previously:

> Et Carthaginem quidem cum eloqui uolo, apud me ipsum quaero ut eloquar, et apud me ipsum inuenio phantasiam Carthaginis. Sed eam per corpus accepi, id est per corporis sensum quoniam praesens in ea corpore fui et eam uidi atque sensi memoriaque retinui.... Sic et Alexandriam cum eloqui uolo quam numquam uidi praesto est apud me phantasma eius. Cum enim a multis audissem et credidissem magnam esse illam urbem sicut mihi narrari potuit, finxi animo imaginem eius quam potui...atque ipsam intuens in animo meo, id est imaginem quasi picturam eius.

> [And in fact when I wish to speak of Carthage, I seek for what to say within myself, and find an image of Carthage within myself; but I received this through the body, that is, through the sense of the body, since I was present there in the body, and have seen and perceived it with my senses, and have retained it in my memory.... So, too, when I wish to speak of Alexandria which I have never seen, an image of it is also present within me. For I had heard from many people and believed that it is a great city; so in accordance with the description that could be given me, I formed an image of it in my mind as I was able...[and] I gazed upon it in my mind, that is, upon the image as if it were a picture of it.][7]

Steven Kruger elaborates on this creative process, noting how viewers draw on memories to construct images of unfamiliar objects: "In the absence of an actual body, its image can be recalled from memory, and such remembered images can be combined to create composite pictures—conjectural likenesses of bodies that exist but that have never been seen, or even likenesses of non-existent bodies."[8] Augustine notes elsewhere that under certain circumstances images could be lifelike: "Cum autem vel nimia cogitationis intentione, vel aliqua vi morbi, ut phreneticis per febrem accidere solet, vel commixtione cujusquam alterius spiritus seu mali seu boni, its corporalium rerum in spiritu exprimuntur imagines, tanquam ipsis corporis sensibus corpora praesententur" [it may sometimes be that by an excessive application of thought, or by the influence of some disorder...or by the agency of some other spirit, whether good or evil, the images of bodies are produced in the spirit just as if bodies were present to the senses of the body].[9] Augustine's observation can be applied to any act of concentrated thought that is motivated by a strong desire to see something or someone.

Augustine gives additional examples of how a reader/listener may respond to a text: "Quis enim legentium uel audientium quae scripsit apostolus Paulus uel quae de illo scripta sunt non fingat animo et ipsius apostoli faciem et omnium quorum ibi nomina commemorantur" [For who, upon reading or listening to the writings of Paul the Apostle, or of those which have been written about him, does not draw a picture in his mind of the countenance of the Apostle himself, and of all those whose names are there mentioned].[10] In claiming that anyone can engage in this imaginative process Augustine suggests that special skills are not needed in order to visualize textual subjects. He also addresses the idea of reading visually in a letter to Nebridius, noting that we form a mental image "qualia figuramus cum legimus historias, et cum fabulosa vel audimus vel componimus vel suspicamur" [when we picture a situation while a narrative is being read, or while we hear or compose or conjecture some fabulous tale].[11] He offers a specific example: "Ego enim mihi ut libet atque ut occurrit animo, Aeneae faciem fingo, ego Medeae cum suis anguibus alitibus junctis jugo" [When it pleases me or when it comes to my mind, I can picture to myself the appearance of Aeneas, or of Medea with winged serpents yoked to her chariot].[12] Later writers also describe reading/listening as a visual process. When Richart de Fournival, writing in the mid-thirteenth century, refers to the "painture" of a text he is speaking of *both* the illustrated image in the manuscript *and* the mental image that the text prompts readers/listeners to conjure in their minds: "Car quant on voit painte une estoire, ou de Troies ou d'autre, on voit les fais des preudommes ki cha en ariere furent, ausi com s'il fussent present. Et tout ensi est il de parole. Car quant on ot .i. romans lire, on entent les aventures, ausi com on les veïst en present" [When one sees painted a story, whether of Troy or something else, one sees those noble deeds which were done in the past exactly as though they were still present. And it is the same thing with hearing a text, for when one hears a story read aloud, listening to the events one sees them in the present].[13] All of these examples demonstrate that readers may freely construct vivid mental images of subjects or scenarios never physically observed.

According to Augustine, mental images formed while reading/listening are in some way based on memory: "Ita fit ut omnis qui corporalia cogitat, siue ipse aliquid confingat, siue audiat aut legat uel praeterita narrantem uel futura praenuntiantem, ad memoriam suam recurrat" [everyone who conceives corporeal things, whether he himself forms an image of them or whether he hears or reads what someone relates about the past or foretells about the future, returns to his memory].[14] By insisting that memories derived from corporeal vision are the foundation upon which a reader constructs a new image, Augustine leaves open the possibility that emotions—or even an attraction—a reader felt toward the original object may inform the imagined one. Augustine acknowledges that images formed while reading/listening are not identical to those that are stored in the mind: "uisiones tamen illae cogitantium ex his quidem rebus quae sunt in memoria, sed tamen innumerabiliter atque omnino infinite multiplicantur atque uariantur" [the visions which take place in thought are drawn, it is true, from those things which are in the memory, yet they are multiplied and varied innumerably and altogether infinitely].[15] He elaborates on the process of creating new images out of remembered ones: "Sed quia praeualet animus non solum oblita uerum etiam non sensa nec experta confingere ea quae non exciderunt augendo, minuendo, commutando, et pro arbitrio componendo" [But because the mind possesses the great power of forming images, not only of things that it has forgotten, but also of those that it has not felt or experienced, while enlarging, diminishing, changing, or arranging at its pleasure those things which have not slipped away].[16] A newly evolved image may trigger off emotions more intense than those generated by the original physical sighting. Readers can exercise their will to fashion new images depending on what they wish to see/experience, piecing together different remembered images into new, improved, ideal images that may in turn attract them passionately.

Augustine describes the vivid intensity of inner vision:

> Voluntas. . .si ad interiorem phantasiam tota confluxerit atque a praesentia corporum quae circumiacent sensibus atque ab ipsis sensibus corporis animi aciem omnino auerterit, atque ad eam quae intus cernitur imaginem penitus conuerterit, tanta offunditur similitudo speciei corporalis expressa ex memoria ut nec ipsa ratio discernere sinatur utrum foris corpus ipsum uideatur an intus tale aliquid cogitetur.

> [But if that will. . .concentrates exclusively on that inner phantasy and turns the mind's eye completely away from the bodies which surround the senses and from the bodily senses themselves, and turns entirely to that image which it sees within itself, then it comes upon so striking a likeness of the bodily species, expressed from the memory, that not even reason itself can distinguish whether the body itself is seen without, or something of the kind thought within.][17]

In the same paragraph, he relates a remarkable example of vivid imaging: "Et memini me audisse a quodam quod tam expressam et quasi solidam speciem feminei corporis in cogitando cernere soleret ut ei se quasi misceri sentiens etiam genitalibus flueret" [I remember once hearing a man say that it was usual with him to see the form of a woman's body so vividly and as it were so solidly in his thoughts that he would as good as feel himself copulating with her and seed would even flow from his genitals].[18] This example of a man habitually experiencing an orgasm as a result of his viewing a mental image demonstrates that visualization potentially can be erotic.

Likewise, might a novice knight—or even a man who simply has a passion for chivalry—reading or listening to a chivalric text conjure up a homoerotically charged image of a model knight whom he desires to be like? *The Life of the Black Prince* stresses ideal qualities that all knights should strive for. The Chandos Herald's intense admiration for the Black Prince—and the implication that readers should likewise admire him—is evident: "cils frans Princes dont je vous dy, / Depuis le jour que il nasquy / Ne pensa fors que loiaute, / ffranchise, valour et bonte / Et se fu garniz de proece" [the noble prince of whom I speak never, from the day of his birth, thought of anything but loyalty, noble deeds, valour and goodness, and was endowed with prowess].[19] The narrator's repetition of "si" before each chivalric virtue suggests his attraction to the subject of his narrative: "Si preus, si hardis, si vaillanz / Et si courtois et si sachanz" [so noble, bold, and valiant, so courteous and so sage].[20] Similarly, Charny invites his readers to envision a handsome, valiant knight like Judas Maccabeus: "il fu preudoms…il fu fors, appers et penibles; il fu beaus entre touz autres…il fu preux, hardis, vaillans et bien combatens" [he was a man of worth…he was strong, skillful, and unrelenting in effort and endurance; he was handsome above all others…he was full of prowess, bold, valiant, and a great fighter].[21] Some male readers prompted by the narrators' enthusiasm may build a vivid, desirable image, drawing on remembered images of knights they have seen. They may engage in a mental process similar to that of Januarie in Chaucer's "Merchant's Tale," who views a parade of images of potential wives in his mind: "Many fair shap and many a fair visage / Ther passeth thurgh his herte nyght by nyght, / As whoso took a mirour, polisshed bryght, / And sette it in a commune market-place, / Thanne sholde he se ful many a figure pace / By his mirour; and in the same wyse / Gan Januarie inwith his thoght devyse / Of maydens whiche that dwelten hym bisyde."[22] Like Januarie, who "shops" for an image that most excites his desire by drawing forth pictures of women of the town, a motivated knight/reader might scan through remembered images of knights, choosing one whom he enthusiastically wishes to emulate. While the goals of Januarie's and the knight's endeavors are different, both processes are erotically informed because in each case the imaginer is seeking a superlative, compelling image.

This process is not merely one of matching a remembered image with a description in a text, however. Neither the Chandos Herald nor Charny gives a precise physical description of a model knight, and thus the reader is left to construct an ideal image based on the vague details provided; he must imagine another male—a perfectly built knight—whom he, consciously or not, desires to be. Particularly for novice knights striving to become model figures themselves, this imaginative reading process can be erotically charged because in order to create an image of a superlative knight, the reader must imagine what a man demonstrating "splendid bearing," handsomeness, physical strength, endurance, and prowess might look like.[23] He must not only hunt through remembered images but also, as Augustine explains, alter these images—enhance them—to suit his taste. This individualized image upon which the reader focuses his inner gaze is thus colored by desire.

Identifying with a (Desired) Knight

Recent psychoanalytical theory has been concerned with the process by which a subject is constructed through identification with desired images. In her influential and often commented upon essay, "Visual Pleasure and Narrative Cinema," Laura Mulvey offers a rigorous psychoanalytical read-ing of cinema spectatorship. She draws on Freud's concept of scopophilia, pointing out that Freud originally defined it as a sexual drive operating independently of the erotogenic zones whereby the observer takes "other people as objects, subjecting them to a controlling and curious gaze."[24] Mulvey adds that Freud considered this gaze to be erotically charged, bringing pleasure to the observer—a pleasure likewise enjoyed by the cinema spectator: "[t]he cinema satisfies a primordial wish for pleasurable looking, but it also goes further, developing scopophilia in its narcissistic aspect."[25] She maintains that "[t]he conventions of mainstream film focus attention on the human form.... [C]uriosity and the wish to look intermingle with a fascination with likeness and recognition."[26] Spectators thus derive pleasure from gazing at an image with whom they identify—someone like them, yet also someone more attractive, powerful, or sexually dynamic whom they wish to be. Mulvey delineates three gazes in associa-tion with films: "that of the camera as it records the profilmic event, that of the audience as it watches the final product, and that of the characters at each other within the screen illusion."[27] We can isolate three corresponding gazes in chivalric texts: that of the external narrator at characters in the text; that of the reader at characters in the text; and that of characters at each other. I take up the first two here and the third in chapter 5.

Mulvey, following Freud's bifurcation of desire and identification—desire for someone of the opposite sex and identification with someone of the same sex—describes the two types of pleasurable looking promoted by conventional films: "The first, scopophilic, arises from pleasure in using another person as an object of sexual stimulation through sight. The second, developed through narcissism and the constitution of the ego, comes from identification with the image seen."[28] Mulvey argues that in mainstream cinema, "the male figure cannot bear the burden of sexual objectification. Man is reluctant to gaze at his exhibitionist like."[29] Paul Willemen justly questions Mulvey's claim by pointing out that, according to Freud, the scopophilic instinct is originally directed at one's own body and only later displaced to another object. Willemen argues that "[i]f scopophilic pleasure relates primarily to the observation of one's sexual like (as Freud suggests), then the two looks distinguished by Mulvey are in fact varieties of one single mechanism: the repression of homosexuality." He concludes that a male spectator identifying with a male character could at the same time gaze *at* the male hero, which would "be a substantial source of gratification for a male viewer."[30] Likewise, Steve Neale, summarizing D. N. Rodowick, maintains that "the [narcissistic] male image can involve an eroticism, since there is always a constant oscillation between the image as a source of identification, and as an other, a source of contemplation."[31] The actor on the screen is not an exact copy of the spectator but likely someone the spectator desires to be.

The distinction between active scopophilia and identification collapses in situations where the spectator is gay. Earl Jackson cogently analyzes how a gay male spectator may respond to a male character in a film: "The gay male spectator...regularly identifies with the figure he sexually objectifies. In other words, he experiences a coalescence of drives that are radically dichotomized in his heterosexual male counterpart. For the gay male spectator, the pleasure of looking at the male object of desire potentially merges with an erotic identification with that object; scopophilia and identification become interanimating components of a specifically ego-erotic subjectivity."[32] Drawing on Freud's theory regarding the primordial autoeroticism of the scopophilic instinct, Teresa de Lauretis further articulates the eroticism informing a same-sex spectatorial interaction: "the film would address the spectator as a subject of its fantasy in its different levels and forms, would provide at once the fantasy and the means of access to it, would make a place for the spectator as subject in its fantasy, by the solicitation of her 'primordial' autoerotic and scopophilic instinct in its reflexive form."[33] The spectator viewing the film scenario as a fantasy thus becomes both subject and object—the object being a projection of the subject. While I am not suggesting that male readers of chivalric texts necessarily respond to male figures as gay men would, the above analyses are relevant for exploring the homoerotics of reading/imagining model knights. In a late medieval chivalric context characterized in part by normative male–male intimacy, there would be no social mechanism inhibiting same-sex scopophilia. That identification and scopophilia are interlinking processes explains why narrators in chivalric texts at times seem attracted to the male characters they are describing. And because the reader, prompted by the narrator, gazes at a figure that he himself imagines, he is engaged in a potentially eroticized narcissistic act.

In the *Prose Lancelot*, the narrator gazes intently at the youthful Lancelot:

> Et les espaules furent lees & hautes a raison. Et le pis teil que en nul cors ne trouast on ne si large ne si gros ne si espes...& li brac furent lonc & droit. Et bien furent furni par le tor desos...les mains furent de dame tout droitement. se li doit fussent vn poi plus menu. Et des rains & des hanches ne vous poroit nus dire que len les peust miex deuiser en nul cheualier. Droites ot les cuisses & les iambes & voltis les pies. Ne nus ne fu onques plus drois en son estant.

> [his shoulders were broad and conformably high, and never was there a chest that was so broad or so full or so deep.... And his arms were long and straight, and they were well supplied by the body beneath.... His hands had been those of a lady, had the fingers been somewhat more delicate. And for his loins and his hips, they might not be called better fashioned in any knight. His thighs and his legs were straight, and his feet arched, and no man ever stood more erect.][34]

The narrator does more than recite the ideal physical characteristics of a model knight. His eyes move over Lancelot's body, measuring the width of his shoulders, the full depth of his chest; he pauses over his fingers and admires his loins, hips, thighs, and legs. His description has much in common with that of a courtly lover's enthusiastic, point-by-point examination of his beloved lady's body.[35] The narrator is emotionally invested in his description, claiming that Lancelot's physique cannot be surpassed. Might some male readers prompted by the narrator's enthusiasm construct an image of Lancelot that is likewise erotically charged? Following Augustine's concept of how one comprehends descriptions visually, the reader grasps the meaning of the narrator's words by drawing forth memories of knights actually observed (or remembered images of knights previously envisioned). In remembering knights in armor, the reader must look at the body beneath the armor.[36] He must picture a man with a broad, deep chest, perfectly formed loins, hips, and legs. The reader may enhance these memories, creating an ideal image of a knight—one that surpasses all other knights. The reader cannot merely borrow the narrator's description; he must produce a mental picture of a knight from his imagination, one exhibiting what he considers to be a perfect physique. As a novice knight (or someone dreaming of becoming a knight), he identifies with the image of Lancelot he has created in his mind; and he also gazes at him. Identification and scopophilia thus converge on the same object. And since the body the reader sees before his mind's eye—a body that on some level he desires to have—is actually a projection of himself, this image is potentially autoerotic.

Elizabeth Cowie maintains that "[i]dentification does not involve a simple matching of self and image. What we are dealing with here is the desire for such images, so that through these images, narratives, etc. we come to know ourselves as we truly are...[but] only discovering all this in the moment of reading, in the act of watching, the novel or film."[37] Cowie's blurring of the distinction between reading and watching relates well to the medieval understanding of reading as a visual process. She also points to the spectator/reader's desire to both *be* and *have* the image.[38] Likewise, Diana Fuss maintains that "the desire to be *like* can itself be motivated and sustained by the desire to *possess*: being can be the most radical form of having."[39] "Having" the image implies that the desiring subject in some way unites with the imagined figure. While I am not suggesting that a male reader/subject attempts to engage in a sexual act with the image before his mind's eye, in seeking to take hold of the desired image he may be erotically drawn to it.

In their writings about love and lovesickness, medieval physicians note a connection between the imagination and emotions. Mary Wack points out that according to Urso of Calabria, "all the passions of the soul originate in the imagination and are completed in the heart."[40] She goes on to summarize Urso: "when we sense something pleasurable, the mind's attention turns toward it, and the *spiritus* moves to the 'instrument of the fantasy,' which is the first cell of the brain where the imagination is localized. Immediately imagination moves us to conceive the pleasurable effects of the sensed thing 'with a thirsting appetite.'"[41] While the active imagination of the lovesick sufferer is by doctrine confined to heterosexual eroticism, medieval mystics experienced both heterosexual and homoerotic imaginings.[42] Wack reports on Rupert of Deutz who, in a dream where he is worshipping Christ on the Cross, is prompted by Christ's return of his gaze to rush to the altar and engage in a remarkably homoerotic encounter with Christ:

> Non satis hoc mihi erat, nisi in manibus apprehenderem, amplexumque deoscularer.... Sensi enim ego, quia voluit...apprehendi, quem diligit anima mea, tenui illum, amplexatus sum eum, diutius osculatus sum eum. Sensi quam graviter hunc gestum dilectionis admitteret, cum inter osculandum suum ipse os aperiret, ut profundius oscularer.

> [I wanted to touch him with my hands, to embrace him, kiss him.... I sensed that he wanted me to hold him, embrace him, kiss him for a long time. I sensed how seriously he accepted these love-kisses when while kissing, he himself opened his mouth so that I might kiss more deeply.][43]

The image of Christ Rupert sees is evidently so vivid and his desire to "possess" this image so intense that he rushes toward it. Rupert's interaction with the imagined figure of Christ is autoerotic—the entire scene is a fantasy occurring within his mind. Religious fervor notwithstanding, this passage exemplifies the erotic potential of images. Like Rupert, novice knights/readers who are passionate about "being" the model knight they imagine—even just for a moment—may be erotically drawn to this image.

Cowie observes that "fantasy has come to mean the making visible, the making present, of what isn't there, of what can never *directly* be seen."[44] Chivalric treatises, biographies, and romances invite the reader to imagine the model knights who are described. These men cannot be directly seen because they are not physically present. Chivalric texts are directed at the emotions of some readers, offering an enticing view of the rewards (honor, respected social status) enjoyed by men-of-worth. They also indicate how model knights attract the admired gazes of both men and women. The image of a model knight the male reader constructs is a product of his past vision and his current emotional state—a fantasy image he desires to possess, yet this image is unattainable. That the imagined figure exists only in the mind of the viewer does not diminish the homoerotic potential of the desired image; and this image is desired ever more intensely as it eludes the grasp of the desiring subject. As demonstrated by Rupert of Deutz or the man, cited by Augustine, who reached orgasm while having sex with an imagined woman, one may respond erotically to a vivid image.

Cowie explains that fantasy is not a static image but rather an imagined sequence of scenes in which the fantasizing subject is a protagonist. And the subject identifies with the "player(s)" in the scene.[45] Jean Laplanche and Jean-Bertrand Pontalis elaborate: "Fantasy. . .is not the object of desire, but its setting. In fantasy the subject does not pursue the object or its sign: he appears caught up himself in the sequence of images. He forms no representation of the desired object, but is himself represented as participating in the scene...."[46] In a chivalric context, a novice knight may imagine a scenario where a model figure is performing and, in a sense, participate in the scene. That the model knight/performer is invested with qualities the novice knight deems worthy of emulation underscores the erotically charged relationship between the two knights, regardless of the fact that it is an "imaginary" one. Judith Butler articulates the interrelationship between the subject and object in a fantasy scenario: "[F]antasy seeks to override the distinction between a desiring subject and its object by staging an imaginary scene in which both positions are appropriated and inhabited by the subject. . . . Insofar as fantasy orchestrates the subject's love affair *with itself*, recovering and negating the alterity of the lost object through installing it as a further instance of the subject, fantasy delimits an auto-erotic project of incorporation."[47] The subject thus does not desire the object per se because this object is merely an extension of the fantasizing subject. However, it is only while the fantasized scene is playing that the subject experiences a sense of "wholeness." A fantasy sets up the *possibility* of recovering full pleasure—a possibility that is in a sense realized during the sequence of images moving toward but never actually reaching a union between subject and object. A novice knight/reader who constructs a fantasy scenario of a model knight performing a series of actions thus does not actually incorporate the desired image but may experience an auto-erotic fulfillment.

A male reader might in fact form what Kaja Silverman refers to as a "sodomitical identification," which "permits the fantasizing subject to look through...[the imagined] figure's eyes and to participate in his sexuality by going 'behind' him."[48] Since the model knight exists only in the subject's mind, he is an extension of the subject; and thus the subject does in effect "see" and perform *through* him. How might a description of the bathing ritual a novice knight undergoes just prior to the knighting ceremony play out in the mind of an attentive male reader? In the *Ordene de Chevalerie*, Saladin, who is holding Hugh, a model knight, captive in the Holy Land, requests that Hugh knight him. Although Saladin, being a non-Christian, is not the typical man-of-worth celebrated in chivalric texts, he must be suitable for knighting otherwise Hugh would have declined Saladin's request. Hugh performs the following actions: "l'a du baing osté, / Si l'a couchié en un biau lit, / Qui estoit fez par grant delit / . . . / Quant el lit ot un poi geü, / Sus le dresce, si l'a vestu / De blans dras qui erent de lin" [Hugh took him (Saladin) out of the bath and laid him in a fair bed, which was delightfully wrought. . . . When Saladin had lain a little while on the bed, Hugh raised him up and clad him in white sheets made of linen].[49] In imagining this scenario, a reader may identify with Hugh and thus look "through" him as he acts upon the naked body of Saladin. He would perform Hugh's actions with him, taking Saladin out of the bath, laying him on a bed and then dressing him. The fantasizing subject does not "unite" with Hugh but approaches very close from behind, leaning when he leans, lifting when he lifts and all the while gazing at—and acting on—a naked knight-to-be. The reader may also identify with Saladin and whether or not the reader imagines himself naked as well he would be in a sense "under" Saladin as he is lifted out of the bath and dressed. The reader may possibly identify with both men simultaneously. Terrell Scott Herring points out that "fantasy enables the subject to occupy multiple positions in its framework."[50] For male readers passionately caught up in the above narrative, touching or being touch by an imagined model knight might have a homoerotic valence.

Pleasure, Pain, and the Reader

Chivalric romances often present scenes where knights are brutally fighting one another. In imagining—and participating in—these scenes, the reader may derive pleasure. Cowie aptly describes how fantasy informs both reading and film spectatorship:"Films and stories offer us a contingent world for their events and outcomes, and, just as we draw on the events of the day to produce our own fantasies, so too we can adopt and adapt the ready-made scenarios of fiction, as if their contingent material had been our own."[51] Likewise, chivalric narratives offer readers ready-made scenarios to imagine—fantasy scenarios informed by the readers' own emotions and, possibly, unconscious wishes for fulfillment. Charny suggests that listening to stories about knights' adventures is pleasurable:

> Et de telx gens qui sont ainsi faisanz et faiz et parfaiz en tele bonté come dessus est dit, bien les doit l'en volentiers oïr et escouter et raconter de grans biens, de bons faiz et de bonnes paroles qui en celle maniere ont esté faiz et diz par pluseurs bons.

> [And one should take pleasure in hearing about, listening to, and recounting the good deeds, the great feats, and the admirable utterances of such people who are thus striving to achieve, have achieved, and have perfected themselves in such knightly qualities.][52]

Such stories undoubtedly contain details of violent acts committed by, and possibly against, a heroic knight. A listener/reader may derive pleasure from vicariously participating in the action unfolding before his mind's eye. Unlike the static portrait of Lancelot examined above, a narrative's description of knights engaged in brutal fights might not instill a reader with the desire to be one of these knights but rather, as Cowie explains, invite him to "identify with the character's position of desire in relation to other characters."[53] In a fantasy fight scenario certain male readers might *feel* pleasure imagining the heroic knight inflicting pain on his adversary; the reader might also derive pleasure from vicariously experiencing the pain inflicted by the adversary on the heroic knight.

Freud defines masochism as "sadism turned around upon the subject's own ego."[54] He describes three stages in this process: in the sadistic first stage, there is an "exercise of violence or power upon some other person as its object.... This object is abandoned and replaced by the subject's self...[t]ogether with...[a] change from an active to a passive aim in the instinct.... [Then] another person is sought as an object...[who] has to take over the original role of the [active] subject."[55] A masochist is thus actually the original sadist only now he is the passive object being tortured by someone else who occupies the subject/sadist position. According to Laplanche, "sexuality emerges only with the turning round upon the self, thus with masochism."[56] Before this "turning round" the attacker may display heteroaggressive sadism, or sadism that is not sexually charged. In chivalric fight scenes then, it is only when the attacking subject "allows himself" to be attacked that the fight becomes in a sense sexualized. Laplanche and Pontalis elaborate on Freud's definition of masochism: "[in] masochism proper, the subject has pain inflicted upon himself by another person [i.e. it is not self-inflicted]."[57] Freud describes a fourth stage in the process whereby "once the suffering of pain has been experienced as a masochistic aim, it can be carried back into the sadistic situation and result in a sadistic aim of *inflicting pain*, which will then be masochistically enjoyed by the subject while inflicting pain upon others, through his identification. . .with the suffering object."[58] Sadistic pleasure is thus, according to Freud, actually informed by masochism. Or, as Laplanche puts it, "it is within the suffering position that the enjoyment lies."[59] In a chivalric context, a wounded knight attacking his opponent can identify with—and derive pleasure from—the pain he is now inflicting. For Freud maintains that "sensations of pain, like other unpleasant sensations, extend into sexual excitation and produce a condition which is pleasurable, for the sake of which the subject will even willingly experience the unpleasantness of pain."[60] He refers to this particular form of masochism as "erotogenic masochism."[61] By imagining a protracted fight scenario described in a chivalric text and identifying with one or both of the protagonists—each of whom occupying at some point the positions of attacker and attacked—male readers can experience the eroticized pleasure of pain.[62]

In his essay, "A Child Is Being Beaten," Freud distinguishes three phases in the female beating fantasy:

Phase 1: "My father is beating the child [whom I hate]."
Phase 2: "I am being beaten by my father."
Phase 3: "Some boys are being beaten [I am probably looking on]."[63]

The subject of the fantasy moves from a nonsexual sadistic identification with the father in phase 1 to a masochistic subject position in phase 2, and then in phase 3, the subject forms an sexualized sadistic identification with the beater—sexualized because having previously "experienced" the masochistic position, the subject identifies with both the beater and those being beaten. We can draw a similar scenario for a fantasizing subject/reader of a chivalric text:

Phase 1: knight A is beating knight B [whom the reader hates].
Phase 2: the reader fantasizes being beaten by knight A.
Phase 3: knights A and B are beating each other, which the reader is observing.

In the first phase, the reader's identification with heteroaggressive knight A "turns round" into a sexually charged masochistic identification with knight B. This is particularly compelling in chivalric texts where both knights in a struggle are "men-of-worth." In the third phase, the reader might identify with whichever knight gains the upper hand, thus forming a sadomasochistic identification with the beater; for, having previously identified with the beaten knight, the reader identifying now with the beater derives masochistic pleasure by also identifying with the one being beaten. My rearticulation of the beating fantasy offers a framework for examining how male readers imagining violent encounters between knights in the fourteenth-century *Stanzaic Morte Arthur* may form homoerotic masochistic and sadomasochistic identifications.[64]

The following scene illustrates Freud's stages of masochism. Lancelot attacks Ewain, exhibiting heteroaggressive (i.e. non-sexualized) sadism. He gives him a "dint...with mikel main," causing Ewain to be "wounded wonder sore."[65] However, Ector then takes Ewain's place and attacks Lancelot: "Ector smote with herte good / To Launcelot that ilke tide; / Through helm into his hed it yode / That nighe lost he all his pride" (305–08). In thus "turning round," Lancelot illustrates masochism in its proper form; for the pain he has formerly inflicted on Ewain is now inflicted on himself by Ector. But then, "Launcelot hit him [Ector] on the hood / That his horse fell and he beside" (309–10). And so we have an illustration of the next stage in which the masochist becomes once again a sadist. However, unlike the nonsexual initial stage, this time the sadistic instinct is sexualized—or, as Freud puts it, "masochistically enjoyed"—because Lancelot, having been wounded, identifies with the knight now occupying the masochistic position. In fact, Lancelot is bleeding after he wins the fight: "Launcelot blindes in his blood; / Out of the feld full fast gan ride" (311–12). The idea that a masochist finds pleasure-in-pain is illustrated in Lancelot's comments to Ector: "Though thou have sore wounded me / There-of I shall thee never wite [blame], / But ever the better love I thee, / Such a dint that thou can smite" (500–03). The love that unites the wounded knight with his attacker eroticizes the physical combat that has just transpired, and this in turn informs the relationship between the fantasizing reader and the protagonists in the imagined scenario. The text therefore invites the reader to experience not only Lancelot's pleasure-in-pain but also an eroticization of the entire fight scenario.

Another scene involves a fight between Lancelot and Mador, the brother of a Scottish knight who was accidentally poisoned at Arthur's court. The narrator whets the reader's appetite: "The batail for to *see* and lithe [hear]; / *Saw* never no man stronger fight!" (1582–83; emphasis added). In drawing attention to the fight as an exceptional spectacle to be observed, the narrator invites readers to summon forth vivid images, which would in some cases be informed by actual chivalric encounters previously experienced—thus fantasy images based on "real" knights. The fight begins with both knights occupying the position of heteroaggressive sadist: "There was so wonder strong a fight, / O foot nolde nouther flee ne found" (1592–93). Each knight then slips into the position of masochist: "From lowe noon til late night, / But given [i.e. they give each other] many a woful wound" (1594–95). The text offers readers two opportunities for masochistic identification in that both knights are presented as exemplary models of chivalric prowess; and while the text may lead a reader to identify more with Lancelot and thus "hate" Mador, it is not unlikely that, as in the second phase of the beating fantasy, a reader/observer might also form a masochistic identification with the "hated" knight—since he is after all avenging the death of his brother. Although the fight continues into the third phase of the beating fantasy, only Lancelot offers the reader an eroticized sadomasochistic identification: "Launcelot then gave a dint with might; / Sir Mador falles at last to ground; / 'Mercy!' cries that noble knight, / For he was seke and sore unsound" (1596–99). As in the earlier fight with Ector, Lancelot gives an eroticized blow to Mador because having been wounded he derives masochistic pleasure from identifying with the knight upon whom he is inflicting pain. For some male readers, vicarious homoerotic pleasure is realized through a sadomasochistic identification with Lancelot or a masochistic one with Mador. It is also possible that both can occur simultaneously, thus intensifying the erotic effect. The beaten knight has evidently experienced pleasure; he tells Lancelot: "I have fought in many a land, / With knightes both less and more, / And never yet ere my match I fand" (1605–07). In other words, there is nothing as pleasurable as being beaten in a good fight. The text again reveals the homoerotic foundation upon which a fight scenario is played out: "Launcelot him [Mador] kist with herte free, / And in his armes gan him up take" (1622–23). The body language here is striking. The victor receives the defeated one like a lover in a display of affection that in a way parallels the happy turn of events in a courtly (or modern) love story. Except in this case the union of "lovers" is based on shared pleasurable experiences of pain. And the fantasizing reader, having vicariously experienced the pleasure-in-pain of both knights, also derives satisfaction from this male–male kiss and embrace.

In the third and final scene I will explore, Gawain, who swears revenge on Lancelot for killing his brother, engages him in a protracted fight. For Gawain at least, future pleasure motivates this fight, suggested by his vow: "Ere either of us shall other slayn, / Blithe shall I never be" (2410–11). Either as sadomasochistic slayer (with the assumption that in the process of slaying Lancelot he will himself be wounded) or masochistic slain (assuming that before succumbing to his wounds he inflicts pain on Lancelot), Gawain expects to be "blithe." As the scene unfolds, Lancelot, too, is in a position to be "blithe." And the reader can identify with the pleasure-in-pain experienced by either knight. The fight begins with both knights attacking each other, and the narrator invites the reader to view the scene along with the implied male spectators: "The knightes met, as men it sigh [saw] / How they set their dintes sore" (2800–01). Lancelot's initial heteroaggressive sadist position "turns round" into a purely masochistic one: "Again twenty strokes he gave not one" (2809); after previously striking Gawain, Lancelot now merely accepts blows. That he "[m]any a dint…gan well endure" (2812) suggests that he might indeed enjoy the pain of being repeatedly struck. How might a reader identifying with Lancelot fantasize this? Would he not situate his fantasmatic self in an eroticized, submissive position vis-à-vis Gawain? Having focused on Lancelot's masochistic position, the text then offers a brilliant dramatization of the emergence of sadomasochism. Lancelot, who is evidently in a crouched position as he is being beaten, straightens up and gives Gawain "a wounde wide" (2815). The beating Lancelot now administers to Gawain is thus informed by an eroticized masochistic identification. The narrator's description of Gawain's wounded condition invites the engaged reader to envision a truly formidable action on Lancelot's part: "The blood all covered his colour / And he fell down upon his side. / Thorough the helm into the hede / Was hardy Gawain wounded so / That unnethe was him life leved" (2816–20). While it is admittedly difficult to comprehend how either of the depicted beatings might be pleasurable, not to mention erotic, for a reader forming a sado-masochistic or, simply, masochistic identification, the text reveals that in a chivalric context it is indeed just that. Gawain, who is barely alive, cannot wait to continue the fight. He assures Lancelot: "When I am hole and going on high; / Then will I prove with might and main" (2830–31). When the fight continues a fortnight later, Gawain's masochistic pleasure-in-pain is briefly transformed into sadomasochism as he beats Lancelot so "bitterly" that Lancelot "all for-wery was" (2900–01). But then Lancelot delivers a mighty blow, and Gawain "grisly groned upon the ground" (2912). He refuses to yield, however. Because he will be "blithe" only when one of them is slain—which at present seems like a death-wish—his repeated experiences of being grievously wounded in effect lead him toward content-ment; his wounds are informed by the pleasure he awaits. And the reader forming a masochistic identification with Gawain would likewise derive pleasure from vicariously experiencing his repeated bouts of pain.

Jackson notes how reading narratives in general can be erotic: "The act of reading for pleasure indeed makes an easy analogy with sexuality, in the ambivalent relations between appetite and satisfaction that characterize them both. Both experiences are typically cognized as a pursuit of a goal, a pursuit pleasurable in itself, but ultimately a means to an object the desire for which initiated and motivates the process."[66] He goes on to point out that "[t]he attainment of the goal (Freud's 'end pleasure') extinguishes the pleasure of the approach (Freud's 'forepleasure')."[67] But a chivalric text like the *Stanzaic Morte Arthur* offers multiple pleasures. Readers who follow the protagonists through the stages of eroticized sadism/masochism in each of several fight scenarios are afforded multiple "forepleasures." And *each* fight scenario offers an "end pleasure." Robert Scholes highlights both forms of pleasure in his observation about fiction: "what connects fiction...with sex is the fundamental orgastic rhythm of tumescence and detumescence, of tension and resolution, of intensification to the point of climax and consummation. In the sophisticated forms of fiction, as in the sophisticated practice of sex, much of the art consists of delaying climax within the framework of desire in order to prolong the pleasurable act itself."[68] The masculine-based analogy in both observations speaks clearly to my examination of a male reader's homoerotic sadomasochistic identifications with knights engaged in a protracted conflict. In the last scene, although the fight between Gawain and Lancelot approaches a climax on several occasions, it is not actually attained. The fantasizing reader identifying with Gawain's pleasure-in-pain is propelled ever forward toward the desired goal, experiencing pleasure along the way.

I have concentrated on (sado) masochistic identification because the pleasure afforded a reader is perhaps less apparent than that suggested by an identification with the figure who is the "beater." In chivalric romances, the hero does not merely perform the beating but also often suffers "beatings." Identifying with the wounded hero is the other half of the reader's pleasurable spectatorial experience. Freud's concept of sadism/ masochism—particularly regarding the pleasure-in-pain informing erotogenic masochism—and its dramatization in the beating fantasy provide a methodological tool for uncovering potential homoeroticism in the reading of chivalric texts.

Chivalric texts thus reveal an underlying discourse in their presentation of model knights whether in statuesque portraits or vivid fight scenarios: namely, an invitation to readers to imagine and, particularly for novice knights or male readers who are enthusiastic supporters of chivalry, to identify with these heroic characters. The ostensible discourse of ideal knightly qualities can best benefit the novice knight/reader when he imagines the model knights and the actions in which they demonstrate these qualities. While authors might not consciously invite male readers to form homoerotic identifications this is a potential combined effect of vivid descriptions, an apparent cultural mode of visualizing what one reads, and the fervor some male readers have for chivalry. Even the violent acts depicted in some texts serve a sociopolitical agenda because they illustrate how model knights enjoy fighting—how they find pleasure in both beating and getting beaten—and, moreover, the eroticized pleasure a reader may derive from imagining such actions may propel him actually to pursue them himself.

CHAPTER 5

MALE–MALE GAZING

In chapter 4 I explored how some male readers might respond to chivalric texts' tacit invitation to envision model knights. Although the conjured images might be based on actual knights the reader has seen, I focused on the imaginative visual process. In this chapter, I continue to explore homoerotic spectatorship in chivalric contexts, but now examine the visual dynamics of a knight looking closely at another knight using his corporeal sight rather than his imaginative faculty. In *The Book of Chivalry*, Charny advises novice knights to study *actual* model men-at-arms: "regarder les meilleurs. . .et a teles genz fait bon prendre exemplaire et mettre paine de faire les ouvres pour eulz resembler" [one should observe those who are best. . . . And it is good to take such men as examples and to strive to act in such a way as to resemble them].[1] That chivalric treatises urge novice knights to study the physical bearing and skills of true men-of-worth—men who are living in the novice knights' contemporary world—and to strive to be just like them suggests the existence of an economy of male–male spectatorship in late medieval chivalric society whereby men not only imagine other men but also gaze at "real" men. In recommending that a novice knight (or any interested spectator) direct his gaze at a model figure—one who apparently neither acknowledges nor returns the gaze of the observer—chivalric treatises are promoting unidirectional spectatorship. This does not however preclude a homoerotic interaction from occurring between the observer and the observed. Although film theory offers a useful language for studying eroticism in visual encounters, chivalric contexts problematize the gendered spectatorial positions that some film theorists delineate. As we shall see, male–male gazing blurs the distinction between activity and passivity.

Theorizing the Viewer

Christian Metz explains the relationship of the observer to the images on the screen: "At the cinema, it is always the other who is on the screen;

as for me, I am there to look at him. I take no part in the perceived, on the contrary, I am *all-perceiving*. All-perceiving as one says all-powerful."[2] Understood in Metz's formulation is that the observer, in identifying with the controlling gaze of the camera, occupies a subject position that only looks, thus denying the possibility of being looked at. Heteronormative readings of chivalric texts likewise position a male spectator of a model knight as "all-perceiving," impervious, and thus outside the erotically charged visual field; he "controls" the visual act and thus cannot be acted upon—stimulated— by the object of his gaze. But does the observer maintain a purely active position in the spectatorial scenario even when the model knight does not return his gaze? In claiming that a model knight demonstrates admirable physical strength and prowess—undoubtedly more than many of his male spectators do—chivalric texts suggest that he attracts and captures the gaze of his male spectators. Who is then controlling whom?

Mulvey's most contentious claim is that "[i]n a world ordered by sexual imbalance, pleasure in looking has been split between active/male and passive/ female. The determining male gaze projects its phantasy on to the female figure which is styled accordingly."[3] According to Mulvey, looking is an active, male process, being looked at a passive, female one. She maintains that "[i]n their traditional exhibitionist role women are simultaneously looked at and displayed, with their appearance coded for strong visual and erotic impact so that they can be said to connote *to-be-looked-at-ness*."[4] This modern, heterosexual binary of active-male-observer/passive-female- observed is problematic in situations where the compelling object of the male spectator's gaze is male. Commenting on Mulvey's theory, Cowie points out that "[v]isual pleasure is not a straightforward affair. It always implies specularising the object. . .[a]nd this is as true of women as of men."[5] Cowie thus suggests that the male figure in a film is not immune from objectification by the spectator; and, I would argue, likewise the model knight being observed in tournaments and battles. This does not imply that the performing knight/object is "passive." A hardy man-of-worth demonstrating exemplary martial skills attracts the gaze of his spectators from a position of power; at the same time, this "active" object/model knight is vulnerable in that he is "styled" by the fantasies of his observers. He cannot control *how* his observers see him or respond to him: they may aggrandize his appearance and actions; they may even become attracted to him.

Sarah Stanbury takes issue with some film theorists' bifurcation of spectatorship into active/male and passive/female positions. She rightly asks: "Since the very concept of a 'phallic gaze' emerges from a regime of the visual that splits vision as male and the object of the gaze as paradigmatically female, can we speak of a 'phallic gaze' in medieval representation—if the central body in that system of representation is not female at all?"[6]

According to Stanbury, a late medieval spectacle focused on the body of Christ has "[a]n investiture of power in the body displayed, rather than in the subject that views the body."[7] She maintains that this "is consistent with the workings of visuality that Foucault describes for pre-nineteenth century Western regimes. To be seen, to be the center of collective visibility, once defined power, Foucault has argued; to be unseen, unrepresentable, defined one's status as powerless."[8] This is also true for spectatorship in chivalric contexts. Charny suggests that exemplary knights enjoy an admired, privileged social status as a result of their actions having been viewed and positively evaluated by the public gaze. Stanbury delineates a late medieval visual economy: "The dominance of the image in fourteenth-century spectacle supports and even, we might say, fleshes out Foucault's analysis of modernist regimes of visuality, allowing us to suggest that the structure of the gaze in premodern England reverses or inverts the 'scopic regime of modernity.' Visibility, to-be-seen-ness, is not to be exposed, known, focused under the lens of a distanced and controlling eye, but quite the reverse: to be seen and to command the gaze of others is to control visual relations."[9] In a chivalric context, however, the model knight not only commands the gaze of his observers but also in a sense exposes himself to the eyes of the novice knight/interested male spectator, who, following Charny's advise, closely examines him in order to emulate him. Even in a visual economy that privileges the observed, the observer's role cannot be ignored.

In theorizing the act of vision, ancient and medieval writers favored either intromission, whereby the observed object was thought to be a source of light that travels to the eye, or extromission, where the eye was said to emit a ray or power that reaches the light object, seizes it, and then returns to the eye.[10] Augustine describes the process as a combination of both:

> Gignitur ergo ex re uisibili uisio, sed non ex sola nisi adsit et uidens. Quocirca ex uisibili et uidente gignitur uisio ita sane ut ex uidente sit sensus oculorum et aspicientis atque intuentis intentio; illa tamen informatio sensus quae uisio dicitur a solo imprimatur corpore quod uidetur, id est a re aliqua uisibili.

> [The vision, therefore, is produced by the visible thing, but not by it alone, unless the one who sees is also present. Wherefore, vision is produced both by the visible thing and the one who sees, but in such a way that the sense of sight as well as the intention of seeing and beholding come from the one who sees, while that informing of the sense, which is called vision, is imprinted by the body alone that is seen, namely, by some visible thing.][11]

While delineating the active role both observer and observed play in a visual act, Augustine seems to privilege the visible object. For the content of sight—the "information"—touches the seeing subject, making an imprint. The object may thus affect or stimulate the observer; whereas the observer, although controlling the gaze has no effect on the observed object.

Collette points out that "the most influential late medieval thinking about optics assumed a degree of power in the object of vision itself. As a result, the subject one looked at was thought to be as important as the act of looking itself, and the act of looking always a dynamic interchange between viewer and viewed."[12] One of the major writers on optics in the thirteenth century, Roger Bacon, explains his theory of vision in some detail in his *Opus maius*. Central to Bacon's theory is the understanding that rays or "species" are emitted from the visible object in the form of a pyramid reaching the observer's eye as the apex of the pyramid.[13] The object and the viewing eye are thus linked together through the species emanating from the object. David Lindberg summarizes Bacon: "an object produces its likeness or species in the adjacent transparent medium, which in turn produces a further likeness in the next part of the medium, and so forth."[14] While Bacon subscribes to the theory of intromission, he identifies activity on the part of the observer: "sed operatio videndi est certa cognitio visibilis distantis, et ideo visus cognoscit visibile per suam virtutem multiplicatam ad ipsum" [the process of seeing concerns the cognition of a distant visible object, and therefore sight perceives the visible object through the multiplication of its own power to the object].[15] In fact, the observing eye exerts itself on the species emitted from the object:

> species rerum mundi non sunt natae statim de se agere ad plenam actionem in visu propter ejus nobilitatem. Unde oportet quod juventur et excitentur per speciem oculi, quae incedat in loco pyramidis visualis, et alteret medium ac nobilitet, et reddat ipsum proportionale visui, et sic praeparet incessum speciei ipsius rei visibilis, et insuper eam nobilitet, ut omnino sit conformis et proportionalis nobilitati corporis animati, quod est oculus.
>
> [The species of the things of the world are not suited to act immediately and fully in sight because of the nobility of the latter (i.e. the observing eye). Therefore these species (coming from the observed object) must be aided and excited by the species of the eye, which proceeds through the locale of the visual pyramid, altering and ennobling the medium and rendering it commensurate with sight; and thus it prepares for the approach of the species of the visible object (itself), so that it is altogether conformable and commensurate with the nobility of the animated body, i.e. the eye.][16]

There is thus a union of sorts between the species of the observing eye and the species reaching the eye from the observed object. In noting that the eye excites the incoming species, Bacon suggests that the object eventually registered in the viewer's senses is altered in some way by the viewer's eye. And I pose the possibility that this alteration could be linked to the emotional state of the viewer or the viewer's attitude toward the object. Might not a process occur similar to the one Augustine outlines for reimagining a remembered image, whereby the stored image is increased or altered as the viewer pleases? While the observer plays an active role in the process Bacon describes, the scenario also renders the observer a passive player receiving the species, which, after the necessary preparations have been made, is then admitted into the eye. Moreover, the incoming species approaching the eye initiates the eye's response. Bacon neatly sums up the concurrent active and passive roles occupied by the viewer in a visual act: "visus est activus et passivus. Nam recipit speciem rei visae, et facit suam virtutem in medium usque ad visibile" [vision is active and passive. For it receives the species of the thing seen, and exerts its own force in the medium as far as the visible object].[17]

John Pecham's *Perspectiva communis* draws heavily on Bacon and, according to Lindberg, was widely read in universities and commented upon during the late Middle Ages.[18] Pecham elaborates on the interaction between the observed object and the seeing eye: "Pyramis enim radiosa a visibili oculo impressa rem oculo representat, sed certificatio fit de visibili per rotationem oculi super rem que basis est pyramidis" [To be sure, the pyramid of radiation, impressed on the eye by the visible object, manifests the object to the eye; but the visible object is certified by a turning of the eye (all about) over the object, the latter being the base of the pyramid].[19] Pecham's language suggests a momentary intimacy between the eye and the observed object. The manifested object is *impressed* on the eye; the eye *moves over* the object in order to "certify" it.

Thus, according to medieval theories of vision, neither the observer nor the observed object occupies an exclusively active or passive position. While the observer indeed actively gazes at the observed and in a sense controls the image received, the observed plays a more active role than that recognized by some film theorists. Given the fact that in a chivalric visual economy the observed object—the model knight—is likely to be more physically powerful than the observer, medieval optical theory affirms the potency and attraction of the objectified male without reducing the observing male to a passive, "mastered" position. Although authors of chivalric texts did not necessarily read treatises on vision, theories of intromission were undoubtedly "in the air," finding expression for instance in the courtly love convention of a lover being struck through the eye by something emanating from the beloved object. Bacon, Pecham, and others describe vision as an intimate encounter—a form of copulation—between object and observer and thus provide a framework for exploring visual acts within a chivalric context. In light of a novice knight's motivation for studying a model figure—his desire to be an admired man-of-worth— these visual encounters are potentially erotic.

Pleasure in the Eyes of the Beholder

Understood in medieval theories of vision is the significant role volition plays in the act of seeing—we see something often because we wish to look at it (true for both medieval and modern visual economies). We should therefore not ignore or underestimate the desire propelling a novice knight/male observer to look closely at a model knight either for purposes of emulation or simply as a pleasurable pastime. And this desire informs how he will see and be affected by what he sees. Some enthusiastic male observers may even become stimulated or aroused by the exemplary knights they are studying. The following optical moments in *Troilus and Criseyde* and *Sir Gawain and the Green Knight* dramatize how a visual act can be erotically charged for the observer.

In book 1 of *Troilus and Criseyde*, at the palladium, Troilus's "eye percede, and so depe it wente, / Til on Criseyde it smot, and ther it stente" (1.272–73). The object of Troilus's gaze apparently emits a powerful "species"; for "sodeynly he [Troilus] wax therwith astoned" (1.274). The scenario continues to illustrate the potent effect the viewed object has on the viewer: "And of hire look in him ther gan to quyken / So gret desire and swich affeccioun, / That in his herte botme gan to stiken / Of hir his fixe and depe impressioun. / And though he erst hadde poured up and down, / He was tho glad his hornes into shrinke; / Unnethes wiste he how to loke or wynke" (1.295–301). Noting how agency is obfuscated in this visual act, Stanbury rightly asks: "Who, in fact, is looking? And does that look (with its rays or arrows) have power over the body of the other, or is it simply an elaborate conceit for a kind of erotic solipsism?"[20] I suggest that Troilus's "processing" of the look he receives produces the erotic effect. Criseyde's "look," or, to use Bacon's term, "species"—not her return gaze—becomes deeply impressed on Troilus's "herte botme." As admired object of Troilus's gaze, Criseyde is in an ocular position similar to that of a model knight who is keenly observed by a novice knight/male spectator. Like the model knight in chivalric treatises, she does not acknowledge her spectator, or, more precisely, spectators.[21] Stanbury points out that "even though he [Troilus] seems victimized, that victimization occurs through his own action: *his* gaze pierces the crowd and smites Criseyde."[22] Yet we can delineate Troilus's role even further. According to Bacon, the species of the observer's eye "aids" and "excites" the species coming from the observed object, "rendering it commensurate with sight." Thus, Criseyde's "look" would have no effect on Troilus unless his eye alters it in some way. If the deep impression made on Troilus by the species emanating from Criseyde is in part his own doing, then his subsequent reaction is *auto*erotically charged.[23]

Although I am not suggesting that a novice knight would gaze at a model figure in the same manner, the above scene dramatizes the potential eroticism of spectatorship. After Troilus "wax. . .astoned," he continues to gaze at Criseyde more intently: "And gan hir bet biholde in thrifty wise" (1.275). He finds her "feyr and goodly to devise" (1.277). The observed object thus draws the observer to it. After the first physical effect, the observer cannot take his eyes off of the object. He is mesmerized by it. Might a highly motivated novice knight, dreaming of becoming an admired man-of-worth, study a model figure with equal rapture? After his initial awe, would he not keep his eyes glued on the knight performing before his eyes? Would the species impressed upon—and certified by—his sight not be colored by his attraction to that object? And would that not be a pleasurable sensation? Like Troilus, in this putative scenario the novice knight creates, in part, the eroticized visual effect.

In book 2, Troilus's celebratory ride through Troy bears some similarities to a chivalric event where spectators eagerly view performing knights. In a sense speaking for the men who race down the street to see Troilus, the narrator gushes: "So lik a man of armes and a knyght / He was to seen, / fulfilled of heigh prowesse, / For bothe he hadde a body and a myght / To don that thing, as wel as hardynesse; / And ek to seen hym in his gere hym dresse, / So fresh, so yong, so weldy semed he, / It was an heven upon hym for to see" (2.631–37). Troilus is presented here as a model knight who is being observed and evaluated primarily by men: "men criden in the strete, 'Se Troilus' "; "men myghte many an arwe fynde [in his shield]" (2.612, 641).[24] Criseyde hears the people cry, "Here cometh oure joye, / And, next his brother, holder up of Troye!" (2.643–44), and sees Troilus blush at receiving such a tumultuous reception. She then gazes intently at him: "Criseÿda gan al his chere aspien, / And leet it so softe in hire herte synke, / That to hireself she seyde, 'Who yaf me drynke?' " (2.649–51). Stanbury remarks that "[h]er gaze. . .participates in and is in part constructed by the gaze of a crowd. . . . Troilus is not, in fact, so much the object of her scrutiny as he is the object of a collective look"—one that has a "masculine animus."[25] The crowd's admiring gaze not only informs Criseyde's gaze, however; it also heightens the effect her gaze has on her. As in the palladium scene in book 1, the object of the gaze does not look directly at the observer; for as Criseyde studies closely Troilus's "chere," his eyes are directed downward. Criseyde's position is both active and passive: active in making the incoming species emitted from Troilus's look commensurate with her eyes; passive in letting it "softe in hire herte synke." The crowd's enthusiastic gaze at Troilus's "body and might" gives him an erotic valence, and his "look" carries this charge as it approaches Criseyde's sight. Moreover, the crowds' positive response to Troilus influences how Criseyde's eyes process the incoming species. Would she have been equally attracted to him if he were simply walking down the street unnoticed? Possibly. But the text clearly connects Criseyde's reaction with the public celebration.

This scene thus suggests that a collective, admiring gaze at a knight may intensify the effect on an individual observer.

Criseyde's reaction to looking at Troilus is not only lightheadedness, however: "For of hire owen thought she wex al reed, / . . . / And with that thought, for pure ashamed, she / Gan in hire hed to pulle, and that as faste" (2.652; 656–57). Her "shame," which results directly from gazing at Troilus, is a twofold realization: this celebrated knight is suffering unrequited love for her; and she is attracted to him. She pulls her head in because she knows that her reddening is a physical sign, visible to others, of her infatuation. It is, as Stanbury points out, "as if the dynamics of visual control had completely reversed and she were the object of someone else's gaze. Unseen though she remains, she has become objectified by her own consciousness."[26] Whether or not someone actually gazes at her is beside the point; she reacts *as if* someone were looking at her looking at—and responding to—Troilus. In a public forum this is always a possibility. The "all-perceiving," invulnerable subject position is, as Cowie puts it, "always looked at and as a result the 'omnipotent gaze' is unstable, difficult to sustain."[27] In a chivalric context, a male viewer's recognition that he is possibly the object of other spectators' gazes might heighten his interaction with the model knight at whom he is directing his gaze. While a novice knight may not blush when observing a man-of-worth, he may indeed become enraptured and even on some level erotically stimulated by the object "impressed" upon his eyes. In a cultural environment that affirms and even promotes male–male intimacy, a male observer may be expected to become enraptured by an exemplary knight performing for a crowd. And knowing that his reaction is possibly being watched may instead of embarrassing him actually intensify his response.

These scenes illustrate the potent effect an observed, desired object may exert on the observer—an effect that is in part autoerotic. Moreover, the second scene demonstrates that a knight whose exemplary status is affirmed by cheering crowds may become more desirable, heightening— and eroticizing—the visual effect he has on an attentive and motivated observer. In these scenarios the observer and the observed are distant from each other. In *Sir Gawain*, we can examine the effects on the observer when subject and object are in close proximity.

After Gawain arrives at Bertilak's castle, and the two men embrace, he gazes at his host: "Gawain glyght on the gome that godly hym gret, / And thought hit a bolde burne that the burgh aghte, / A hoge hathel for the nones, and of hyghe eldee; / Brode, bryght was his berde, and al bever-hwed, / Sturne, stif on the stryththe [striding firmly along] on stalworth schonkes, / Felle face as the fyre, and fre of hys speche."[28] Bertilak does not return Gawain's gaze, yet he is undoubtedly aware that Gawain is studying him.

In fact, he is in a sense posing for a moment as Gawain's eye takes in his shape, face, and legs. Having just embraced, they are standing close together. And Bertilak's "look" pleases Gawain: "And wel hym semed for sothe, as the segge thught, / To lede a lortschyp in lee of leudes ful gode" (848–49). The previous embrace adds an erotic charge to Gawain's visual act— a charge that is heightened by the continued proximity of Bertilak's body and the positive evaluation Gawain gives it. The pleasure Gawain experiences is not caused by Bertilak's return gaze but rather Gawain's action on and reception of the species emanating from Bertilak. Like a model knight, Bertilak exerts power over Gawain, who at least in part because he is enraptured by Bertilak's appearance places himself under his command. Bertilak's first command is that Gawain be attended by male servants who go on to undress and dress him. Gawain is now the object of men's admiring gazes: "Sone as he on hent, and happed therinne, / That sete on hym semly, with saylande skyrtes, / The ver by his visage verayly hit semed / Welnegh to uche hathel, alle on hwes, / Lowande and lufly, alle his lymmes under, / That a comloker knyght never Kryst made, / hem thoght" (864–70). He thus becomes a model figure himself, attracting the gaze of other men who favorably evaluate his body at close proximity.[29]

These two spectatorial moments illustrate not only the pleasurable effect a male object has on his male observer(s) but also that a model knight is both gazed at and evaluated by his observers. Stanbury rightly points out that "the gazes of Gawain and the servants are in fact interpretive *and* evaluative, acts of vision that provoke subjective commentary couched in qualifiers."[30] I would add that these subjective interpretations and evaluations are shaped by the particular taste of the observer. Bertilak is a suitable lord of a castle, according to Gawain, because of his powerful, manly physique; Gawain is very handsome, in the servants' view, because his clothed body is spring-like. And the more the observed knight satisfies the observer's notion of what the physical characteristics of a model lord/knight should be, the more likely the visual act will have a pleasurable and, possibly, erotically charged effect on the observer. Model knights do not often stand still before their observers, however; they perform for them.

The Homoerotic Dynamics of Performing

The Green Knight bursts into Arthur's hall and the narrator gazes intently at him:

> Fro the swyre to the swange so sware and so thik,
> And his lyndes and his lymes so longe and so grete,
> Half etayn in erde I hope that he were;

Bot mon most I algate mynn hym to bene,
And that the myriest in his muckel that myght ride,
For of bak and of brest al were his bodi sturne,
Both his wombe and his wast were worthily smale,
And alle his fetures folwande in forme that he hade,
          ful clene. (138–46)

While shockingly large, and green, he exhibits the perfect physique of
a model knight such as Lancelot. The narrator's gaze passes over his body—
neck, trunk, loins, legs, waist—and in a sense touches it.[31] He measures the
bulkiness and thickness of his trunk, the length and size of his loins and
limbs, estimating that his overall size must be equivalent to "half etayn." The
Green Knight exceeds the narrator's conception of a model knight—surely
he has never seen anyone comparable. But the narrator does not merely
take the Green Knight's measurements; he evaluates them. His repeated use
of the intensifier, "so," implies that these parts of the Green Knight's body
are *pleasingly* bulky, thick, or great. The narrator evidently finds a slender
stomach and waist "worthy." And in *his* view, the Green Knight is the
"handsomest knight on horseback."[32] His highly subjective positive evaluation suggests that he is attracted to this powerfully built man. The narrator's
fascination with the Green Knight's body is further illustrated in his attention to the knight's close-fitting apparel. His gaze studies the "strayt cote
ful streght that stek on his sides, / . . . / Heme, wel-haled hose. . . / That
spenet on his sparlyr" (152; 157–58). Although the narrator is external to
the scene, his close examination of the Green Knight's body situates him—
or at least his gaze—in the hall together with Arthur and his knights who
are likewise staring at the intruder. Through his detailed and enthusiastic
description, the narrator establishes the Green Knight as a model figure
whom one might desire to be like. Greg Walker observes that the "the narrator almost instantly begins to notice and appreciate a superlative quality
to the knight's manliness, and to afford him the admiring gaze of one
knightly male to another. We learn to admire the Knight for his physical
perfection before we recoil from his most striking abnormality, his color."[33]
Yet his monstrous size and strange color do not necessarily make him less
attractive to his observers. These observers do not respond, however, until
he begins to perform for them.

The Green Knight looks over the assembled guests and demands to
know: "Wher is. . . / The governour of this gyng?" (224–25). He attempts
to find out himself by studying the knights before him: "To knyghtes he kest
his yye, / And reled hym up and doun. / He stemmed and con studie /
Quo walt ther most renoun" (228–31). His direct address and gaze spark
their interest, drawing them nearer to him: "Al studied that ther stod, and
stalked hym nerre" (237). The text suggests that the knights' interpretive

and evaluative gaze on the Green Knight is, like the narrator's, a positive one. Rather than running away or avoiding him, they sit in stunned silence, staring at him, and await his next move. Following medieval optical theory, in order to comprehend—or "certify"—the image of the Green Knight, species from the knights' eyes must make the approaching species commensurate with their sight. This process renders the Green Knight's exaggerated size and green color in human terms. And like the narrator who "certifies" the Green Knight's body as that of a superlative model knight with strong limbs and slender waist, Arthur's knights see the Green Knight as extraordinary but recognizably a knight. We should not forget that while the knights are gazing at the Green Knight, he is gazing at them. Stanbury draws attention to "[t]his narrative hiatus [which] presents us suddenly with two sets of eyes, mutually gazing, mutually exclusive as each works with discrete intent, one to isolate an individual and the other to assess identity and purpose."[34] And in each case the object of the gaze is also being assessed physically. While searching for the identity of the "governour of this gyng," the Green Knight is evaluating Arthur's knights, studying them to see which one conforms with *his* idea of a leader. And his evaluation is not a positive one. He refers to them as "berdles chylder" and concludes that "Here is no mon me to mach, for myghtes so wayke" (280; 282). On the other hand, the knights recognize the Green Knight's powerful form. This unequal evaluation—the Green Knight's negative assessment of the knights' manliness and their being enraptured by his strange, mighty form—establishes a visual arena in which the players are clearly demarcated: namely, an intriguing, intimidating exhibitionist who performs for his receptive observers. And the Green Knight's exhibitionism is, I suggest, homoerotic both for him and his male observers.[35]

Geraldine Heng's articulation of the lady's seductive exhibitionism in her bedroom encounters with Gawain is useful for delineating the homoerotic valence of the Green Knight's performance. Heng writes: "Tapping the mutually bound libidinal processes of scopophilia and exhibition, the Lady's calculated projection of an erotic feminine body fuels excitation by playing off Gawain's desire to see, his impulse to look, against her provision of something that desires to *be* seen, a desirable self-display for her own private purposes."[36] Uninvited, the lady walks into Gawain's bedchamber and attempts to seduce Gawain through crafty words and the exposure of her body. Similar dynamics occur in Arthur's hall. The Green Knight purposely barges into the hall knowing that his enormous, green form will stun his observers. His exhibiting of his powerful frame and his bullying the knights—and there is no suggestion that this is unpleasant for him—is inextricably linked to the knights' eagerness to look at him. The narrator's scrutiny and eroticized appraisal of the Green Knight's body as well as the implied examination by the knights suggest male desire to study another male body. And the

Green Knight makes no attempt to hinder this male–male scopophilic act. Quite the contrary. He uses his body to test Arthur and his knights.[37]

The Green Knight's exhibitionism is not only characterized by intimidation. After Gawain agrees to the terms of the beheading game, he displays himself vulnerably for his spectators: "The grene knyght upon grounde graythely hym dresses: / A little lut with the hede, the lere he discoveres; / His longe lovelych lokkes he layd over his croun, / Let the naked nec to the note schewe" (417–20). The Green Knight is carefully staging himself for the key act in his performance: he bends his head forward, laying—not simply tossing—his hair over his crown; he *lets* his bare neck show. The narrator's attention to the Green Knight's "lovelych lokkes" again suggests what is human and aesthetically pleasing about the Green Knight's body. Moreover, the Green Knight's voluntary exposure of his naked flesh renders him vulnerable to the fantasizing gaze of his observers. His powerful and intimidating body is approachable, becoming malleable "raw material" that his observers' eyes can mold into a desired image.[38] Similarly, knights in a tournament who suffer wounds while demonstrating exemplary prowess expose their vulnerability to their observers; and this exposure of their humanness—that they are after all flesh and bone—makes them more readily objects of identification for those male observers desiring to be admired, performing knights.

Jackson's delineation of gay male exhibitionism offers another means for articulating the homoerotic dynamics at this stage of the Green Knight's performance. Jackson explains that in "intersubjective narcissism. . .the subject has to be accounted for in its expressions as both spectator *and* spectacle."[39] Likewise, the Green Knight is both spectator and spectacle. From a "phallic" position of power, he gazes at Arthur's knights, evaluating their manliness. At the same time, he is an object of desire, attracting the gaze of his observers. But the moment he bows his head and bares his naked neck, he consciously—and invitingly—surrenders himself to the knights' gaze. The homoerotic appeal is his transgressive masculinity. Jackson explains that a narcissistic exhibitionist "constitut[es]. . .himself as subject by positing his body as image-object in the consciousness of the other. Through the deliberate presentation of his body to the desiring gaze of the other. . .[he] constitutes himself to himself as a desirable object for the other."[40] The Green Knight intentionally constructs himself not as a subject who gazes—which as powerful male he has previously done and will do again—but one who "sustains the desiring look of the other."[41] His role reversal from intimidating and awe-inspiring subject to passive, vulnerable object excites because it is unexpected; his unmanly observers find themselves in control of the manly form before their eyes—a positioning they could not have foreseen.

After the Green Knight receives Gawain's blow he becomes again an active, intimidating exhibitionist. Headless but decidedly masculine, he approaches the knights: "*stythly* [stoutly] he start forth upon *styf schonkes*, / And *runyschly* [fiercely] he raght out, there as renkkes stoden" (431–32; emphasis added). His spellbound observers stare at him as he "his hede by the here in his honde haldes" (436). He then directs his wide-eyed gaze at Guinevere but addresses Gawain, reminding him of the oath he swore to him.[42] His performance ends, as it began, in a stunningly dramatic manner: "With a runisch rout the raynes he tornes, / Halled out at the hal-dor, his hed in his hande, / That the fyr of the flynt flawe fro fole hoves" (457–59). His final action—his grand finale—intertwines the repulsive with the appealing. Although riding out of the hall headless and bleeding, he is at the same time a knight whose manly physique is highly esteemed in the chivalric culture of the text.

The Green Knight's entire performance is erotically charged in that it captivates, mesmerizes, empowers, and, significantly, does not fully satisfy his observers. Heng summarizes Bertilak's wife's seductive performance: "Voluntarily, deliberately, she submits herself to the prospective mastery of the gaze, seeming to let Gawain take the full measure of what he surveys, but only to turn potential mastery into something else, and in other directions, when she manipulates its compulsions to subserve another aim than that of which it is aware: the inculcation and maintenance of a strategically conditioned state of agitation in Gawain."[43] We can likewise summarize the Green Knight's eroticized performance. Throughout his stay in Arthur's hall, but most obvious in the moments just prior to his beheading, the Green Knight is "submitting" himself to the gazes of his observers. Simultaneously titillating and horrifying the knights who are studying him, his body attracts their gaze. Shifting from an active to passive and back to an active position, he manipulates their "compulsions" to interpret and evaluate what they see; he frustrates their efforts to "certify" in their sight the monstrous with the perfect, the green color with the powerfully built torso, the bully with the vulnerable human. And his calculated exit occurs before they have had the opportunity to fully comprehend his performance. Like an effective, captivating performer, he leaves the stage with his audience desiring to see more of him.

The Green Knight's performance at Arthur's court is a dramatized diagram of the potentially homoerotic exhibitionism in chivalric society. It also draws attention to shifting subject/object positions of the performing model knight and his observers during a performance, illustrating how male–male desire circulates in ways that defy modern notions of exclusive activity or passivity. The dramatized exhibitionism in *Sir Gawain* notwithstanding, chivalric treatises and romances generally do not illustrate the visual dynamics of a model knight's performance nor his reaction to being closely studied by admiring (male) observers. Yet even if he fails to acknowledge or respond to those who are enthusiastically watching him, his performance is still potentially homoerotic. In his reading of Rainer Werner Fassbinder's film, *Querelle*, Steven Shaviro articulates a male–male spectatorial relationship that parallels the dynamics I have been examining. Shaviro notes that the "glorious body [of Querelle] is an image that attracts the gaze of Seblon, and of the spectator, precisely because it does not *need* to be looked at; it arouses desire by virtue of its apparent absence of desire."[44] Similarly, a model knight may attract the gaze of his observers because he does not *need* to be looked at or admired, nor is he emotionally invested in being the object of the observer's desire. Shaviro goes on to delineate a homoerotic interaction: "Querelle arouses Seblon's (and the spectator's) desiring glances to the precise extent that he remains unaffected by them, indifferent and inaccessible. Thus, being desired, while himself not experiencing desire, invests Querelle with an aura of intense erotic power. But since this power is a function of unawareness and indifference, it is not something that its bearer can wield or possess. . . . His erotic aura is all the more splendid and seductive in that it cannot be used or touched."[45] A novice knight who enthusiastically desires to be a man-of-worth and examines the body of the performing knight, evaluating it as excitedly as the narrator does the Green Knight, may experience an erotic charge because he knows that the performing knight is indifferent to or perhaps unaware of him. That knights normally perform in armor does not hinder the observer's evaluative act. His eyes would penetrate the knight's armor, imagining the body beneath that is demonstrating such admirable prowess. From this empowering, voyeuristic position, the observer is free to fantasize or fashion the knight's manliness and skill in a manner that is satisfying to him. Of course, a knight in full armor may conceal his enjoyment of performing for admiring male observers, in which case the observer and observed would—unknowingly—be linked in a homoerotic scenario.

★ ★ ★ ★ ★

But why do chivalric treatises urge novice knights to closely observe model men-at-arms? And what would motivate young men enthusiastically to follow this recommendation? The following passage from Charny's *Book of Chivalry* regarding novice knights who have already begun to study the art of chivalry provides an answer to both questions:

> et de plus en plus leur acroist leur cognoissance tant qu'il voient et cognoissent que les bonnes gens d'armes pour les guerres sont plus prisiez et honorez que nul des autres gens d'armes qui soient. Dont leur semble de leur propre

cognoissance que en ce mestier d'armes de guerre se doivent mettre souverainement pour avoir la hautre honnour de proesce.

[Their knowledge increases until they see and recognize that the men-at-arms who are good in war are more highly prized and honored than any other men-at-arms. It therefore seems to them from their own observation that they should immediately take up the practice of arms in war in order to achieve the highest honor in prowess.][46]

The political agenda behind Charny's urging of novice knights to observe model men-at-arms closely is apparent: study the best fighters and then become one. France is after all engaged in a protracted war with England.[47] Charny's prediction (or hope) that young men desiring to be honored men-at-arms will *immediately* take up the practice of chivalry suggests that they would enthusiastically approach this learning task—a task that involves examining and evaluating the men they wish to emulate. These putative acts of male–male spectatorship unfolded in a medieval visual economy that recognized the powerful attraction of the object being viewed; this visual economy also understood spectatorship as a kind of "copulation" between species from subject and object. Knowingly or not, Charny (or any chivalric writer celebrating model knights) is urging young men to engage in visual intimacy with another man. And a young knight's enthusiasm, awe, and possible attraction to the knight performing before his eyes could eroticize the image he processes. The performing knight's pleasure in proving that he is indeed exemplary and the observer's emotional investment in the model's worthiness might further infuse the spectatorial scenario with a homoerotic charge.

Troilus and Criseyde dramatizes visual acts whereby the observer reacts with pleasure, astonishment, or fascination to someone directly observed. Although subject and object are not exclusively male in these scenarios, these visual acts are paradigmatic and, as *Sir Gawain and the Green Knight* illustrates, men could become attracted, stimulated, or mesmerized by the man they are closely studying. Charny urges young men to become esteemed men-at-arms by examining and emulating exemplary knights. These discourses of male–male gazing, both dramatized and suggested, together reveal a fourteenth-century visual economy that is potentially homoerotic.

PART TWO

DENIGRATIONS OF MALE SAME-SEX DESIRE

INTRODUCTION

SODOMY AS A DISCURSIVE WEAPON

Part 1 indicates that there were a variety of discourses that affirm or suggest eroticized intimacy between men in chivalric contexts. The line separating acceptable and unacceptable male–male intimacy is a nebulous one, however; and in societies where strong homosocial attachments were common, an accusation of sodomy was a convenient weapon to hurl at one's political opponent. While scholars are not in agreement regarding when "sodomy" acquired its current meaning—the act of anal sex between men—they do generally concur that the biblical citizens of Sodom were not guilty of indulging in this particular form of same-sex behavior. Referring to the men of Sodom wishing to "know" the visiting angels, Derrick Bailey observes that the Hebrew word, *yadha*, is rarely used in the Old Testament to denote sexual activity, and when it does occur it generally refers to heterosexual intercourse.[1] Boswell supports Bailey's view and offers as further evidence a passage from the New Testament where Jesus apparently relates the Sodom story to inhospitality.[2] Mark Jordan also agrees that the moral lesson of the Sodom story in Genesis 19 is about hospitality to strangers and not same-sex copulation.[3] Jordan maintains that " 'sodomy' is a medieval artifact," a term that was "invented" during the Middle Ages uniting under one rubric "desires, dispositions, and acts, that had earlier been classified differently and separately." He adds, " 'Sodomy' is also a judgment."[4] Whether or not one agrees with Jordan's argument that "sodomy" first took on its current meaning in the high Middle Ages, there is little doubt that by the fourteenth century accusations of "sodomy" referred to sexual acts between men; moreover, the term had become an effective weapon to be used against one's political opponents.

Boswell observes that "[p]erhaps the single most prominent aspect of the period from the later twelfth to the fourteenth century was a sedulous quest for intellectual and institutional uniformity and corporatism throughout Europe. . . . The Inquisition arose to eliminate theological loose ends and divergences of opinions.... Secular and ecclesiastical concerns were melded in the interests of uniformity."[5] James Brundage finds that in the late twelfth century, "[s]exual practices and preferences...commenced to be taken as indicators of doctrinal orthodoxy; deviance form the dominant sexual preference was thought to manifest deviance from accepted doctrine."[6] By this logic it followed that groups such as the various "Manichean" sects that the orthodox church considered heretical must also be guilty of committing acts of sexual deviance. Boswell notes that "[i]t became a commonplace of official terminology to mention 'traitors, heretics, and sodomites' as if they constituted a single association of some sort."[7] An early linking of heresy and sodomy is made by Guibert de Nogent who targets heretics living near Soissons in around 1114:

> conjugia damnant, et fructificare coitibus. Et certe...videas viros mulieribus cohabitare sine mariti conjugisque nomine, ita ut vir cum femina, singulus cum singula, non moretur, sed viri cum viris, feminae cum feminis cubitare noscantur, nam viri apud eos in foeminam coitus nefas est.

> [They condemn marriage and propagation by intercourse. Clearly...you may see men living with women without the name of husband and wife in such fashion that one man does not stay with one woman, each to each, but men are known to lie with men and women with women, for with them it is impious for men to go to women.][8]

While Guibert's charges of same-sex intercourse may be accurate, it is also possible that he is merely discrediting the sect because it rejects a basic tenet of the Roman Church: namely, lawful procreation. Similar accusations were leveled against the Cathars and Vern Bullough suggests that "[s]ince the medieval people recognized the sexual nature of man, they undoubtedly used this aversion to procreation to ascribe to the Cathars every kind of nonprocreative sex."[9]

Heretics were not the only ones accused of practicing sodomy. Boswell observes that during the period of the Crusades, Christian writers increasingly portrayed Muslims as engaging in deviant sexual acts.[10] The political motivation of this defamation is evident in a letter originally thought to have been written by Alexius I Commenus of the Eastern Church but now believed to have been composed (i.e. forged) in the West shortly before the First Crusade:

> Totius aetatis et ordinis viros, id est pueros, adolescentes, juvenes, senes, nobiles, servos, et, quod pejus et impudentius est, clericos et monachos, et heu proh dolor! et quod ab initio non dictum neque auditum est, episcopos Sodomitico peccato deludunt. et etiam unum episcopum sub hoc nefario peccato jam crepuerunt.

[They (i.e. Muslims) have degraded by sodomizing them men of every age and rank: boys, adolescents, young men, old men, nobles, servants, and, what is worse and more wicked, clerics and monks, and even—alas and for shame! something which from the beginning of time has never been spoken of— bishops! They have already killed one bishop with this nefarious sin.][11]

While one should not doubt that sexual acts between men took place in Muslim society, and that Christian and Muslim men possibly had both consensual and non-consensual sex together, the political invective of the quoted text is apparent. Because the list of alleged victims is so sweeping it would appear that no type of Christian male escaped sexual attack from a Muslim. Jacques de Vitry is even more venomous in his *Historia Orientalis*, claiming that Mohammed, "Per hoc latenter vitium Sodomiticum hostis nature in populo suo introduxit. Unde ipsi ex maxima parte non solum in utroque sexu, sed etiam in brutis turpitudinem abusiue operantes" [the enemy of nature, popularized the vice of sodomy among his people, who sexually abuse not only both genders but even animals and have for the most part become like mindless horses or mules].[12] Although de Vitry is apparently using sodomy in its broader definition—including heterosexual anal intercourse as well as the sexual abuse of animals—since much of the anti-Muslim literature focuses on male–male intercourse, we can assume that most Christian readers of de Vitry's book would probably understand sodomy to mean, at least in part, sexual acts between men. Boswell observes that as a result of connecting Christian Europe's most feared enemy with "minority sexual preferences," antipathy of Christian sodomites increased in the popular mind.[13] Thus, a mere charge of sodomy, without conclusive proof, could harm one's reputation and/or economic status. Against this trend of accusing heretics and Muslims of performing deviant sexual acts, we find in the early fourteenth century two European kings attacking their political opponents by leveling charges of sodomy against them.

After nearly ten years of continuous conflict and animosity between King Philip IV (the Fair) of France and Pope Boniface VIII, Philip called a great assembly together at the Louvre on June 13–14, 1303 attended by nobles and high church officials. Guillaume de Plaisians read charges against the pope, which included heresy, sodomy, and other crimes.[14] Joseph Strayer maintains that "the truth or even the reasonableness of the charges was of little importance to the assembly."[15] It was simply a political maneuver by Philip against the pope. Brundage points out that in the popular mind sodomy was considered a common vice among the clergy.[16] It is possible then that Philip merely included sodomy among the other charges *because* it was reasonable. The political effectiveness of Philip's action thus hinges on a social context in which acts of sodomy were imagined to be commonly practiced by officers of the church but nevertheless not tolerated.

The following incident, cited by Brundage, clearly illustrates how an accusation of sodomy is used to harm a political foe. On August 6, 1311, King James II of Aragon accused his political enemy, Pons Hugh IV, Count of Ampurias, of committing sodomy:

> Cum ad audienciam nostram Jacobi...per famem...et c[lam]orem...quam et quem diuicius sine scandalo dissimulare non possemus vel sine periculo tolerare sepe ac sep[iu]s pervenisset ut nonullos in diocesis Gerundensis illa incontinentia laborare que contra naturam est.

> [Since through (common) fame and (general) knowledge certain matters have come to the attention of Us, James,...(w)e can no longer ignore (this situation) without scandal or tolerate (it) without danger. (We have learned that) it has happened often, indeed, very often, that some persons of the Diocese of Gerona cultivate that sort of debauchery which is against nature.][17]

The evidence consists of a number of witnesses who maintained that Hugh made sexual advances to them. Only one, who was threatened with torture, acknowledged having sexual intercourse with the Count. Although the accusations could be true, one must be skeptical of the claim made by witnesses that they were merely innocent victims in the alleged encounters. Whatever James thought personally about sodomitical acts—consensual or not—it is unlikely that his actions were motivated solely by moral indignation.

Brundage notes that Hugh offended James when he captured a Venetian ship and moreover proved that he was a formidable opponent to James by procuring the pope's support for his action. Earlier, Hugh had earned the king's disfavor by resisting his persecution of the Knights Templar. Brundage thus suggests that James drew up the sodomy charge against Hugh in order to wrest Hugh's lands away from him, because a person convicted of sodomy "was tainted with infamy" and subsequently could lose all the public offices he held.[18] James was evidently playing on the popular association of sodomy and divine retribution when he warned that such acts of "debauchery" that are "against nature" cause destruction of cities and their inhabitants.[19] Brundage assumes that James, whom he refers to as a "seasoned skeptic," probably did not himself believe that acts of sodomy "caused earthquakes or that the cities of Aragon and Catalonia were in imminent danger of destruction because of the deviant sexual preferences of the Count of Ampurias."[20] Brundage thus concludes that James's prosecution of Hugh "represents another episode...in the political use of sodomy."[21]

In chapters 6 and 7 I examine in depth "discursive sodomy," that is, verbal articulations of illicit conduct between men. I am using "sodomy" in its medieval sense, denoting same-sex behavior deemed sinful, abominable, and against nature. This negative sodomitical discourse strategically focuses on the disparate power relations between the two partners, rendering one an active aggressor and the other a passive victim. A positively valued sodomy—if that is not a contradiction in terms—would not stigmatize the positions in male–male intimate interactions but rather afford "activity" and pleasure to both partners. While "sodomy" itself seldom surfaces in the trial testimonies of the Knights Templar or the chronicles concerning Edward II and Richard II (and never in *Troilus and Criseyde*), it is always hovering nearby as a hint, a suggestion, a possibility. The discourse I explore sexualizes male–male encounters such as kisses and conversations—acts that are generally understood as asexual (or the potential homoeroticism is unacknowledged). This discourse builds on both the specificity of sodomy—illicit male–male sexual intercourse—and what Barbara Weisberger aptly describes as "the undefined and indefinable nature of the sodomitical."[22] She points out that the unnamed sin of sodomy is "infinitely expansive and highly contaminating."[23] Thus, it can contaminate manipulative or persuasive actions between men that unfold in a secluded and secretive environment; it can taint normative homosocial behavior when it occurs between the wrong men. In other words, discursive sodomy has the potential for *sodomizing* a wide range of male–male intimate acts. The texts I examine deploy associative meanings of sodomy as a political weapon, vilifying those male–male relations deemed a threat to a king, influential nobles, or the realm.

CHAPTER 6

SODOMY, POLITICS, AND MALE–MALE DESIRE

Persecuting The Knights Templar: A Discourse of Indecent Acts

The Order of the Knights Templar, once a highly respected military order, came under serious attack in the early fourteenth century and in the course of a few years was disbanded.[1] Historians unanimously agree that the motivation of Philip IV of France, who led the persecution of the order, was economic and political. Boswell notes that with the Templars' "international treasury" sitting in Paris, it is not surprising that Philip "cast his eye hungrily upon the prosperous order."[2] Malcolm Barber sums up Philip's position: "the Templars were particularly obnoxious to Philip the Fair as a wealthy, exempt and predominantly aristocratic enclave in a country whose king had made considerable progress towards subduing the pretensions of the feudal nobility."[3] Barber also observes that because charges of heresy and indecent acts were at the center of the subsequent trials of the Templars, Philip was evidently tapping into the ongoing persecution of "sodomitical heretics."[4] Boswell maintains that the current harsh penalties for those found guilty of committing sodomy made it the most politically effective accusation to bring against the order. He goes on to point out that in France, "mere suspicion of the act was considered sufficient to warrant such torture that many of the knights died under it."[5] James Given asserts that "King Philip the Fair . . . used and abused inquisitorial procedures to destroy the Knights Templar."[6]

In his excellent study of the medieval Inquistion in Languedoc, John Arnold remarks: "Inquisition documents were not made for 'us': the logic that informed their production is part of the historical situation under analysis. . . . [T]hey must be understood not as passive reflectors of events occurring 'elsewhere,' but as sites of discourse that are inextricably part of the performance of power and authority. As texts, they must be analyzed not only in terms of what they *say*, but also of what they *do*: their functions, their effects, their textuality."[7] The texts of the Templar trials create a discourse of illicit sexuality—a written proof of the Templars guilt, even though there is a paucity of actual cases where indecent acts took place. The narratives re-presented in the authoritative hand of the trial notaries collectively perform the task Philip of France and his allies set out to do: namely, justifying the dissolution of the Order of the Knights Templar and confiscation of their considerable assets.

Anne Gilmour-Bryson summarizes the most important accusations made against the Templars:

1. That the members denied Christ, God, the Virgin or the saints during a secret ceremony.
2. That the members committed a variety of sacrilegious acts upon the cross or the image of Christ.
3. That the members practised obscene kisses.
4. That the members encouraged and permitted the practice of sodomy.
5. That the priests of the Order did not consecrate the Host.
6. That the members did not believe in the sacraments.
7. That the members practised various sorts of idolatry.
8. That the grand master, or other dignitaries, absolved brethren from their sins.[8]

There has been much discussion among historians regarding whether or not the Templars were guilty of these charges. Gilmour-Bryson has recently suggested that since it was standard practice during the medieval Inquisition to include sodomy with charges of heresy, then perhaps "homosexual accusations [were] added to the other charges simply because the authors of the allegations hoped that some of them would fit."[9] That charges of obscene kisses and incitement to commit sodomy are sandwiched between other charges typically directed at heretics supports Gilmour-Bryson's suggestion. Both of these charges were also associated with accusations of witchcraft. Vern Bullough points out that the charge regarding obscene kisses performed during the initiation ceremony relates to acts allegedly performed during heretical or witchcraft ceremonies that involved kissing the anus of an animal.[10]

The articles of accusation against the Templars that I want to examine are the following:

> Item, quod in receptione fratrum dicti ordinis vel circa interdum recipiens [et] receptus aliquando [se] deosculabantur in ore, in umbilico seu <in> ventre nudo et in ano seu spina dorsi.

Item, aliquando in umbilico.
Item, aliquando in fine spine dorsi.
Item, aliquando in virga virili....
Item, quod fratribus quos recipiebant dicebant quod ad invicem poterant
unus cum al[io] com[misceri] carnaliter.
Item, quod hoc licitum erat eis facere.
Item, quod debebant hec facere ad invicem et pati.
Item, quod hec facere non erat eis peccatum.
Item, quod hec faciebant ipsi vel plures eorum.
Item, quod aliqui eorum.

[Item, that in the reception of the brothers of the said Order or at about that time,
sometimes the receptor and sometimes the received were kissed on the mouth, on
the navel, or on the bare stomach, and on the buttocks or the base of the spine.
—Item (that they were kissed) sometimes on the navel.—Item, (that they
were kissed) sometimes on the base of the spine.—Item, (that they were kissed)
sometimes on the penis....
Item, that they told the brothers whom they received that they could have
carnal relations together.
Item, that it was licit for them to do this.
Item, that they ought to do and submit to this mutually.
Item, that it was not a sin for them to do this.
Item, that they did this, or many of them (did).—Item, that some of them
(did).][11]

Gilmour-Bryson notes that "there is a very close correlation between the
use of torture, which appears to have been widely used in France and Italy,
and confessions of guilt."[12] Regarding the charges that newly initiated
brothers were given permission to practice sodomy, even after torture had
been applied only two out of 138 witnesses questioned in the Paris trials
admitted to having actually engaged in same-sex activity. However, 107
admitted that such sexual behavior was permitted but they themselves never
took part in it.[13] Each witness who confirmed the validity of the charge,
even without confessing his own guilt, suggests that illicit same-sex behavior
is occurring somewhere; multiplying this confirmation 107 times produces
a narrative of sodomy seemingly occurring *everywhere*.

The testimony given at the trials in Poitiers offers diverse accounts of
the indecent kisses taking place during the initiation ceremony. Gilmour-
Bryson notes that the trials at Poitiers were very important in that they
were intended to convince Pope Clement V that Philip was justified in
demanding the prosecution of the Templars. She explains that torture was
used and "[t]he witnesses appearing seem to have been handpicked, perhaps
trained in their answers, in order to convince the pope of the Templars'
guilt."[14] If this is the case, then why do the witnesses offer different versions of the initiation ceremony—particularly in light of the fact that the

overwhelming majority of testimonies at different trials offer strikingly similar responses?[15] I would suggest that because the witnesses wished to placate the inquisitors, they made sure they provided the *right* answers by drawing on rumors circulating among the various Templar households or, possibly, their own experiences; in either case, these diverse testimonies—whether they represent the truth or not—together form a discourse of illicit male–male conduct.

Johannes de Joviniaco, a witness at the Poitiers trial, reports that the normal procedure at the initiation ceremony involved the initiated knight kissing the receptor on the mouth, the navel, and the base of the spine (anus).[16] Another witness, Clemens de Pomar, offers quite a different version of his own initiation ceremony: "Duxerunt eum retro altare, ubi fecerunt eum [exire] suis vestibus secularibus, quo denudato dicti magistri et alii fratres, qui erant ibidem, osculati fuerunt [in] ore, et ipse postea eum in fine spine dorsi, secundo in virga virilli, tertio in umbilico et quarto in ore" [they (i.e. the brothers who received him) led him behind the altar where they made him take off his secular clothes, and the other brothers who were there kissed the master on the mouth, and afterwards, he, himself (Clemens), naked, kissed the master first on the anus, second on the penis, third on the navel, and fourth on the mouth.][17] Two additional witnesses present accounts of the initiation ceremony that deviate from both the "normal" procedure and that described by Clemens de Pomar. Iohannes de Villaribus claims that he was undressed and then kissed by two brothers on the mouth, navel, and anus, and afterwards led to the preceptor with whom apparently no kisses were exchanged. Iacobus de Castilhione states that the receptor kissed him on the anus, navel, and mouth, in that order.[18] The official charges brought against the Templars do not explicitly state that the initiate was naked at the initiation ceremony, although it is implied in that either the receptor or initiate was allegedly kissed on the navel or "bare stomach." Thus, in claiming that they were undressed and then brought to the preceptor naked, Clemens and Iohannes offer testimony that in effect eroticizes the initiation ceremony. Each of these novices is in a sense "raped" by experienced Templars, and the fact that he is made to take off his clothes/undressed suggests he is not naked by choice. The conflicting testimony at this trial forms a multifarious discourse of illicit male–male interactions, which implies that individual preceptors drew up their own initiation ceremony—based on their own taste or proclivity—rather than follow a standard procedure. That personal agency plays a role implicates the Templars more deeply in sexually informed conduct.

There is also a great deal of conflicting testimony regarding the accusation that statutes of the order permitted and even encouraged sexual acts among the brothers, and that some knights allegedly took advantage of this.

Typical of the testimony given at the Poitiers trial is that offered by Hugo de Guamaches, who maintains that although he was given permission to satisfy his natural urges with brothers of the order, "Set ipse dixit, quod non faceret nec unquam fecit nec fuit requisitus, nec audivit, quod fratres abuterentur se ipsis" [he said that he never did this, nor did anyone require him to do this, nor did he hear of anyone taking advantage of this].[19] His testimony nevertheless adds to the discourse of alleged sexual misconduct because in admitting that permission was given, Hugo suggests the possibility that, unknown to him, some brothers of the order might have "required" their fellow knights to engage in sexual acts. And evidently some did. Clemens de Pomar states that the master commanded him not to refuse other brothers of the order who wished to have sex with him. Interestingly, rather than presenting himself as a victim of the master's command, he says that he in fact engaged in sexual acts with brothers whenever he wished.[20] Clemens offers a narrative of apparently one-sided sexual conduct between men because he gives no indication that the knights derived pleasure from having sex with him. At the Auvergne trial, Guillaume de Born claims that, following the statute, he often engaged in sexual acts with the brothers with whom he shared a dwelling. And like Clemens de Pomar, he presents a one-sided sexual scenario. Guillaume describes how the brothers would lie face down on the floor, holding themselves up with their feet and hands, and he would then climb on top of one of them and anally penetrate him. He admits to having done this more than fifty times.[21] Guillaume's narrative depicts same-sex activity as being carried out between an "aggressor" and a "victim" (or "victims") with no indication that the victim willingly assumed his position or that these roles ever were reversed. Guillaume does not admit that he himself at any time lay on the ground on all fours while another brother penetrated him. While the "victim" might very well derive pleasure from this apparently regularly occurring encounter, the narrative does not offer that as a possibility. Both narratives present same-sex conduct between knights as an aggressive, "unchivalric" act in which evidently only the desire of the knight initiating the encounter is considered. (Not that mutually initiated sodomy would be acceptable but it would at least be more consistent with the ideal that brother knights in a chivalric order were equals.) Despite the fact that Guillaume's and Clemens's testimonies differ markedly from that given by the majority of witnesses at the Auvergne and Poitiers trials, their narratives serve to substantiate the validity of the charges.[22] They explicitly describe sexual scenarios that most of the witnesses affirmed were occurring somewhere.

The trials in England did not produce damaging testimony on a par with that provided by witnesses on the Continent. One witness after the other denies the charge of indecent kisses, admitting only to a kiss on the mouth, and each also denies having been given permission to have sexual relations with other knights of the order.[23] Of course, the series of repeated questions itself creates a narrative of alleged illicit behavior. Moreover, a trace of potential guilt remains in the denials recorded at the English trials because, since some knights on the Continent admitted to wrongdoings (or having been given permission to engage in sexual activities with one another), there is the possibility that the English Templars were lying. Nevertheless, some sensational testimony regarding sexual acts surfaces in the documents of the trials in England; but this comes from witnesses who are not members of the order. Some historians dismiss these testimonies as hearsay. Clarence Perkins vehemently attacks these "stories," describing them as "extremely fantastic and improbable in character, remarkable productions of overheated imaginations."[24] Konrad Schottmüller gives little credence to such "old wives tales" and rumors spread by a few members of minority orders who did not report firsthand experiences but rather what they had heard from someone else.[25] While Perkins and Schottmüller might be correct in finding the English Templars innocent of these charges, the "stories" are significant in that they illustrate the discourse regarding same-sex behavior that might circulate within clerical and secular circles in early fourteenth-century England.

Robertus le Dorturer, a notary in London, offers testimony based on direct experience. He claims that Guido de Foresta, the high preceptor of the English order, wanted to sodomize him but he ran away.[26] This is especially interesting because the alleged statute permitted sexual intercourse only between knights of the order. Robertus thus raises the possibility that same-sex encounters took place between Templars and outsiders. Like similar accusations made by knights on the Continent, Robertus's testimony depicts potential male–male sexual relations as a failed act of sexual violation—the failure of an "aggressor" to penetrate his "victim"—thus underscoring the violence or aggression that informs these narratives. Another non-Templar witness, Johannes de Presbur, a member of the Carmelite order, reports that a Templar wanted to sodomize a relative of his. Although he produces the name of his relation and specific information about the Templar, he neglects to mention if the act was consummated.[27] It is possible that the inquisitor did not pursue the matter since the charge that the Templar propositioned Johannes's relation alone was considered damaging testimony. Whether true or simply made up in order to please the inquisitors, these two testimonies describe illicit sexual encounters and thus add to the negative discourse of same-sex behavior that all of the Templar trials were generating.

The prosecution of the Templars for allegedly performing obscene kisses and engaging in—or attempting to engage in—sexual acts with one another builds on a long-standing association between heresy and sodomy. Records of the various Templar trials together form a denigrating discourse of male same-sex desire. The attack on the Knights Templar by the King of France and his allies was certainly politically motivated and illustrates the expediency of hurling charges of sodomy and sodomitically inflected acts at a formidable opponent. Despite the fact that the majority of damaging testimony contain unsubstantiated allegations, not to mention the number of conflicting accounts from witnesses, the prosecutors succeeded in bringing down the entire order.[28]

Vilifying Same-Sex Intimacy: The Attack on Edward II and Piers Gaveston

Modern historians have, in various ways, addressed the intimate personal relationship that evidently existed between Edward II and Piers Gaveston, the son of a Gascon knight.[29] Anthony Tuck concedes that Edward's "emotional obsession with his favourite" aroused the wrath of the nobles.[30] While not convinced that Edward and Gaveston actually engaged in homosexual acts, Caroline Bingham acknowledges that Edward's behavior encouraged accusations of sodomy.[31] Mary Saaler, however, concludes that "the evidence points to a homosexual relationship between these two men."[32] My purpose is not to settle this question once and for all, but rather to examine the negative discourse concerning the relationship between Edward and Gaveston found in chronicles of the period. Alan Smith articulates the issues that are at the center of my investigation: "in what way does sodomy menace political institutions, and, more specifically, the absolute monarchy?. . . . Explanations based on social relations, such as the anxiety over political friendships between the king and his courtiers suspected of 'unnatural' influences, define this problem in terms of access to power, embodied by the monarch's self. In such scenarios, real or imagined intimacy with the king's body threatens the social order by circumventing the court's highly structured means of access."[33] In the case of Edward II and Gaveston, as well as the very similar case later in the century involving Richard II and his favorites, the motivating factor for the nobles' criticism and subsequent attack was their perception that the favorite had exclusive access to the king. I want to examine how those who felt excluded and threatened by the king's intimate association with a particular courtier generate a discourse that negatively sexualizes these relationships.

There are a number of chronicles covering the reign of Edward II that were written either contemporaneously or shortly after the events they are recording. These include *Annales Londonienses, Annales Paulini, Vita Edwardi secundi,* Trokelow's *Annales,* and Robert of Reading's continuation of the

Flores historiarum.[34] Voicing the concerns of the influential nobles, these chronicles do not wage an attack on same-sex relations per se but rather on the "immoderateness" and, above all, the exclusive nature of Edward's relation with Gaveston. In excluding the nobles from his inner circle of advisers, the king did not make decisions that served the nobles' best interests. Charles Wood notes that the reason we do not find explicit accounts of Edward's sexual behavior in the chronicles is because "sexual acts are normally private, hidden from the gaze of others; further, medieval chroniclers, despite a frequent willingness to purvey the most wild and unlikely tales, generally displayed a remarkable restraint when dealing with such matters."[35] Wood's explanation is plausible, and historians rightly observe that the chronicles do not explicitly state that Edward and Gaveston had a sexual relationship. However, the chronicles often articulate this relationship in sexually inflected language and always cast it in a negative light.

One chronicler describes how Edward, then prince, became enraptured with Gaveston: "Quem filius regis intuens in eum / tantum protinus amorem iniecit quod cum eo firmitatis fedus iniit, et pre ceteris mortalibus indissolubile dileccionis vinculum secum elegit et firmiter disposuit innodare" [when the king's son gazed at Gaveston, he immediately felt so much love for him that he entered into a compact of brotherhood with him and chose and decided to tie himself to him, against all mortals, in an unbreakable bond of affection].[36] Edward's prompt recall of Gaveston following the death of Edward I, who had banished Gaveston from England because of what he saw as his son's dangerous attachment to his friend, suggests that he could not bear the absence of his "brother." And the chroniclers were quick to comment on the inordinate intimacy between the reunited friends.

Contemporary chroniclers note that Edward II "immediately" summoned Gaveston back to England, keeping him close at his side and loving him exclusively.[37] And the chronicler cited earlier remarks that after Edward recalled Gaveston from exile in 1307, the "flame of love" between the two friends was renewed.[38] The months immediately following Edward's reunion with Gaveston provoked a great deal of negative commentary. A major accusation made against the young king was that he "clung" to the advice of his intimate friend, Gaveston, rejecting the traditional sources for counsel, namely, the nobles. While the Saint Paul chronicler notes that Edward also turned to young men with whom he had association since his youth, the nobles felt most threatened by Gaveston's privileged position at court and access to the king.[39] The author of the *Vita Edwardi secundi* clearly states the nobles' position regarding Gaveston's intimate bond with the king: "Inuidebant enim ei magnates terre, quia ipse solus haberet gratiam in oculis regis et quasi secundus rex dominaretur, cui subessent omnes et par nullus" [For the magnates of the land hated him, because he alone found favour in the king's eyes and lorded it over them like a second king, to whom all were subject and none equal].[40] At the base of the nobles' charges is the suggestion that Edward was blinded by his excessive love for Gaveston. Johannes de Trokelowe observes: "Petrum de Gavestone, quem a primaeva aetate prae omnibus hominibus mundi rex dilexerat ultra modum" [from an early age, of all the men in the world, Edward loved Gaveston beyond the bounds of moderation].[41] He also reports how Edward, upon returning to England following his marriage to Isabella of France, greeted Gaveston with unrestrained affection before the eyes of the nobles who were also present: "Inter quos Petrum occurrentem, datis osculis & ingeminatis amplexibus, familiaritate venerabatur singulari" [running to meet Gaveston, who was among them (i.e. the nobles), he gave him kisses and repeated embraces; He (Edward) adored him with a singular familiarity].[42] It is this perceived "singular familiarity" between Edward and Gaveston that greatly disturbed the nobles. As Alan Bray and Michel Rey point out regarding James I and his friend, Robert Carr, "public displayed intimacy" between a king and his favorite advertised the influence and privileged position enjoyed by the king's favorite.[43] Although none of the chronicles contemporary with Edward II specifically accuses Edward of committing sodomy with Gaveston, they imply that this was an illicit relationship.

After Edward married Isabella, the Saint Paul chronicler reports that Edward sent the wedding gifts received from the King of France (Isabella's father) to Gaveston. Among these gifts was an extremely beautiful marriage bed.[44] The chronicler thus implies that Edward was going to consummate his marriage with Gaveston rather than with Isabella. Somewhat later, the nobles refused to attend a parliament, fearing it was unsafe for them because "capitalis inimicus eorum. . .regio lateret in thalamo" [their chief enemy. . .was lurking in the king's (bed)chamber].[45] The author's use of *thalamus*, with its connotation of marriage bed, implies that Gaveston is not merely the king's valet or chamber knight but also his bed-companion. The Saint Paul chronicler also indirectly chastises the king for his behavior during the coronation banquet, noting that after the queen's uncles observed how on the dining-couch (*triclinium*) Edward paid more attention to Gaveston than to Isabella, they indignantly returned to France.[46] The chronicler thus paints a picture of Edward reclining with Gaveston at the banquet, openly displaying intimate affection. He goes on to report that a rumor was spreading everywhere that the king loved "an evil sorcerer" more than his beautiful wife.[47] The idea that Gaveston held Edward under a spell and thus "seduced" him from reason is a central charge made by the nobles, which I will turn to shortly. The Saint Paul chronicler's commentary on Gaveston's prominent role at Edward's coronation further vilifies Edward and Gaveston's relationship. He remarks that Gaveston carried the crown in his "foul/sordid hands,"[48] which in light of widespread criticism of Edward's excessive love for Gaveston and implications that the two men slept together suggests that Gaveston's relationship with Edward is somehow "foul" or "sordid." Robert of Reading (at Westminster) also condemns the relationship between Edward and Gaveston as a result of what was witnessed at the coronation and banquet: "Angliae et caeteros similiter habuit in abhominationem et totaliter in despectum, quia praedictus novus rex eum ultra modum et rationem amavit" [the English, and other men similarly, considered it an abomination and completely contemptible that the new king loved him beyond measure and reason].[49] I suggest that the chronicler is deploying "abomination" in its biblical sense—an act extremely odious to God—and since he is referring here to the relationship between two men, he is possibly interpreting Edward and Gaveston's bond as sodomitical.[50]

These thinly veiled allegations that the king was involved in an illicit relationship with his favorite are inextricably linked to political concerns. If Edward had merely kept Gaveston as a minion and maintained good relations with the nobles, it is unlikely that anyone would have strongly objected to the king's sexual life. After all, he did what was expected of him in producing a male heir. However, he antagonized the magnates of England by naming Gaveston earl of Cornwall, and perhaps even more infuriating to the nobles, he excluded them from his inner circle of advisers and confidants. Chroniclers suggest that Edward's inseparable attachment to his favorite worked against the interests of the nobles because Gaveston, a foreigner who often demonstrated his contempt for the English aristocrats, turned the king away from them. And as far as the nobles were concerned, Gaveston's relationship with the king had to be permanently severed.

In 1311 the king's opponents drew up a list of ordinances demanding an extensive reform of royal policy. The denigrating discourse regarding Edward and Gaveston generated by the chroniclers finds expression in ordinance #20: "quod Petrus de Gauestone dominum regem male duxit, domino regi male consuluit, et ipsum ad male faciendum deceptorie et multiformiter induxit…de die in diem dominando supra statum regis et corone in destructione regis et regni; specialiter elongando cor domini regis a suis legiis omnibus" [that Piers Gaveston has led the lord king astray, counselled him badly and persuaded him deceitfully and in many ways to do evil,…dominating from day to day the state of the king and of the crown to the destruction of the king and kingdom; more especially by turning away the lord king's heart from his liege men].[51] Building on contemporary criticism of Edward's excessive love and affection for Gaveston, the ordinance's presentation of Edward as a victim—dominated, acted upon, and led astray by his male beloved—casts this relationship under a shadow of aggressive, illicit same-sex conduct. Another chronicler refers to Gaveston as a *seducer* of the king.[52] Gaveston's alleged deceptive manipulation of Edward is inextricably linked to the personal—possibly sexual—nature of their bond. The label, "seducer," enters a discursive arena that interprets Edward and Gaveston's relationship as intimate, exclusive, and one-sided— a relationship characterized by the king's blind, immoderate love for his (manipulating) companion. And Edward, who is the one being *seduced*, occupies the passive position in this sodomitical scenario.[53]

Robert of Reading interrupts his narrative of events occurring in 1324 to lash out at the king: "O versana stultitia regis Anglorum, a Deo et hominibus cunctis reprobanda, qui sibi proriam infamiam et concubitus illicitos peccatis plenos non dilexisset, nequaquam tam generosam regni consortem et dulces amplexus conjugales in contemptum generis sui a latere suo removisset!" [Oh! the insane stupidity of the king of the English, condemned by God and men, who should not (have) love(d) his own infamy and illicit copulations, full of sin, and should never have removed from his side his noble consort and her gentle wifely embraces, in contempt for her noble birth].[54] Heterosexual love was undoubtedly far less threatening to the nobles than same-sex love. Robert offers a sweeping view of Edward's behavior, one that includes Gaveston, Hugh Despenser, the younger, and possibly other men as well. In painting this summary portrait of Edward, Robert suggests that the current political turmoil in England— and Edward's increasingly precarious position—is directly linked with the king's "illicit copulations, full of sin."

Chronicles that were written later in the fourteenth century also vilify Edward's relationship with Gaveston. The *Gesta Edwardi de Carnarvan*, first composed probably in the 1360s but, according to Stubbs, not finally shaped before 1377, describes how the earls condemned Gaveston for *seducing* his feudal lord and king.[55] The chronicler is evidently drawing on earlier sources, which claimed that because Edward was so in love with Gaveston and clung to his advice in all matters, Edward was *seduced* into actions that were not in the interests of the nobles. Thomas de Burton, writing at the very end of the fourteenth century or early fifteenth century, does not use such vague terms as "excessive" or "immoderate" to describe Edward's love for Gaveston; rather, he states very clearly: "ipse quidem Edwardus in vitio sodomitico nimium delectabat" [Edward, indeed, took too much delight in the sodomitic vice].[56] Thomas's chronicle is first and foremost a history of the Meaux monastery and other events are provided merely as historical background. While Thomas undoubtedly drew on earlier chronicles for his comments on the reign of Edward II, it appears that his conclusion regarding Edward's sexual habits is his own. While they certainly imply it, the major chronicles contemporary with Edward II do not *directly* state that Edward committed sodomy. Thomas's observation thus reflects a late fourteenth-century view of Edward II.

Another chronicler contemporary with Thomas de Burton, but writing in a very different part of England, was Thomas Walsingham. Walsingham generally relies on Trokelowe's *Annales* for his depiction of the early years of Edward's reign (and Edward's relationship with Gaveston) but varies the language and occasionally adds his own comments. For instance, after presenting a description of how Edward's love for Gaveston resulted in the king "clinging" exclusively to him, which follows Trokelowe nearly verbatim, Walsingham inserts what appears to be his own reading of Gaveston: "Ille vero, etsi eum facie tenus reamaret, ejus, ni fallor, munera plus amavit" [Truly, although as far as his outward appearance he loved Edward in return, but, not to be mistaken, he loved rewards more].[57] In viewing Gaveston as a type of male prostitute—pretending to love Edward in exchange for gifts and favors—Walsingham situates this same-sex relation in the realm of the sexual. By not merely copying information from previous sources but also expanding on the events he was reporting, Walsingham adds to the still current discourse denigrating Edward and Gaveston's relationship.

Thus, in the late fourteenth century, during the reign of Edward II's great grandson, Richard II, at least three chronicles were being written, which in varying degrees reinterpreted reports of a notorious same-sex relationship from the early part of the century. Another notorious case of alleged illicit sexual behavior from the early fourteenth century, namely, the trials of the Knights Templar, apparently had currency at this time as well. In reporting on the Templars, Walsingham does not merely copy information gleaned from earlier chronicles but rather summarizes the events in his own words, drawing his own conclusion regarding the charge of sodomy. While the actual accusations (#40–45) listed in the *Annales Londonienses* state that brothers of the order were permitted to practice sodomy, and many in fact did so, Walsingham reports: "depositum est contra eos, quod vitio foedabantur sodomitico" [it was charged against them, that they were defiled by the sodomitical vice].[58] He not only suggests that the entire order was guilty of this sin but also adds that they were "defiled" by it.

Chroniclers of the late fourteenth century did not only generate a negative discourse regarding illicit male–male relations during the early years of the century; they also had much to say about the same-sex friendships of the present king, Richard II, who in some ways followed the footsteps of his great grandfather.

Richard II and his Court Favorites: Tales of Seduction and Perversion

The year 1388 was a sobering one for the twenty-one-year-old Richard II. For it was at the parliament early that year—the parliament that came to be known as the "Merciless" Parliament—that the party of nobles, the Lords Appellant, succeeded in removing all of Richard's court favorites from his side.[59] The underlying theme of the thirty-nine articles of appeal was that Richard was unduly influenced by his favorites. Thus, the king's personal relations with other men was at the center of the nobles' charges. Anthony Tuck draws a parallel between Richard II's development of a "personal government" in the years between 1382 and 1386 in which he relied solely on the counsel of his close associates, excluding the high nobles, and the policy of Edward II: "Once again, as in Edward's reign, men who thought themselves the natural counsellors of the king found their place usurped by others."[60] He goes on to point out that Richard's close associates monopolized access to the king and "Richard, like Edward, rewarded his closest friends and supporters with lavish grants of land, offices, and titles."[61] The nobles at the Parliament of 1386 make a chilling reference to the fate of Edward II, who was deposed and subsequently murdered in 1327:

> Habent enim ex antiquo statuto, et de facto non longe retroactis temporibus experienter (quod dolendum est habito), si rex ex maligno consilio quocumque. . .se alienauerit a populo suo, nec uoluerit per iura regni et statuta. . .set capitose in suis insanis consiliis propriam uoluntatem suam singularem proterue exercere, extunc licitum est eis cum communi assensu et consensu populi regni ipsum regem de regali solio abrogare, et propinquiorem aliquem de stirpe regia loco eius in regni solio sublimare.

> [They have an ancient law, which not long since, lamentably, had to be invoked, which provides that if the king, upon some evil counsel. . .estrange himself from his people, and will not be governed and guided by the laws of the land. . .but wrong-headedly, upon his own unsound conclusions, follows the promptings of his untempered will, then it would be lawful with the common assent and agreement of the people of the realm to put down the king from his royal seat, and raise another of the royal lineage in his place.][62]

The nobles' invoking of Edward II's fate reveals that his fall from power—and the cause of that fall—was circulating in the 1380s. Moreover, Richard's same-sex attachments were being compared to Edward's and, likewise, they generated a negative, politicized discourse.

Richard's court favorites during the 1380s included Michael de la Pole, Simon Burley, and Robert de Vere; but it was to the youngest member of the group, de Vere, to whom Richard was evidently most emotionally attached.[63] Tuck observes that "of all the king's favourites, he was the most lavishly rewarded."[64] Nigel Saul points to what was clearly the central issue: namely, the favors bestowed on de Vere in the way of land grants "contrasted sharply with the parsimony shown by the king to other more deserving lords."[65] What further fueled the lords' rage was that Richard blatantly favored a young man who in their view was not exceptional on account of high social rank or military prowess, and thus one who did not deserve the rewards that historically belonged to them.[66] It is not surprising that the nobles' envy of the privileges Richard's friends received, together with their frustration at being excluded from the king's inner circle, escalated to a full-blown attack on the king's favorites in 1388. Modern historians have not focused on what is clearly implied in the nobles' agenda: the severance of Richard's most personal ties with other men. The nobles (and the chroniclers reporting the events) did not disregard the intertwining of personal and political affairs; Richard rewarded those men whom he cared for, and in the case of de Vere, evidently loved.

The major historical sources for the reign of Richard II during the 1380s include the *Westminster Chronicle*, Thomas Walsingham's *Chronicon Angliae* and his later *Historia Anglicana*, Henry Knighton's *Chronicle*, and the *Historia vitae et regni Ricardi secundi*.[67] With the exception of the *Historia Anglicana*, which reflects revisions Walsingham made to his earlier *Chronicon Angliae*, the other chronicles were written soon after the events they recorded.[68] My purpose is not merely to restate the events leading up to the Parliament of 1388 but rather to examine how the chroniclers' reports of these events create a sexually charged discourse that depicts Richard's same-sex relations as dangerous to the well-being of the realm. The chroniclers' venomous attacks on Richard and his companions echo the views of the powerful nobles—views that may or may not reflect the actual situation.

The Westminster chronicler's report of two incidents illustrates the social acceptability of close bonds between the king and particular male subjects. He notes that while the king was at Ely in the spring of 1383, a knight who was traveling in the royal party, one "who was on terms of the closest intimacy with" the king, was struck by lightening and blinded. Richard immediately ordered the clergy to lead a procession to a nearby holy site and pray for the knight's sight to return.[69] Richard's response indicates that this man was indeed someone to whom he was particularly close, and the chronicler's parenthetical information explains—and justifies—the king's reaction. Apparently, the king would not have responded in this concerned manner had another one of his knights with whom he was not so "intimate" been similarly injured. The chronicler offers no indication that this relationship, or the king's reaction to his friend's mishap, was negatively viewed. The chronicler also reports the king's reaction to the murder of a longtime friend, the son of the earl of Stafford, in 1385: "Publicata vero morte filii comitis predicti rex diucius vacavit in lacrimis et lamentis, quia illum quasi coevum et sodalem sue juventutis in flore magis corditer diligebat" [When the death of the earl's son was made known the king abandoned himself for some time to tears and mourning, since he had loved the lad all the more tenderly for having been a contemporary and comrade in the heyday of this own youth].[70] Here again there is no hint of condemnation of the king for shedding tears upon learning that he lost a friend whom he had loved "tenderly [corditer]." Both incidents highlight Richard's proclivity for forming intimate ties with men and reveal that when these relationships did not threaten the interests of the nobles, no one apparently objected.[71]

The chronicles do however clearly express criticism of Richard's actions concerning Robert de Vere. The *Historia* states that at the parliament held on October 20, 1385, "dominus rex, cupiens dominum comitem Oxon', dominum Robertum de Veer, quem intime diligit, honorare, ad tumulum sui honoris ipsum marchionem Dublinie in Hibernia constituit atque fecit" [the king, desiring to honor the earl of Oxford (i.e. de Vere), whom he loved intimately, and to add to the hill of honors (already received), established and made him marquis of Dublin in Ireland].[72] The writer undoubtedly voices the nobles' indignation by noting that the king desired to add to the "hill of honors" that had already been bestowed on de Vere. Also, in adding the parenthetical information that Richard "loved" de Vere "intimately," the chronicler links the promotion with the king's intense feelings for de Vere. While it is not uncommon for a king to love his subjects, this particular love posed a threat to the nobles because they perceived it as being exceptionally strong or "intimate." In the following year, when Richard raised de Vere even higher, naming him to the position of duke of Ireland, the nobles condemned the promotion of a man they considered "mediocre," one who did not stand out because of lineage or "virtuous qualities."[73] In the nobles' view, the king was blinded by his love for de Vere to such an extent that he could not see what was best for the realm. What they are saying in a sense is that the king loved and rewarded the wrong man.

The Westminster chronicler reports that at the parliament of November 1383, "inter regem et dominos temporales magna dissencio est exorta; nam prout eis videbatur rex insano consilio adherebat et propter hoc bonum regimen circa se non admisit" [a serious quarrel arose between the king and the lords temporal, because, as it seemed to them, he clung to unsound policies and for this reason excluded wholesome guidance from his entourage].[74] Richard's exclusion of the nobles from his inner circle of men was a highly contentious issue. The political motivation for the nobles' charge is evident from the qualifying clause, "as it seemed to them." The nobles' own interests defined the distinction between "unsound" and "wholesome" counsel. Although ostensibly they were concerned about the well-being of the realm, pointing out that in following the good counsel of the lords former illustrious kings made England "a land of plenty and brilliant prosperity,"[75] one cannot doubt that in a prosperous England the upper nobility prosper as well. Moreover, echoing their predecessors who levied similar charges against Edward II, the nobles accuse Richard's favorites of monopolizing access to the king, thereby supplanting the lords from the position they traditionally occupied. It is not surprising then that the lords "nitebantur totum onus gubernacionis supra se assumere" [strove to take the full burden of control upon themselves].[76]

In reporting the events leading up to the Merciless Parliament of 1388—the culmination of the nobles' campaign to wrest Richard's court favorites from their powerful influence on the king—chroniclers describe the relations between Richard and his intimate friends in a sexually charged discourse that presents the king as the passive, "seduced" victim of the machinations of evil, perverse men. Knighton refers to the king's closest friends in 1387—Robert de Vere, Michael de la Pole, Alexander Neville, Robert Tresilian, and Nicholas Brembre—as "quinque nephandi seductores regis" [the king's five (abominable) seducers].[77] And, commenting on de la Pole's influence on the king during the French invasion scare of 1386, the author of the *Historia* observes: "rex circumquaque delusus, seductus et subplantus est" [the king was completely deluded, seduced, and overthrown].[78] Even more revealing is Walsingham's rubric for his report on the events directly following the Parliament of 1386: "Rex a seductoribus circumvenitur" [the King is encircled by seducers].[79] He writes: "rex, contra vota procerum, fecit eum [Michael de la Pole] cohabitare sibi, una cum duce Hiberniae et archiepiscopo Eboracensi, domino Alexandro Nevyle; qui extunc commoverunt regem contra dominos" [the king, against the wishes of the nobles (who voted to impeach de la Pole because of illegal acts he committed), made him (de la Pole) live with him, and with the duke of Ireland and the archbishop of York, Alexander Neville, who then incited the king against the nobles].[80] Walsingham's language not only suggests that the king is harboring a criminal but also that this criminal is sheltered under the king's roof together with de Vere and Neville. In describing the king "encircled" by his favorites, Walsingham creates a scenario where Richard is physically in the presence of his intimate friends who assume an active role toward him—inciting him against the nobles. Physical contact between Richard and his companions is suggested in that *commovere* means not only "to incite" but also "to move violently," "to shake."

Walsingham's scenario also includes a report of how these men "seduce" the king: "susurrantes regem non in effectu esse regem, sed nomine tenus, futurumque, ut nihil sui juris exsisteret, si domini tanta potestate gauderent" [they whispered that the king was not, in effect, king but only in name, and in the future, none of his own laws would come forth if the nobles were to enjoy so much power].[81] Walsingham implies that de Vere and the others were "whispering" the above *to* the king, suggesting a secretive communicative environment where the interlocutors are in close proximity with one another; that they manage to "incite" the king assumes that these intimately spoken words are emotionally charged. Walsingham thus constructs a picture of Richard surrounded by his most intimate friends who, while positioning themselves very near the king, convince him to follow their advice—advice from men who are depicted elsewhere as "traitors." Since it is unlikely that Walsingham (or his source) was present during these conversations, he is concocting a particularly negative scenario of male–male intimacy.

Walsingham goes on to observe: "Ab illo ergo tempore abalienavit se rex a coetu procerum, et cum istis jugiter gradiebatur, jocabatur, et consilia exercebat" [from that time the king estranged himself from meeting together with the nobles, but with those men (i.e. his favorites) he walked and jested continuously and cultivated unions].[82] Here again Walsingham renders Richard's relations with his companions in language that highlight male–male intimacy. *Coetus* (or *coitus*) not only means "meeting together" but also "sexual union." Walsingham is not necessarily suggesting that instead of having sexual unions with the nobles Richard is cultivating such unions with his favorites; however, that the king is said to have "estranged" himself from the nobles implies that a king should normally be coupled with his advisers in a form of marriage. Also, by noting that at the same time the king was engaging in playful activities with these men he was also forming "unions" with them, Walsingham draws attention to the very personal and intimate nature of these relations. As in the case of Edward II and Gaveston, Richard is not being condemned for cultivating close unions with other men, but rather with the *wrong* men.

In his narrative of the events surrounding the Merciless Parliament, Thomas Favent describes the actions of Richard's companions/counselors: "eorum serpentini oris colloquiis, ambicionibus, adulacionibus, laciuiis verbis, et blandimentis indolem regem obcecarunt in tantum quod omnibus eorum venenosis conspiracionibus et desideriis illaqueatus" [they blinded the natural character of the king with their snakelike mouths, their desires for office, their flatteries, wanton words, and allurements to such an extent that (the king) was entrapped in all of their poisonous conspiracies and desires].[83] Like Walsingham, Favent creates an erotically charged scenario where Richard's favorites employ "wanton words" and "allurements"—words with strong romantic or sexual connotations—to manipulate him. The young king's "natural"—untainted, pure—character is corrupted—even, in a sense, violated—by the cunning, "poisonous" desires of his intimate friends. He is helpless, "entrapped" in their self-serving plans. Although Richard's position as seducer is implied in this narrative because as king he can distribute offices and other favors, Favent's scenario positions Richard as a passive, seduced victim.

Some of the articles of appeal brought forth by the Lords Appellant at the Merciless Parliament focus on the personal relations between Richard and his favorites. While the articles do not actually state, or even imply, that sexual acts transpired, they "taint" the interactions between the king and his closest friends with sodomitical associations. The first article accuses these men of taking advantage of the young, innocent king, "entirely engross[ing] in all things his love and firm faith and belief," and turning him against his "loyal lords."[84] Furthermore, the article states: "emblemissantz et amenussantz sa roial prerogative et regalie, luy firent si avant obeiser qil fuist jurre destre governe, conseille et demesne par eux. Par vertue de quele serement eux luy ont si longement tenuz en obeisance de lour faux appensementz et ymaginacions et faitz" [impairing and diminishing his royal prerogative and regality they made him so far obey them that he was sworn to be governed, counselled, and guided by them. By virtue of which oath they kept him so long in obedience to their false thoughts and imaginations and actions].[85] Thus, the opening article sets the scene: the youthful king is acted upon by more experienced men. The language suggests that force of some kind was used to make Richard yield to their "false thoughts and imaginations." While this force need not have been physical (or sexual), these men apparently exercised some power of persuasion on the impressionable young king. Since chroniclers observe that Richard was beguiled by flattery, this article accepts as given that the king's favorites used pleasurable means to "keep him" so long under their control.

The relationship between Juan II, king of Castile and his intimate friend/adviser, Alvaro de Luna, in the fifteenth century offers an enlightening parallel. One contemporary writer comments: "Tanta e tan singular fue la fiança que el rey fizo del condestable e tan grande e tan exçesiva su potençia. . . [L]a inclinaçión natural pudo en él aver tanto vigor e fuerça que de todo punto sin algunt medio se sometiese a la hordenança e consejo del condestable" [So great and extraordinary was the trust the king placed in his *condestable* and so great and excessive the *condestable's* power. . . . So strong a hold did his natural inclination have on him that he gave himself over entirely and without reserve to the charge and counsel of the *condestable*].[86] Gregory Hutcheson observes that "the site of perversion shifts from the king to Luna and back again—from the utter passivity (*nigligençia*) of the one to the absolute control (*potençia*) of the other—and ultimately it never anchors itself. . . . It is precisely in this in-between space—a space of tension and irresolution—that Juan II and Luna's relationship is at its most provocative, and sodomy, though unnamed, is most graphically enacted."[87] Likewise, the quoted article suggests that Richard's youthful, "natural" vulnerability is corrupted—perverted—by his favorites and he is subsequently involved in an "unnatural" relationship. It states that the king "of right"—properly, naturally—"ought to have been governed" by his "loyal lords,"[88] whereby "governed" should be understood as choosing to accept wise counsel. In shifting between the king's power ("royal prerogative"; "regality") and the actions performed on the king by his companions/advisers ("obey"; "keep"), the article attempts to delineate a relationship that is incomprehensible, unstable, and unnamable.

The subject of oaths between Richard and his intimate friends is taken up again in the second article, stating that de Vere, de la Pole, and Neville "ont fait luy jurrer et asseurer envers eux qil les meintiendra et sustiendra a viver et a morir ove eux. Et. . .ils liy ont mys pluis en servage encountre son honour, estat et regalie" [made him (Richard) swear and assure them that he will maintain and support them, to live and die with them. And so. . .they have put him more in servitude against his honour, estate, and regality].[89] As in the first article, Richard is depicted as a passive partner in the relationship, having been "made" to enter into a lifelong bond—a bond expressed in terms associated with chivalric brotherhood. However, chivalric bonds, as presented in romances and treatises at least, stress mutuality; knights swear to support *each other*. The bonds described in the article focuses solely on the needs of Richard's companions. Moreover, in chivalric texts a knight is not generally coerced into entering this type of relationship.

The fourth article further vilifies this bond and elaborates on the dynamics between Richard and his companions:

> par lour faux covyn et accrochement de lour faux malveistes mesnerunt et mal conseillerent nostre seignur le roy si qe sa presence quell' il doit de soun devoir moustrer a les grandes seignurs. . .ne le fist point forsqe a la volunte et a la taille des ditz Alexandre ercevesqe Deverwyk', Robert de Veer etc., Michel de la Pole etc., Robert Tresilian etc., Nichol Brembre etc.

> [by their false covin and accroachment of their false wickedness, (they) led and evilly advised our lord the king so that his personal presence which he ought of his duty to show to the great lords. . .was not so shown save at the pleasure and allowance of the said Alexander archbishop of York, Robert de Vere, etc., Michael de la Pole etc., Robert Tresilian etc., Nicholas Brembre etc.][90]

The modifier, "false," connoting something unlawful and contrary to what is "proper," stigmatizes this putative agreement or assembly.[91] The article creates a scenario whereby these men not only control the movements of the king but also place themselves constantly in his physical presence. Otherwise, how could they prevent the lords from approaching the king at some time? They thus have exclusive access to the king's body—both physical and political. The article gathers the previous accusations under one roof so to speak, situating Richard at a vague place isolated from the nobles where his companions make him obey them or yield to them. And in this secluded environment, shrouded in conspiratorial secrecy, Richard's closest friends are said to perform their "wicked" deeds *on* him. This purported scenario suggests, as in the case of Juan II and de Luna, "open complicity in the sodomizing at the very least of...[the king's] political body."[92] A further examination of how some chroniclers describe Richard's companions will illuminate the sodomitical inflection in the discourse.

Walsingham implies that Richard's favorites are other-than-manly, men who cannot appreciate—let alone carry out—an exemplary act of military prowess such as that performed by the earl of Arnudel who destroyed French forts at Brest in 1387: "invidebant tantae probitati qui cum rege erant, dux Hiberniae, et comes Southfolchiae, M[ichael] atte Pool, et Symon de Burleya, depravantes acta sua, et dicentes eum nullum opus egregium perpetrasse" [those men who were with the king, the duke of Ireland, the earl of Suffolk, Michael de la Pole, and Simon Burley, cast an evil eye at so much uprightness, while perverting their own actions and telling him (the king) that he (the earl of Arundel) performed no extraordinary work].[93] *Depravare* can mean "to corrupt/pervert" in a verbal or moral sense, and Walsingham conflates both senses of the word. Similarly, Favent refers to the king's nearest friends/advisers as men who were "living perversely [*viciose*]" and "deluding the king."[94] The perverse acts that Walsingham and Favent name do not necessarily suggest perverse *sexual* acts. However, in both instances the writers are charging Richard's companions with diverting from what they and, by implication, the noble faction, consider respectable, "natural" behavior for men of their rank.[95] In using "perverse" within a discourse that accentuates the intimate association between Richard and his friends—an association whereby these men *seduce* the innocent king into opposing what is good and right for England—the chroniclers are clearly suggesting "perverse" in its immoral sense. Richard, too, was viewed as "perverse." Writing about the removal of Richard's favorites in 1388, John Gower observes that the Lords Appellant "Sic emendatum Regem faciunt renouatum" [thus molded a reformed and reinvigorated King].[96] Gower implies that the king, no longer the passive, seduced victim of "abominable" men, is now "manly" according to the standard imposed by the nobles.

In the revised version of his *Chronicon Angliae*, Walsingham adds the following sentence to his commentary on Richard's elevation of Robert de Vere to the position of duke of Ireland in 1386: "tantum afficiebatur eidem, tantum coluit et amavit eundem, non sine nota, prout fertur, *familiaritatis obscoenae*" [he (Richard) was pleased with him (de Vere) so much, he worshipped and loved him so much, not without the disgrace, as it is said, of an *obscene intimacy*].[97] Why did Walsingham insert this sentence at least ten years after the fact?[98] Walsingham now blatantly accuses Richard of engaging in behavior that he and other chroniclers have implied right along in their denigrating, sexualized discourse. How could homosocial relations be more stigmatized, how could one taint the image of a political foe more than to raise the possibility of sodomy? That the pro-Lancastrian Walsingham alluded to the unnamable sin during the time when Richard was waging a campaign against the former Appellants cannot be overlooked.[99]

The *Historia* offers the following summary description of Richard's social behavior: "cupiditate detentus, luxurie nimis deditus, uigilator maximus, ita ut aliquando dimidiam noctem, non nunquam usque mane totam noctem in potacionibus et aliis *non dicendis* in sompnem duceret" [occupied exclusively with desires, devoted to excessive and riotous living, he was a great reveler so that sometimes he spent half the night without sleeping, sometimes even the entire night until the early morning in drinking bouts and other *unnameable things*].[100] By ending his summary portrait of the (soon-to-be-dethroned) king with a reference to "unnamable things," the author suggests that the final word on Richard—what will be remembered most about him—is a hint of sodomy.

In 1399, Adam of Usk was evidently present when "a number of doctors, bishops and others" discussed the reasons for deposing Richard II.[101] He reports: "Per quos determinatum fuit quod periuria, sacrilegia, *sodomidica*, subditorum exinnanitio, populi in seruitutem redactio, uecordia, et ad regendum inutilitas, quibus rex Ricardus notorie fuit infectus...deponendi Ricardum cause fuerant sufficientes" [they decided that perjuries, sacrileges, *sodomitical acts*, dispossesion of his subjects, the reduction of his people to servitude, lack of reason, and incapacity to rule, to all of which King Richard was notoriously prone, were sufficient reasons...for deposing him].[102] The charge of "sodomitical acts" is not given any more prominence than "perjuries" or "sacrileges"—it is merely another example of the misconduct of which Richard was "notoriously prone." Like in the case of the Templars, where indecent acts are included among other charges such as heresy and the worship of idols, the accusation of sodomy here is used to further denigrate the character of an opponent. Chris Given-Wilson notes that Usk is quoting from the deposition of Federick II by Pope Innocent IV at the Council of Lyons in 1245, but Usk has substituted "sodomitical acts" for "heresy."[103] While Usk might very well have taken the initiative in making this substitution, it is more likely that the officials at the meeting included the charge of sodomy in their discussion of Richard's misdeeds, and Usk, as *notator*, merely reported what was said. In the actual process of deposition, reported in the *Annales Ricardi secundi*, there is no mention of sodomy.[104] Openly stating what is strongly suggested in the other chronicles of the period, Usk's text is a logical endpoint for the denigrating discourse concerning Richard's same-sex relations.

★ ★ ★ ★ ★

Trial testimonies and chronicles in the fourteenth century illustrate that in certain situations a king or powerful nobles construe intimacy between men as illicit, perverse, and threatening to the realm. These texts offer evidence that there was a richly varied language readily available for expressing the unnamable—a language that was all the more effective in maligning the alleged offenders because it arose within a cultural context partly defined by strong homosocial bonds. The forms of male–male intimacy stigmatized in the discourses I have examined are in a sense one end on a continuum of chivalric normative same-sex conduct.

The Templar initiation ceremony, where allegedly a naked initiate kisses (or is kissed by) another knight on the mouth, navel, and anus, is not categorically different from the traditional bathing and dressing of a squire by a knight immediately before he is knighted. In each case one knight comes into contact with—and acts upon—the naked body of another knight. The former instance is rendered "obscene" because of the political/economic motives of the persecuting authority. And the charges that in accord with statutes of the order some Templars sought to engage fellow knights in sodomitical acts—and the witnesses' suggestions that only one partner actually desired to engage in these acts—are not entirely inconsistent with the tenets of chivalry. In an ideal chivalric bond knights swear to aid and support each other, and while the treatises do not suggest that knights satisfy one another's sexual needs, the Templar testimonies illustrate merely an extreme and one-sided interpretation of this ideal.

Both Edward II and Richard II conceived their most intimate male bonds in chivalric terms. In romances such as *Amys and Amylion*, the *Prose Lancelot*, and *Troilus and Criseyde*, knights demonstrate and express their "truth" and love for each other. Likewise, Edward is said to have entered into "a compact of brotherhood" with Gaveston, tying himself to him "in an unbreakable bond of affection." Richard wrote a letter to de Vere stating that he "pledged [literally, placed his heart near] to live and die with him."[105] At a time when kings were expected to be exemplary knights, taking part in military campaigns along with their knight-subjects, although not renowned for their prowess Edward and Richard logically would view their personal ties in chivalric terms. Lee Patterson points out that Richard might have commissioned the chivalric biography of his father, the Black Prince, and during the 1380s he "was engaged in the process of fashioning a chivalric identity."[106] In the eyes of their respective nobles, however, each king entered into a chivalric bond with the wrong man. The ordinance against Gaveston or the articles against Richard's companions evoke a perverse form of chivalric fidelity, presenting these intimate bonds as one-sided relationships, whereby the seduced or deluded king swears to support and obey the advice of his favorite(s). The chronicles stigmatize these bonds, highlighting their intimacy and exclusivity—characteristics that in other circumstances would be tolerated and even celebrated—and delineating interactions between the king and his companions in language that suggests illicit conduct.

Claire Sponsler's observation regarding Froissart's report of the events leading up to the execution of Edward II's favorite, Hugh Despenser, in 1326 applies to all the chronicles I have examined: "Froissart's narrative attests to at least partial acceptance of homosocial and homoerotic behavior among men at court, implicitly recognizing that male affectional and associational structures did not just lurk hidden within the government but in fact constituted it and were necessary for the operation of courtly culture."[107] When a king's personal associations were conceived as not the *right* ones, however, or when a politically and economically motivated campaign was being waged against a knightly order, chroniclers and trial recorders generated discursive sodomy. Spanning the fourteenth century, sodomitical discourses proved to be effective weapons. While not directly responsible for the dissolution of the Knights Templar or the execution of Edward's and Richard's intimate companions, in documenting alleged illicit conduct these texts provided a justification for the conclusive actions that were taken.[108]

CHAPTER 7

DRAMATIZED SODOMITICAL DISCOURSE:
THE CASE OF TROILUS AND PANDARUS

In addition to positively depicting an eroticized relationship between two knights—an affirmation found in other fourteenth-century chivalric texts—Chaucer's *Troilus and Criseyde* also reveals a discourse that denigrates male–male intimacy. During the years Chaucer was composing his text, namely, 1382–86, he was an esquire in Richard II's household and controller of petty customs; he was also acquainted with, in varying degrees, most of Richard's "seducers."[1] Although *Troilus and Criseyde* was most likely completed by the time of the Parliament of 1386, which Chaucer attended as M.P. for Kent, he had undoubtedly caught wind of the storm of protest by the powerful nobles—the murmurings referred to by Walsingham—against Richard's favored treatment of his intimate friends. Derek Pearsall suggests that Chaucer was well-informed of the political situation, speculating that "Chaucer was 'elected' as a reliable king's man in anticipation of some difficult passages in the October Parliament."[2] Of course, even if Chaucer was viewed "as a reliable king's man" it does not necessarily mean that he wholeheartedly and consistently supported the king's faction or that he sympathized with the victims of the nobles' campaign. My reading of Troilus and Pandarus's relationship does not hinge on settling the question of Chaucer's affinity, but rather I propose that the tumultuous political events that Chaucer himself witnessed or at least heard about find expression in his work.[3] That *Troilus and Criseyde* is in part a translation of an earlier work does not diminish its topicality. Given the long association between England (and London) and Troy, Chaucer's "translation" of Boccaccio's *Filostrato* would have a political relevancy different from that of the original text.[4] Patterson notes that "[s]ubstantial and specific political value was...invested in the idea of Trojan origins—a fact that gives the literary initiative undertaken by Chaucer, who remained loyal to his beleaguered monarch throughout the factional 1380s, an inevitably political dimension."[5]

Without questioning Chaucer's loyalty to Richard II, the discourse in *Troilus and Criseyde* that I examine assumes a different position. Chaucer's text enters the contemporary political arena by depicting Pandarus and Troilus as, respectively, manipulating adviser and passive advisee—roles that suggest the highly criticized relationship between Richard II and his court favorites (as well as that between Edward II and Gaveston).[6] Like the chronicles that vilified Edward II's and Richard II's personal ties, Chaucer's text exposes the potentially dangerous intermingling of homosocial intimacy and political influence. And it, too, generates a sodomitical discourse by sexualizing—or *sodomizing*—a normative male–male bond, rendering one man as the active-aggressive-seducer and the other as the passive-vulnerable-seduced. Chaucer's text goes one step beyond the chronicles, however, in that it vilifies the active partner in the sodomitical bond while delineating how the passive/seduced one extricates himself from his seducer.

A Diagram of Seduction, Power, and Influence

Troilus and Criseyde dramatizes the process by which an adviser/friend seduces and influences a royal prince. In book 1, Pandarus attempts to wrest out of Troilus the truth of his secret love by stating his credentials: "Though I be nyce, it happeth often so / That oon that excesse doth ful yvele fare / By good counseil kan kepe his frend therfro" (1.625–27). Like Richard II's court favorites who advised the young king generally against the interests of the nobles, Pandarus is presented as an unsuitable adviser for Troilus. Although he claims that because he is "nyce" and prone to "excesse" in matters of love he can help Troilus avoid making similar mistakes, this same admission depicts him as someone decidedly unqualified to give sober counsel. And Pandarus's consistent failure to find satisfaction in love suggests that his motivation for aiding Troilus is in part informed by his own need to experience (at least vicariously) love's pleasures.[7] More incriminating still is Pandarus's quest for power over Troilus—power to influence his trusting friend in a way that is not always consistent with the interests of the royal family and Troy in general.

In order to obtain the personal information he desires, Pandarus must "seduce" Troilus twice: first make Troilus trust him and then, once he knows everything, make him believe that he can help him. Throughout this scene Troilus is positioned as a victim, not only of love but also of Pandarus's relentless badgering. He is physically vulnerable, lying "stylle" in bed while Pandarus hovers over him. Troilus implicitly acknowledges Pandarus's coercive power in that he asks his friend to *allow* him to bemoan his misfortune: "But suffre me my meschief to bywaille" (1.755). Although Troilus's rejection of Pandarus's "proverbes" might be interpreted as defiance, his begging

Pandarus to cease taunting him with "olde ensaumples" indicates that his resistance is actually weak (1.756; 760). And this weakness is underscored by Pandarus's refusal to grant Troilus his wish: "No,. . .therfore I seye, / Swych is delit of foles to bywepe / Hire wo, but seken bote they ne kepe" (1.761–63). He in effect walks right over Troilus's pleas. Yet Pandarus has not yet achieved his desired goal, and so he assumes a tactic that is both more aggressive and manipulative. He strengthens his power position by denigrating Troilus's resistance: "But oones nyltow, for thy coward herte, / And for thyn ire and folissh wilfulnesse, / For wantrust, tellen of thy sorwes smerte" (1.792–94). He dismisses Troilus's heartfelt suffering as "cowardly," his willful stubbornness and, by association, his anger, as "folissh." Moreover, he accuses him of distrusting his "felawe" (1.696) and "brother" (1.773). Obtaining Troilus's trust is at the center of Pandarus's efforts because in gaining Troilus's trust he also gains power over his friend. Pandarus's skill as a clever manipulator is evident in the following scenario he offers Troilus: "If thow dost deye, and she not why it is, / But that for feere is yolden up thy breth, / For Grekes han biseged us, iwys? / Lord, which a thonk than shaltow han of this! / Thus wol she seyn, and al the town attones, / 'The wrecche is ded, the devel have his bones!'" (1.800–05). This passage posits a friend advising a royal prince to take a course of action that would, according to him, benefit his public reputation. While acknowledging Troilus's higher social position, Pandarus's counsel also demonstrates dangerous intellectual superiority in that he taunts his friend by making an improbable situation sound plausible. Although there is no indication that Troilus is receptive to this painted picture, the fact that Pandarus presents it suggests that he *thinks* Troilus might believe it.

Pandarus then changes his tactic, using soothing words of promised requited love to wear down Troilus's resistance and bring him closer to his grip. He persuades Troilus of the need to make his love known to the lady in question, offering a tempting picture of a lover who is "evere in oon. . .fressh and grene / To serve and love his deere hertes queene, / And thynke it is a guerdon hire to serve" (1.816–18). And, at last, Troilus succumbs: "Of that word took hede Troilus, / And thoughte anon what folie he was inne, / And how that soth hym seyde Pandarus" (1.820–22). Pandarus has thus established himself as a qualified adviser. In response to Troilus's question, "What is me best to do?" (1.828), Pandarus, not surprisingly, suggests "if the like, / The beste is that thow telle me *al* thi wo" (1.829–30; emphasis added). In giving Troilus the impression that the decision to reveal all the details of his secret is his own, Pandarus demonstrates clever manipulation. His tactic reveals a key component of seduction, namely, the promise of pleasure, which he offers to Troilus cloaked in the formal language of chivalric oaths: "And have my trouthe, but thow it fynde so / I be thi boote, er that it be ful longe, / To pieces do me drawe and sithen honge" (1.831–33). The seduction is however not yet successful. Pandarus needs to take a more physical approach.

Pandarus states his desire to be Troilus's "leche," telling him that he can only heal him if he "first unwre his wownde" (1.857–58). Although Chaucer echoes Boethius here, the context is quite different. For Pandarus's role is not as benevolent as Lady Philosophy's in that his wish to heal Troilus is inextricably linked to his desire to exert control over Troilus's pursuit of love.[8] By revealing his "wownde" to Pandarus, Troilus would not only expose his secret but also leave himself vulnerable to Pandarus's "healing" technique. Given their respective active and passive roles throughout this scene, Pandarus's positioning himself as a healer about to take some action on Troilus's body has sodomitical associations. Pandarus badgers Troilus into letting him see his wound: "Look up, I seye, and telle me what she is / Anon, that I may gon about thy nede" (1.862–63). Without being asked, he assumes control over Troilus's affairs. He persists: "Knowe ich hire aught? For my love, telle me this. / Thanne wolde I hopen rather for to spede" (1.864–65). He finally elicits a physical response from Troilus: "Tho gan the veyne of Troilus to blede, / For he was hit, and wax al reed for shame" (1.866–67). This brief passage offers a step-by-step illustration of a seduction about to be successfully performed. Pandarus begins by insisting that Troilus look at him. And with the eyes of his "victim" focused on him he makes a tempting offer to take care of his "nede." Given the fact that Troilus's "nede" are sexually informed, Pandarus's promise eroticizes the moment. Having secured Troilus's gaze, Pandarus pushes further, adding the incentive of offering his love if Troilus reveals the lady's identity.[9] Troilus's blush is certainly in part a reaction to Pandarus's stumbling so near the truth; however, it is also an indication of the heightened eroticism between the seducer and his object. Troilus's eyes are evidently focused on Pandarus as he closes in on his secret. Pandarus's excited reaction to Troilus's blush, "A ha!...Here bygynneth game" (1.868), paves the way for his final maneuver. He does not wait for Troilus to reveal his "wownde"; instead, "with that word he gan hym for to shake, / And seyde, 'Thef, thow shalt hyre name telle'" (1.869–70). Pandarus's seductive power building up over the last 240 lines reaches its climax in an expression of physical force, and Troilus at last succumbs, trembling, as he reveals Criseyde's name (1.871–74). Despite the role heterosexual desire plays in Pandarus's successful action, Troilus is unwillingly seduced by a male friend into revealing secret, personal information because he is not powerful enough to resist him. Pandarus obtains what he so diligently seeks and now, as trusted counsel, is about to assume complete control over Troilus's pursuit of love.

Pandarus's seduction involves manipulating Troilus into confessing an erotically charged secret. In the first volume of his *History of Sexuality*,

Foucault notes that "[o]ne confesses—or is forced to confess. When it is not spontaneous or dictated by some internal imperative, the confession is wrung from a person by violence or threat."[10] Foucault describes the intermingling of pleasure and power: "pleasure...comes of exercising a power that questions, monitors, watches, spies, searches out, palpates, brings to light; and on the other hand, pleasure...kindles at having to evade this power, flee from it, fool it, or travesty it.... [P]ower...lets itself be invaded by the pleasure it is pursuing; and opposite it, power assert[s]...itself in the pleasure of showing off, scandalizing, or resisting."[11] Like an inquisitor, Pandarus questions, "searches out" the truth of Troilus's secret love. His excited exclamation, "A ha!...Here bygynneth game" (1.868), illustrates that he might derive pleasure from wringing out Troilus's sexually related confession. After giving in enough to ask Pandarus what he should do (1.828), might Troilus's continued resistance (he does not name Criseyde until line 874) be informed by pleasure—pleasure in keeping his friend/examiner in the dark? While Troilus is indeed the passive partner in this sodomitically inflected confession scenario—Pandarus is invading Troilus's private space—we see (incriminating) suggestions that Troilus might *enjoy* his position.

Foucault goes on to point out that "confession is a ritual of discourse... that unfolds within a power relationship, for one does not confess without the presence...of a partner who is not simply the interlocutor but the authority who requires the confession, prescribes and appreciates it."[12] A politically informed reading of Pandarus's actions draws attention to his desire to influence his friend in ways that somehow serve his needs. Pandarus's quest for knowledge about Troilus's inner secret can thus also be viewed as a quest for power/authority. Although Pandarus fails to clearly establish his role as adviser/recipient of a confession during the early stages of the seduction/confession scene, evident from his failure to convince his friend that his advice is sound, he displays a certain authority in that Troilus eventually confesses to him. Pandarus then uses the confession to bolster his position as adviser. By securing Troilus's trust as well as privileged knowledge, he solidifies his power to influence his young friend. Immediately after receiving Troilus's confession, Pandarus chides him for his former disparaging view of lovers and then orders him to ask the god of love for forgiveness (1.932–34); and Troilus does what he is told: "A, lord! I me consente, / And preye to the my japes thow foryive, / And I shal nevere more whyle I live" (1.936–38). His submission to the god of love is also a submission to Pandarus.[13]

How might the following words that Troilus, on his knees, addresses to Pandarus read when viewed through a sodomitical lens: "thow wis, thow woost, thow maist, thow art al! / Mi lif, my deth, hol in thyn hond I leye. / Help now!" (1.1052–54)? Does the fact that Troilus begs Pandarus to "help" him conduct a clandestine love affair limit its political relevance? Quite the contrary. Far from his earlier resistance to Pandarus's counsel, Troilus now embraces it but also, more significantly, submits fully to his adviser. Having confessed "al," Troilus puts his life in Pandarus's hands. This newly established power relationship is not without an homoerotic component. Troilus's acceptance of Pandarus's help in obtaining Criseyde's love effects a growing intimacy between the two friends. While this intimacy is socially acceptable it can also be interpreted as dangerous. For the advisee, a royal prince, is emotionally dependent on his adviser—one whose interests are not necessarily compatible with other members of the royal family, and Troy in general. In fact, he might influence his young, inexperienced charge to engage in deceptive activities. The power dynamics between the two is evident in the following statement Pandarus makes to Troilus: "I have evere yit / Ben redy *the to serve*... / ... / *Do now as I shal seyn*, and far aright" (2.995–96; 999; emphasis added). The lines neatly juxtapose the dual roles of an adviser who is socially inferior to his advisee; to serve yet to command/influence. After writing the letter to Criseyde, as Pandarus counsels him to do, Troilus, "with his salte teris gan he bathe / The ruby in his signet, and it sette / Upon the wex deliverliche and rathe" (2.1086–88). While the ruby itself, as Windeatt points out, may signify healing qualities, Troilus's deftly closing the letter with his wax seal implies royal authority.[14] By drawing attention to Troilus's royal status here, the text suggests a negative view of Pandarus's newly established authority over Troilus.

When Pandarus explains to Troilus his plan for bringing him secretly together with Criseyde at Deiphebus's house, he assures Troilus that his brother will be helping him "unwist of it hymselve" (2.1400). While the text presents Pandarus simply offering to do a good deed for a loyal friend, it also illustrates that this "good deed" undertaken for Troilus involves manipulating another member of the royal family of Troy. Although Deiphebus is Pandarus's "grete frend" whom "[s]ave Troilus, no man he loved so" (2.1403–04), he addresses him in a formal manner ("sire," "youre lordship," "my lord" [2.1416; 1420; 1431]). In addition, he consistently uses the formal pronoun of address while Deiphebus speaks to him using the familiar form (a convention that underscores their disparate social positions). In offering two illustrations of intimate friendships between a knight/nobleman and a royal prince the text draws attention to their differences; and it casts a suspicious shadow over one of them.[15] As a result of Pandarus's intimate bond with Troilus—a bond that is clearly *more* intimate than that between Pandarus and Deiphebus—Pandarus is in the process of deceiving someone whom he considers a "grete frend." And since Troilus does not indicate his disapproval when Pandarus informs him "how that he Deiphebus gan to blende" (2.1496), he becomes in effect an accomplice in the deception. Troilus does in fact later feign physical illness, "[h]is brother and his suster for to blende" (3.207).

We could dismiss this deception as harmless because it is motivated by a young knight's pursuit of love if it were not for the potential significance of the rumors that Pandarus interjects into his scheme. He presents a fabricated story to Deiphebus and Helen in a serious manner: "He rong hem out a proces lik a belle / Upon hire [Criseyde's] foo that highte Poliphete, / So heynous that men myghten on it spete" (2.1615–17). Pandarus's false charges brought against a fellow Trojan have a powerful effect on his listeners: "Poliphete they gonnen thus to warien: / 'Anhonged be swich oon, were he my brother! / And so he shal, for it ne may nought varien'" (2.1619–21). Pandarus's "harmless" scheme thus stirs up dangerous divisiveness at a time when Troy is under siege. Although Chaucer's text does not follow up on the consequences of these charges, it illustrates a prince's intimate adviser concocting a potentially dangerous rumor to serve the erotic needs of his advisee (and the vicarious pleasure he derives from satisfying those needs); it also illustrates to what length an adviser will go to maintain his hold on his advisee. By invoking the historical subtext of the poem (i.e. Criseyde's status in a city-state at war) the text invites a reading of Pandarus's influence on Troilus that in some ways parallels the perceived negative influence of court favorites on Edward II and Richard II. Like Gaveston, de Vere, and the others, who were accused of turning the king's heart away from the nobles by excluding them from the king's inner circle, Pandarus in effect draws Troilus away from his family by engaging him in a deceptive—and potentially dangerous—scheme. Admittedly, Pandarus does not instruct Troilus to support this rumor; yet the fact that Pandarus is in a position to spread false information that serves Troilus's needs, without bothering to secure Troilus's approval first, indicates that he wields significant power and influence over Troilus.

While Pandarus's seduction of Troilus is not explicitly a sexual one, he does succeed in *penetrating* Troilus's privacy using manipulation, temptation, and aggression. Chaucer's text also illustrates the direct relationship between successful seduction and the power to influence the seduced. Directly after Pandarus draws out Troilus's confession, he proceeds to dominate him, assuming the role of an adviser whose counsel is unquestioningly followed. Before dramatizing the disintegration of Troilus's dangerous relationship with Pandarus, the text more clearly renders this bond sodomitical.

Taints of Sodomy

The depicted intimate moments shared by Troilus and Pandarus in the seclusion of Troilus's bedchamber deviate significantly from the *Filostrato*, suggesting that Chaucer's text intentionally raises the *possibility* of sodomy. I examined earlier how in book 2 after Troilus returns home from his triumphant ride through the city Pandarus seems to enjoy making Troilus sweat, prolonging his friend's agony before telling him the good news that Criseyde is willing to accept him—news that he gives when they are both in bed. Boccaccio presents the scene as follows: "[Pandar]... / A Troilo diritto se n'era ito, / E *di lontano* gli cominciò a dire: / Confortati fratel, ch' i' ho fornito / Gran parte, credo, del tuo gran disire. / E postosi a seder, gli disse *ratto*, / *Senza interpor*, com'era stato il fatto" [Pandarus...repaired directly to Troilus, and began *from afar* to say to him: "Comfort thyself, brother, for I have, I believe, accomplished a great part of thy desire." And he sat down and *straightway* told him *quickly* what had happened].[16] In expanding into four stanzas what Boccaccio concisely expresses in one, Chaucer's text focuses on the same-sex relationship and in effect marginalizes the heterosexual love story. While the analogy made between springtime awakening and Troilus's reaction to Pandarus's words closely follows Boccaccio, the homoeroticism of the moment is heightened in Chaucer's text as a result both of the deferred, sexually inflected climax and the fact that the two friends are in bed when it occurs.

Chaucer's Troilus is less demonstrative in his thanks to Pandarus than Boccaccio's, instead of embracing and kissing Pandarus "a thousand times" he holds up both his hands to his friend in a formal, feudal gesture and says, "Lord, al thyn be that I have" (2.975).[17] This formality however actually renders their bond more dangerous. Troilus's devotion to Pandarus expressed in the contemporary language of chivalric brotherhood invites an analogy to be made with those brotherly bonds young Edward and Richard forged with their respective favorites; but Chaucer's text goes one step further, tainting this act of devotion by situating it in the bed-chamber, with both men in bed (although not necessarily in the same bed, they are in close proximity to each other). Troilus, whose heart "spredeth so for joie it wol tosterte" (2.979–80), remains in bed alongside Pandarus, while in the *Filostrato* the two friends go immediately to Cressida. While Boccaccio's text is vague regarding the setting of Pandarus's promise to aid his friend, Chaucer clearly places this in the bedchamber. Pandarus tells Troilus, "also siker as thow list here by me, / ... / [I] Ben redy the to serve" (2.991; 996). Moreover, ostensibly serving his friend/royal prince, Chaucer's Pandarus/court favorite primarily gives him orders: "Do now as I shal seyn, and far aright" (2.999). Because the promises, vows, and orders between the two men are exchanged in bed in an atmosphere of inexpressible "joie," the text here brings together homoerotic intimacy and politics. Chaucer's additions to Boccaccio's text thus highlight a homosocial intimacy that is rooted in chivalric tradition while also calling attention to the political subtext. Troilus's pleasurable submission to Pandarus, who is now firmly in control of his fate in love, casts a sodomitical shadow over this interaction.

Pandarus treats Criseyde with far less love and respect than he does Troilus. While the privileging of a homosocial relationship over that of an uncle and his niece might merely reflect the chivalric cultural world of the poem, the text hints that there is something illicit about Pandarus and Troilus's relationship. Criseyde's reprimand of her uncle for having more regard for Troilus's "lust" than for her "estat" (2.1133–34) also in a sense condemns her uncle's involvement with Troilus. The text suggests that Criseyde's charges, presented in a rhetorically sophisticated manner, are to be taken seriously: "And loketh now if this be resonable, / And letteth nought, for favour ne for slouthe, / To seyn a sooth; now were it covenable / To myn estat, by God and by youre trouthe, / To taken it, or to han of hym routhe, / In harmyng of myself, or in repreve?" (2.1135–40). In summoning reason, God, and "trouthe" as her allies, Criseyde is speaking on behalf of orthodox values that are set in opposition to Pandarus's and Troilus's desire. She implies that in having "routhe" on Troilus, Pandarus does not exhibit "resonable" and responsible avuncular behavior. Criseyde thus casts a dubious shadow over this male–male bond.

Following his staged scene in book 2 where Troilus passes Criseyde's window, Pandarus, in an exuberant state ("right for joye he felte his herte daunce"), rushes to Troilus (2.1303–04). Troilus is in bed and the room is evidently dark since Pandarus offers him a light in order to read Criseyde's letter (2.1320). How does this scene read in the context of Criseyde's condemnatory remarks regarding Pandarus's behavior? Having just manipulated his niece into entering a relationship that could jeopardize her safety, Pandarus celebrates this achievement by directing his joyful, dancing heart toward his intimate male friend in the dark, secluded bedchamber. Rather than being concerned about his niece, Pandarus prefers to wield a form of sexual power over his friend—controlling when and how Troilus fulfills his sexual desire. Troilus's desire burns in Pandarus's presence and on this, and subsequent occasions, the two men are alone in Troilus's bedchamber. "[D]ay to day" in a state of heightened desire, Troilus, "by Pandare," writes to Criseyde (2.1343–44); and Troilus, for whom sexual satisfaction is deferred, turns to Pandarus for "reed and som socours" (2.1354). While Pandarus does not offer Troilus sexual relief explicitly, the text eroticizes the relationship between the two friends. Pandarus's pleasure in carrying out work for Troilus is directly linked to Troilus's burning desire, and both are expressed in an intimate setting. Same-sex encounters, even when illustrating culturally acceptable homoeroticism, can raise suspicions of illicit conduct if they are shrouded in secrecy and seclusion.

In my earlier discussion of how the text privileges male homosocial intimacy over the heterosexual love story, I drew attention to the "glade nyght"
Pandarus and Troilus spend together after the scene at Deiphebus's. I con-
cluded that this encounter is eroticized because the two friends exchange
lifelong oaths of affection and fealty and are apparently not fully clothed
when doing so. This normative homoerotic scene is tainted by sodomitical
associations, however, when Pandarus and Troilus are viewed as court
favorite/adviser and vulnerable royal prince. This encounter occurs only
"Whan every wight was voided but they two, / And alle the dores weren
faste yshette" (3.232–33). By calling attention to these necessary precau-
tions, the narrator implies that normally there *are* men around and the
doors are *not* "faste yshette." Unusual security is thus required for the meeting about to take place. While the occasion for this homosocial encounter
is ostensibly Pandarus's clarification and defense of his position as Troilus's
go-between in a heterosexual love affair, the text encloses it within two
expressions of mutually expressed male–male affection. The scene begins
with the narrator's comment that Pandarus "By Troilus...lay, with mery
chere, / To tale; and wel was hem they were yfeere" (3.230–31) and ends
with: "Thus held hym ech of other wel apayed, / That al the world ne
myghte it bet amende" (3.421–22). The text depicts mutual pleasure, yet also
a politicized, sodomitical scenario: Troilus's pleasure with Pandarus comes as
a result of his complete submission to Pandarus's schemes and manipulation
(of Troilus as well as others), while Pandarus reaps the pleasurable rewards
from having taken full charge of Troilus's personal life.

Chaucer's text stigmatizes Pandarus and Troilus's relationship by drawing
attention to the disparate power relations within the bond. The account
Pandarus gives Criseyde of how he first learns of Troilus's secret love reveals
a desire for power over his friend. In both versions Troilus is sleeping, or at
least in a sleeping position, when Pandarus arrives. But in the reworked scenario Pandarus explains: "Tho gan I stalke hym softely byhynde" (2.519).
This fantasized scene, which he "clepe ayein now to...[his] mynde" (2.521),
not only draws a parallel between extracting secret information and anal
intercourse but also in drawing attention to Pandarus's stealth suggests that
the passive partner does not willingly submit. Although Pandarus admits that
he does not easily learn the identity of Troilus's secret beloved (2.570–71),
he does not allude to the aggressive, manipulative tactics he uses to extract
this information from Troilus. In fact, he misrepresents the original "seduction"
scene in that he highlights Troilus's "woful wordes," claiming that merely
repeating them would cause him to swoon (2.572–74). By editing out
details of the persuasive maneuvers he exercises on his "woful"
friend—details that imply he has a personal motivation for possessing
this secret information—Pandarus suggests that he has something to hide.

This re-presentation of male–male seduction again positions Pandarus and Troilus as, respectively, active and (unwilling) passive partners in a sodomitical scenario. And Pandarus's manipulation of the facts to suit his purpose casts a suspicious shadow over his intentions, thus underscoring what is *dangerously* illicit about this relationship.

The end of book 3 further intertwines hints of sodomy with political concerns. In the intimate, secluded setting of his bedchamber and immediately following his consummation with Criseyde, Troilus, "with al th'affeccioun / Of frendes love" (3.1590–91), expresses his gratitude to Pandarus on his knees. And in vowing that he is obliged to Pandarus "for ay" (3.1612–13), Troilus in effect enters into a permanent union with Pandarus. While this scene reflects culturally normative homosocial love, it also depicts the dangerous dependency of a royal prince on his favorite/adviser. In deferring Troilus's repayment for the good deeds he has done, Pandarus assures Troilus's continued indebtedness and attachment to him. Particularly subversive here is that Troilus, as prince, should be the one in control, deferring Pandarus's repayment and thus assuring himself of *his* continued devotion.[18] Troilus's love for Pandarus—a seducer and manipulator of a young, inexperienced prince in a beleaguered city-state—leads to a bond of devotion so intense that it cannot be measured (3.1601–03). When Troilus's excessive feelings are set against the politicized contexts of seduction, secrecy, exclusivity, and suspicious motives, his relationship with Pandarus echoes the denigrated bonds between the young kings Edward and Richard and their respective intimate companions. But Chaucer's text goes one step further than the chronicles. It not only taints a normative intimate friendship with hints of sodomy, it also delineates the freeing of the seduced from the seducer and the ultimate destruction of a "dangerous" male–male bond.

Failed Seduction: Denigrating the Favorite

In book 4, Pandarus begins to lose his influence and power over Troilus. After hearing the parliament's decision to trade Criseyde for Antenor, Pandarus rushes to Troilus, and "Into the derke chambre, as stille as ston, / Toward the bed gan softely to gon" (4.354–55). The text thus again sets up a scene for male–male intimacy. In the dark seclusion of Troilus's bedchamber the two friends share their grief. Upon seeing Troilus weep, Pandarus "Gan for to wepe as tendreliche as he; / And specheles thus ben thise ilke tweye, / That neither myghte o word for sorwe seye" (4.369–71). This passage underscores the intimate union of the two friends, "thise ilke tweye," who are indistinguishable in the sorrow they share. Yet there are clues that this encounter will not be like those earlier occasions where Pandarus successfully seduces Troilus into following his advice. Although Troilus again occupies a passive, vulnerable position, Pandarus is far less commanding in his manner. He is "So confus that he nyste what to seye; / For verray wo his wit was neigh aweye" (4.356–57). In addition, "with his chiere and lokyng al totorne," he directs his gaze at his prostrate friend (4.358; 361). Three important tools Pandarus effectively uses in his earlier seductions—his words, wit, and gaze—are debilitated.

As in book 1, Pandarus's seductive maneuvers involve chiding Troilus for his behavior: "whi listow in this wise, / Syn thi desir al holly hastow had, / So that, by right, it oughte ynough suffise?" (4.394–96). Pandarus attempts to shame him into engaging in "rightful" behavior, summoning him into following his plan of action: "Forthi be glad, myn owen deere brother! / If she be lost, we shal recovere an other" (4.405–06). The text foregrounds homosociality over filial relations, as Pandarus, casting aside his niece, seeks to involve himself in Troilus's search for a new love object. However, as we shall see, a positively valued homosociality is highlighted only to be more effectively undermined. The text illustrates that Pandarus is not merely a bad uncle disregarding his niece but, more significant, an unsuitable adviser to Troilus.

Pandarus's argument that "newe love out chaceth ofte the olde" (4.415) does not achieve the desired effect: "[Troilus] Took litel heede of al that evere he mente— / Oon ere it herde, at tother out it wente" (4.433–34). Pandarus's authoritative, seductive speech is far shorter and less compelling than in book 1 and Troilus's resistance is considerably stronger. Earlier, while initially rejecting Pandarus's "wordes" and "lore," Troilus at least admits to having heard them (1.754). Here, Pandarus's persuasive words pass right though Troilus's ears and, moreover, Troilus proceeds to lecture Pandarus. He adamantly refuses to heed Pandarus's advice and in reprimanding him for offering counsel that is "wel sittyng" for a "fend" (4.436–37), hurls the seducer's weapon of chastisement back at the seducer. Troilus maintains that "syn I have trouthe hire hight, / I wol nat ben untrewe for no wight" (4.445–46). Because Troilus's rebuff is informed by ideal chivalric values— and his rebuff is underscored with two negatives—the text tacitly supports his position.[19] We also have an early sign of the coming rupture of Troilus and Pandarus's chivalric bond in that "wight" refers not only to a female replacement for Criseyde but also in a sense to Pandarus. Whereas in book 1 Troilus does not effectively articulate his resistance to Pandarus's unrelenting persuasive rhetoric, here he appears to be *un*seduceable. Troilus not only rejects Pandarus's counsel but also in acknowledging that he could follow it yet chooses not to ("though I myght, I wolde nat do so" [4.459]), he displays his ability not to succumb to Pandarus's influence. And unlike his earlier feeble attempt to silence Pandarus, he now succeeds—at least temporarily. As a result of Troilus's lengthy rebuff, "Pandarus gan holde his tunge stille, / And to the ground his eyen doun he caste" (4.521–22). Despite his resounding defeat, however, Pandarus does not give up. As in book 1, he attempts a different argument with which to seduce Troilus.

After careful consideration, Pandarus prods Troilus: "Why nylt thiselven helpen don redresse / And with thy manhod letten al this grame? / Go ravysshe here! Ne kanstow not, for shame?" (4.528–30). Pandarus resorts to a method of persuasion that seeks to provoke Troilus into following his advice, offering an image of what Pandarus considers ideal, masculine conduct and at the same time chastising Troilus for not exhibiting it. He provokes Troilus further, challenging him to act: "Artow in Troie, and hast non hardyment / To take a womman which that loveth the" (4.533–34). Similar to his aggressive maneuvers in book 1, Pandarus commands Troilus to follow his counsel: "Ris up anon, and lat this wepyng be, / And kith thow art a man" (4.537–38). Pandarus demonstrates his personal investment in this proposed action by assuring Troilus: "in this houre / I wol ben ded, or she shal bleven oure" (4.538–39). Pandarus seeks to maintain the triangular relationship that would undoubtedly involve his continued directing of Troilus's actions in regard to Criseyde. He attempts to seduce/stimulate Troilus into performing an action that disregards what is ostensibly best for Troy and one that requires him to sever ties with his family.[20]

Troilus strikes a blow at Pandarus's persuasive efforts, rendering them superfluous, by responding, "Al this have I myself yet thought ful ofte, / And more thyng than thow devysest here" (4.542–43). Despite the fact that here as in earlier instances Troilus is passive and vulnerable, lying in bed lamenting his fate, he is no longer a malleable object of Pandarus's machinations. The sodomitical scenario thus stalls. Troilus beats Pandarus at his own game, considering and dismissing those same ideas Pandarus attempts to persuade him into accepting and, moreover, claims to out-think his adviser. We see an empowerment of the seduced. In marked contrast to Pandarus's excitedly delivered speech, Troilus responds "ful softe" and in a formal, well-articulated manner. Troilus is depicted as a prince capable of independent thought yet not closed to receiving Pandarus's opinion; however, rather than having it forced on him, he assumes control over his adviser, telling him when he may offer his counsel: "whan thow me hast yeve an audience, / Therafter maystow telle al thi sentence" (4.545–46). The opening lines of Troilus's rejection of Pandarus's counsel reads like a blueprint for responsible princely conduct: "First, syn thow woost this town hath al this were / For ravysshyng of wommen so by myght, / It sholde nought be suffred me to erre, / As it stant now, ne don so gret unright. / I sholde han also blame of every wight, / My fadres graunt if that I so withstoode, / Syn she is chaunged for the townes goode" (4.547–53). Troilus's remarks have relevance for the fourteenth century. He notes that a prince should (1) be aware of historical events and learn from past errors; (2) respect the laws of the realm; (3) obey a higher authority; and (4) act in the best

interests of the public. Troilus is here a self-reflective prince and despite the
very different contexts, the text invites a comparison to be drawn between
the young Trojan prince and Richard II (who was only around nineteen
when the poem was composed). In contrast to Richard, who evidently did
not learn from the mistakes of Edward II's personal politics, Troilus not only
seeks to avoid repeating an unwise action but also realizes that it is sometimes necessary to reject the counsel of an intimate friend if following it
jeopardizes public interests and his familial ties.[21]

The scene does not end on this triumphant note for Troilus. After deliv-
ering his speech, Troilus breaks down in tears and, reminiscent of book 1,
turns to Pandarus for advice (4.575–81). Yet at the same time that it depicts
Troilus once again as vulnerable to Pandarus's influence, the text denigrates
Pandarus further and illustrates his weakening hold on his friend. Pandarus
dismisses Troilus's concerns for the well-being of the town, claiming that if
he had Troilus's "estat" he would abduct Criseyde "Though al this town
cride on this thyng by note" (4.585); he, unlike Troilus, "nolde sette at al
that noys a grote" (4.586). The two friends hold diametrically opposed
views of what it means to be a royal prince: Troilus is reluctant to privilege
self-interest over the public good because of his "estat," whereas Pandarus
considers Troilus's royal status a license to put self-interest before the wel-
fare of the public. By thus highlighting the differences in their respective
positions, the text not only presents Pandarus as an unsuitable and potentially dangerous adviser but also in effect loosens the ties between them
since Pandarus's influence on Troilus is inextricably linked to his intimacy
with him. The text illustrates Pandarus's desperate attempts to keep Troilus
in his grip. He urges him "to thynk right as a knyght" (4.617) and offers an
imagined scenario where Troilus, displaying model knightly qualities such
as "corage" and "myght" (4.619), performs a daring action: "manly sette
the world on six and sevene; / And if thow deye a martyr, go to hevene"
(4.622–23). Yet the knight that Pandarus envisions exercises his "corage"
and "myght"—and ultimately sacrificing his life—not in the name of a
good cause but rather in an illegal act motivated solely by self-interest and
sexual pleasure. And in his proposed scene, Pandarus fights alongside Troilus
in a bloody confrontation in the streets of Troy (4.624–28).[22] Pandarus
situates himself as a participant in the sexual violence, the abduction of
Criseyde, which sets the imagined action in motion. Although Criseyde
is the motive for this encounter, she is markedly absent from Pandarus's
scenario. He thus envisions an exclusively homosocial interaction with
Troilus that is informed by homoerotic identification and heterosexual
desire—an interaction that would bring the two men closer together.

While Pandarus succeeds in seducing Troilus who "gan with tho wordes
quyken, / And seyde, 'frend, graunt mercy, ich assente' " (4.631–32), unlike

in the earlier episodes, Troilus is not completely under the sway of his seducer/adviser. He complies yet qualifies Pandarus's plan: "for no cas, it is nat myn entente, / At shorte wordes, though I deyen sholde, / To ravysshe hire, but if hireself it wolde" (4.635–37). In contrast to his submissive behavior in book 1, Troilus tells Pandarus that he may neither "priken" nor "peyne" nor "tormente" him into performing this act (4.633–34). In rendering Pandarus's seductive weapons ineffective, Troilus in effect rejects the sodomitical associ-ation in which he has up to now engaged. At the same time that the text *de-sodomizes* Troilus and Pandarus's bond, it depicts Pandarus as a potentially dangerous adviser to Troilus. While the implied sexual violence at the heart of Pandarus's scheme as he originally presents it is abhorrent to modern read-ers, the main thrust of the text's denigration of Pandarus is directed at his advocating deceit and divisiveness at a time of war.[23] He advises Troilus to go to the king and "with wisdom hym and othere blende" (4.648) while he sets the plan in motion. Troilus agrees to follow what is certainly the most polit-ically disruptive piece of Pandarus's advice: namely, disobeying the parliament ruling and subsequently possibly engaging in a bloody conflict against his own family. However, Pandarus's influence on Troilus proves to be far less effective than on previous occasions.

During his visit with Criseyde, Troilus appears to have forgotten Pandarus's counsel. He listens attentively as Criseyde presents her protracted argument of how she will be able to return (4.1254–414) and "verrayliche him semed that he hadde / The selve wit" (4.1424–25). While he questions the practicality of her plan, he makes an unconvincing case for escape, offer-ing a very different version of Pandarus's scheme. He begs her, "lat us stele awey bitwixe us tweye" (4.1503), thus implying a private action that in effect excludes Pandarus. Criseyde, who up to now has not directly offered Troilus advice—particularly regarding sociopolitical matters—here assumes the role of adviser to a royal prince, reminding Troilus of his public responsibilities: "Troie hath now swich nede / Of help" (4.1558–59). And Troilus eventu-ally submits to her counsel. That Criseyde, a woman deemed dispensable by the majority of Trojans, places the city she is forced to leave above her own personal interests and convinces Troilus to do the same highlights by way of contrast Pandarus's unsuitability as an intimate friend/adviser for a royal prince. And by permitting Criseyde to replace Pandarus as his adviser, Troilus takes another step in freeing himself from the submissive/seduced position he has occupied in his sodomitical association with Pandarus.

The Final *De-Sodomization* of Troilus and Pandarus's Bond

In book 5, Troilus moves steadily away from both Pandarus's sphere of influence and his company. For the first time, Pandarus is prevented from

responding immediately to Troilus's call because he is occupied all day with
the king (5.284–86). The text subtly draws attention to Pandarus's duplic-
ity toward the king and other members of the royal family; he apparently
enjoys the king's trust yet at the same time can persuade Troilus to put his
personal desire (and, by implication, Pandarus's) above the interests of
the city-state and engage in an action that defies the king's orders. When
Pandarus visits Troilus the next morning, missing is the erotic charge of his
previous visits. On those occasions, Pandarus stealthily advances into the
dark room where the unsuspecting Troilus lies vulnerable in bed; but now,
Troilus, while apparently in bed (it is not clear whether he is lying or sitting), is fully in command of himself when he addresses Pandarus. Dryly,
without any display of "frendes love," Troilus discusses his funeral and
requests that Pandarus deliver the ashes of his heart to Criseyde (5.309–12).
In every previous encounter between Troilus and Pandarus taking place in
Troilus's bedchamber, the two men strengthen their bond and in some cases
Pandarus spends the night. In the present scene, Pandarus tempts Troilus
into engaging with him in homosocial activity—activity that Criseyde,
despite her removal from Troy, still informs. He urges him: "lat us caste how
forth may best be dryve / This tyme, and ek how fresshly we may lyve /
Whan that she comth" (5.389–91). He wishes to rekindle former pleasurable moments he and Troilus have spent and experience new ones: "Ris, lat
us speke of lusty lif in Troie / That we han led, and forth the tyme dryve; /
And ek of tyme comyng us rejoie" (5.393–95). His repeated command,
"ris" (5.393; 407), echoes his earlier aggressive, seductive tactics but here
Pandarus seeks to stimulate Troilus into engaging in erotically charged
activities *with him*. Textual evidence of the "lusty lif" with Troilus he hopes
to relive points to Troilus's affectionate expression of gratitude to Pandarus
and imparting to him details of his bliss with Criseyde.[24] Pandarus seeks to
maintain his command over Troilus—he must continue to be vitally important for Troilus. He tempts him: "This town is ful of lordes al aboute, / And
trewes lasten al this mene while. / Go we pleye us in som lusty route / To
Sarpedoun, nat hennes but a myle" (5.400–03). Steven Kruger points out
that Chaucer often uses "pleye" to connote sexual activity.[25] Although
women do attend the festivities at Sarpedoun's, Pandarus presents the activity as a homoeroticized one where the "route" apparently consists only of
"lordes." Despite his initial success in persuading Troilus to join him,
Pandarus proves ineffective in holding Troilus's attention when they are there.

Upon their return, Troilus excludes Pandarus from his emotional bond
with Criseyde. There are no more erotically charged moments between
the seducer/adviser and the seduced/advisee, no more taints of sodomy in
the secluded darkness of Troilus's bedchamber. Pandarus is not at his side "As he
rood forby places of the town / In which he whilom hadde al his plesaunce"

(5.563–64). And afterwards, "whan he was from every mannes syghte" (5.635), evidently including Pandarus, he mourns Criseyde's absence. He tells his sorrow to the moon (5.649), not, as so often in the past, to Pandarus. The narrator maintains that "ay bisyde hym was this Pandarus / That bisily did al his fulle myghte / Hym to conforte" (5.682–84), but we are afforded no details of his attempts nor evidence that he succeeds. Although Chaucer follows Boccaccio closely here, his cursory treatment of Pandarus's efforts stands out because it contrasts sharply with his earlier expansion of Boccaccio's text in scenes describing Pandarus's seductive maneuvers.[26] In paying increasingly less attention to Pandarus's intimate interactions with Troilus—reducing them to a summary statement—the text suggests that their bond is diminishing in intensity.

The last time Pandarus spends the night in Troilus's bedchamber, Troilus cries out to him after dreaming that Criseyde is kissing a boar. Chaucer deviates here from the *Filostrato* where Troilus has to send for Pandarus (7.25). Chaucer could merely be saving narrative time, or, in drawing attention to the history of intimacy between Troilus and Pandarus—recalling those erotically charged as well as sodomitically tainted nights—Chaucer, wittingly or not, might be emphasizing the break that is to come. Although Troilus seeks further proof, he announces to Pandarus that Criseyde has betrayed him (5.1247). And in an echo of his helplessness in books 1 and 2, Troilus asks, "What shal I don, my Pandarus, allas?" (5.1268). As on earlier occasions, Pandarus gives Troilus advice that he proceeds to follow, but Pandarus's counsel proves this time to be far less accurate and helpful. He dissuades Troilus from believing the message of the dream and after suggesting that Troilus write Criseyde—recalling his similar advice in book 2— wrongly predicts that "if so is that she untrewe be, / I kan nat trowen that she wol write ayeyn" (5.1297–98). Despite vagueness regarding the chronology of events, according to the narrative, Criseyde has already betrayed Troilus for Diomede (5.1030–57). In narrative time, Criseyde's first letter is received *after* she betrays Troilus. That her letter expresses what Pandarus says it will, namely, "She wolde come, ye, but she nyste whenne" (5.1428), suggests that he is as duplicitous as she is. For Pandarus claims "if she write, thow shalt ful sone yse / As wheither she hath any liberte / To come ayeyn" (5.1299–301). Considering that in the eyes of Troy Criseyde is now in effect an ally of the Greeks, could the text be implying that Pandarus, who is after all her uncle, is likewise a "Greek sympathizer" and therefore an unsuitable, dangerous intimate friend/adviser for Troilus?[27]

In their final encounter, Troilus chastises Pandarus for his false advice and implies that he is somewhat responsible for Criseyde's conduct: "O Pandarus, that in dremes for to triste / Me blamed hast, and wont art oft upbreyde, / Now maistow sen thiself, if that the liste, / How trewe is

now thi nece, bright Criseyde" (5.1709–12). Upbraiding Pandarus for refusing to see earlier his niece's faithlessness despite the "proof" afforded by the
dream, Troilus accuses his once dependable—and depended upon—intimate
friend/adviser of misleading him. And in reprimanding him for his short-
sightedness regarding Criseyde, Troilus in effect attacks Pandarus's credibil-
ity and qualification as confidant/adviser. Troilus then, notably, initiates
his next and final course of action without bothering to ask Pandarus for
advice: "And certeynly, withouten moore speche, / From hennesforth, as
ferforth as I may, / Myn owen deth in armes wol I seche" (5.1716–18).
His refusal to engage in any more "speche" on the matter is a further
blow to his loquacious friend/adviser. Troilus reduces the once manipulative and seductive Pandarus to silence: "He nought a word ayeyn to hym
answerde; / . . . / And stant, astoned of thise causes tweye, / As stille as ston;
a word ne kowde he seye" (5.1725; 1728–29). Pandarus at last speaks and
his review of both the good and bad that has come about from his influence on Troilus can be read as his attempt to continue their former
relationship: "If I dide aught that myghte liken the, / It is me lief; and of
this tresoun now, / God woot that it a sorwe is unto me" (5.1737–39).
Troilus evidently weighs "tresoun"—a politically emotive term with strong
contemporary associations—and Pandarus's guilt in this "crime" more that
the pleasure he has brought him, for no reconciliation takes place.[28] Troilus
does not respond and Pandarus's final words to Troilus, "I kan namore seye"
(5.1743), symbolize the final breaking of this bond. No longer tainted by
his association with Pandarus, Troilus is presented as a "noble knyght" who
heroically fights for his city, killing thousands of the enemy (5.1751–56;
1800–04).[29]

    And how does Criseyde figure into the destruction of this intimate same-
sex bond? Like the chronicles of the reigns of Edward II and Richard II,
as well as the trial records of the Knights Templar, Chaucer's text offers
two readings to explain and in a sense justify the disintegration of this
homosocial bond. The Templars were persecuted and eventually disbanded
ostensibly because of alleged obscene same-sex behavior and heretical acts,
but Philip of France undertook this action for economic and political
reasons. The nobles under both Edward and Richard, according to the
chroniclers, acted against their respective king's intimate friends in order to
protect the king and the realm from such evil "seducers," but one can also
read the real reason motivating their actions: namely, their desire to regain
and assure the continuation of their historical privileges and power. Similarly, in Chaucer's text, Criseyde's removal from Troy and her subsequent
betrayal of Troilus is *ostensibly* the reason for the breaking up of Troilus
and Pandarus's friendship; however, the text also suggests a politicized discourse informed by contemporary events—a discourse that sodomizes and

subsequently *de-sodomizes* Troilus and Pandarus's bond—operating *beneath* this "translation" of an Italian text.

★ ★ ★ ★ ★

Despite the fact that books 4 and 5 dramatize the disintegration of Troilus and Pandarus's relationship, *Troilus and Criseyde* is not exclusively a homophobic poem. Chaucer's text also affirms the cultural normativity of male homosocial intimacy. Chivalric treatises having currency in the fourteenth century encourage close contact between knights in that young men are urged to study the behavior and skills demonstrated by more experienced "model" knights, which left open the possibility for affectionate associations to be formed between student and teacher. These texts also suggest a visual economy of male–male spectatorship whereby exemplary knights perform before the admiring gaze of other men. Chivalric treatises and romances tacitly invite novice knights/readers who are emotionally invested in becoming "true men of worth" (or who are passionate supporters of chivalry) to envision model knights—an activity that might involve conjuring erotically charged fantasy images of perfect knights. In addition, some chivalric romances building on a classical and medieval tradition of ideal male friendship valorize male same-sex love. Fourteenth-century England should thus not be viewed as predominantly homophobic regarding intimate relations between men of the upper class. However, the chronicles of the reigns of Edward II and Richard II, as well as the trial testimonies of the Knights Templar, indicate that sodomitical discourses existed in the fourteenth century that targeted "dangerous" male–male intimacy. The chronicles suggest that intimate associations between a king and his favorites are culturally acceptable as long as these favorites are the *right* men. When a king's personal relations interfere with the interests of the powerful nobles, same-sex love is vilified by the chroniclers of the time who, aligning themselves with the threatened nobles, render male–male intimate associations as the seduction of an innocent, victimized king by evil, perverse men. This stigmatizing, discursive sodomy does not erase the homoeroticism that is strongly suggested in chivalric texts. These two contradictory sociocultural forces—one affirming and celebratory, the other denigrating and homophobic—are inextricably linked to each other because a sodomitical discourse can only arise within a society that encourages or, at least, tolerates the formation of male–male bonds.

Studying the dynamics of male same-sex desire in late medieval chivalric texts does not necessarily involve uncovering evidence of knights engaging in genital sex with other knights—although it is certainly possible that this occurred; rather, we need to be attentive to the subtle workings of desire. Normative male–male desire in the fourteenth century included a nexus of erotically charged interactions—spectatorial acts, fantasy images, kisses and embraces, vows of eternal brotherhood, and expressions of love. A queer reading of chivalric texts thus seeks to recover the cultural codes of this *homoerotic normativity*. The closer we look at these cultural artifacts the more we come to realize the inadequacy and inaccuracy of our modern categories of sexuality and desire.

AFTERWORD

QUEER LESSONS FROM THE FOURTEENTH CENTURY

I have been arguing that knights who kiss, express their mutual love, or form lifelong bonds with each other, or novice knights/male readers who conjure fantasy images of model knights, are engaging in homoerotic acts. If such behavior was not considered "queer" in the Middle Ages, what does it have to do with modern queer studies? If the effectiveness of the critical term "queer" is measured by its ability to "unsettle," as Donald Hall points out, then does normative medieval homoeroticism challenge modern views of "normalcy"?[1] Robert Sturges suggests that we ask "not only what specific constructions of sex, gender, and erotic practice were available in different periods and to different cultures, but also what historical effects such constructions may have had on later ones."[2] I would add, what can we learn about ourselves from studying medieval homoeroticism? And how might an awareness of possible erotic interactions between knights affect our society's views of acceptable/ unacceptable sexuality or eroticism?

The range of homoerotic acts revealed or suggested in chivalric discourses expose nuances of male same-sex desire that could find expression today but are not clearly recognized under the modern rubric "homosexuality" or "homoeroticism." The variety of same-sex encounters in medieval texts also draws attention to the difficulty of weighing or comparing one expression of desire with another. Are autoerotic, imaginative acts more or less erotic than face-to-face encounters? Can homoerotic fantasies be included in the same category with physical acts? Can knights who do not engage in any physical interaction with each other but pledge their "trouth" to each other be placed in the same category as those who "pleye" with casual acquaintances in tournaments or practice matches? And where do knights fit in whose most important emotional bond is to other knights but who still have sexual intercourse with women? Imaginary acts are also not easily equated. Are a reader/spectator's sadomasochistic identifications more or less erotic than those whose imaginings do not involve pleasure-in-pain? We could solve this classification conundrum by pluralizing eroticism, speaking thus of medieval homoeroticisms; but it would not stop there. Uncovering the diversity of medieval homoeroticisms also exposes how the modern categories, "homosexuality," "heterosexuality," and "bisexuality," elide the innumerable differences in the erotic proclivities of those included in them. Do we need to pluralize these categories too? Articulating innumerable "homosexualities" or "heterosexualities" will inevitably lead to scenarios of desire that are found in both spheres.

Even without effecting a pluralizing of modern categories of sexual/erotic orientation, medieval texts blur the boundaries. My examination of competing desires in some chivalric romances illustrated that homoerotic and heterosexual desires could inform each other and it is thus difficult to separate these mutually animating forces. The nuances of desire operating in triangular configurations whereby one approaches an object of desire through a third party—either through mediation (the mediator leads one to the object) or vicarious identification (one aligns oneself with the person whose desire is being fulfilled)—cannot be satisfactorily defined by turning to our predominant tripartite classification of sexual orientation. Scenarios in some medieval texts thus illustrate a fluidity, an *intermingling* coexistence of multiple desires that could liberate us from rigid, modern categories of erotic orientation. Rather than attempting to fit some version of "homosexuality," "heterosexuality," or "bisexuality" to medieval expressions of desire, it might be more productive to explore how versions of medieval homoeroticisms exist today—they only need to be recognized.

Diana Fuss uses the figure of inside/outside to problematize the relationship between normative and marginalized sexuality. She observes: "the binary structure of sexual orientation, fundamentally a structure of exclusion and exterioration, nonetheless constructs that exclusion by prominently including the contaminated other in its oppositional logic. The homo in relation to the hetero, much like the feminine in relation to the masculine, operates as an indispensable interior exclusion—an outside which is inside interiority making the articulation of the latter possible, a transgression of the border which is necessary to constitute the border as such."[3] The chivalric contexts I examined extend Fuss's observation. Substituting "sodomitical" for "homo" and "homoerotic normativity" for "hetero" does not alter the substance of Fuss's important insight, but it indicates that there are binaries at work within one form of sexual orientation. In the fourteenth century, stigmatized same-sex behavior is defined against normative male–male intimacy—a king should by right be close to his male advisers but not those men who dangerously manipulate or *seduce* the king. The tainted acts are thus not outside the realm of male–male relations but rather exist alongside—on a continuum with—those associations deemed acceptable and even affirmed. In offering a contaminated version of the affirming discourses, a sodomitical discourse more clearly defines homosocial normativity. The medieval discourses I examined indicate that the key factor for determining which forms of same-sex intimacy are unacceptable is not the nature of the acts themselves—actual sodomitical acts are in the chronicles and *Troilus and Criseyde* almost beside the point—but rather the political consequences of particular same-sex associations. Today, differences in age, class, race, ethnicity, religion, or the perceived power and influence one partner wields over the other, often overshadow the sexual acts of the "excluded" sexual orientation. The fourteenth century apparently grasped the significant role some of these factors play, and writers defined the border accordingly.

We are still affected by the Middle Ages—it comes to us by way of Hollywood. While not attempting to be historically accurate, recent films such as *First Knight* and *A Knight's Tale*, depict handsome, well-built knights jousting with one another in tournaments. The young men in the film audience may no longer have the option of pursuing a career as a knight, and the chivalric treatises' recommendation to novices that they observe closely model knights would not inform the twenty-first century spectator's interaction with the knights on the screen; yet in depicting eroticized interactions between knights—a knight's feverish thrill at piercing, unhorsing, or wounding another knight, the affection and loyalty between knights or a knight and his lord—the film brings the social codes of medieval homosociality (in an admittedly highly fictional form) into our world. Not only may male spectators of any age identify with the fighting knights and "participate" in the action, thus replicating in a sense a *medieval* homoerotic activity, but also the forms of homoeroticism illustrated in the film and the effect they have on film spectators might disturb, or open up, narrowly defined modern categories of male same-sex desire. A male film spectator viewing eroticized interactions between knights who definitely do not seem "queer" and perhaps even experiencing an erotic attraction himself ("hey, I'm not queer") *could* in however minor way re-form modern categories of desire.

How does an inquiry into medieval homoeroticism—a queer reading of chivalric texts—play out in the classroom?[4] If students are encouraged to look for and comprehend social codes of same-sex interactions in medieval texts, might it not possibly lead to greater tolerance for sexual difference both in the classroom and society in general? Might it even lead further to students' questioning the rigidity of the modern binary of hetero/homosexuality? If students examine expressions, or become aware of suggestions, of normative homoeroticism—knights who kiss one another and declare their mutual fidelity and love in language that approximates modern heterosexual marriage vows—they may reevaluate modern definitions of "gay" and "straight." Medieval illustrations may lead to an understanding that the binary of acceptable/stigmatized sexual orientation is subjective and linked to a specific cultural environment. ("If those knights are not queer than those two guys who seem so close might not be queer either.") Examining sodomitical discourses can also be enlightening for students in that it draws attention to how attitudes toward expressions of desire are politically informed. Students thus come to understand how same-sex desire (or any form of desire) does not exist in a vacuum but rather is inextricably linked to the society in which it is located.

In an often quoted passage, Carolyn Dinshaw notes that "[q]ueerness works by contiguity and displacement, knocking signifiers loose, ungrounding bodies, making them strange; it works in this way to provoke perceptual shifts and subsequent corporeal response in those touched."[5] Dinshaw's important recognition of the potential for a queer dynamics between the past and the present suggests that "queering" can occur in two directions: we extend a queer touch to medieval texts by recovering normative homoeroticisms expressed or suggested in these texts; and, in reverse, we allow the insights we gain to queer our understanding of—and transgress the limitations that modern categories impose on—same-sex desire. A receptive, queer inquiry into medieval sexuality and eroticism may prove that the Middle Ages can indeed unsettle.

NOTES

Chapter 1   Articulating Premodern Male Homoeroticism

1. Richard W. Kaeuper and Elspeth Kennedy, *The Book of Chivalry of Geoffroi de Charny: Text, Context, and Translation* (Philadelphia: University of Pennsylvania Press, 1996), pp. 168 and 169. All English translations are by Elspeth Kennedy.
2. Geoffrey Chaucer, *The Riverside Chaucer*, ed. Larry D. Benson, 3rd ed. (Boston: Houghton Mifflin, 1987) 3.1590–92.
3. *Sir Gawain and the Green Knight, Sir Gawain and the Green Knight, Pearl, Cleanness, Patience*, ed. A. C. Cawley and J. J. Anderson (London: Dent, 1976), ll. 1936–37.
4. Allen J. Frantzen, *Before the Closet: Same-Sex Love from* Beowulf *to* Angles in America (Chicago: University of Chicago Press, 1998), p. 6. Frantzen goes on to note that "[t]he view that sexual identity is an effect of discourse might be said to be the most distinctive assumption of queer theory" (p. 7). See also, Annamarie Jagose, *Queer Theory: An Introduction* (New York: New York University Press, 1996) and Teresa de Lauretis, "Queer Theory: Lesbian and Gay Sexualities—an Introduction," *Differences* 3.2 (Summer 1991): iii–xviii.
5. Glenn Burger, "Queer Chaucer," *English Studies in Canada* 20.2 (1994): 156 [153–70].
6. Burger, "Queer Chaucer," 157.
7. Glenn Burger and Steven F. Kruger, "Introduction," in *Queering the Middle Ages*, ed. Glenn Burger and Steven F. Kruger (Minneapolis: University of Minnesota Press, 2001), p. xvi.
8. Karma Lochrie, "Mystical Acts, Queer Tendencies," in *Constructing Medieval Sexuality*, ed. Karma Lochrie, Peggy McCracken, and James A. Schultz (Minneapolis: University of Minnesota Press, 1997), p. 180 [180–200].
9. Chaucer's Pardoner has been the focus of some excellent studies that articulate queerness as an indeterminate threat to heteronormative society, see Glenn Burger, "Kissing the Pardoner," *PMLA* 107 (1992): 1143–56; Carolyn Dinshaw, "Chaucer's Queer Touches/A Queer Touches Chaucer," *Exemplaria* 7.1 (1995): 75–92, and *Getting Medieval: Sexualities and Communities Pre- and*

Postmodern (Durham: Duke University Press, 1999); Steven F. Kruger, "Claiming the Pardoner: Toward a Gay Reading of Chaucer's Pardoner's Tale," *Exemplaria* 6.1 (1994): 115–39; Robert S. Sturges, *Chaucer's Pardoner and Gender Theory: Bodies of Discourse* (New York: St. Martin's Press, 2000).

10. Bruce R. Smith, *Homosexual Desire in Shakespeare's England: A Cultural Poetics* (1991; repr. Chicago: University of Chicago Press, 1994), p. 18.

11. Roberto J. González-Casanovas, "Male Bonding as Cultural Construction in Alfonso X, Ramon Llull, and Juan Manuel: Homosocial Friendship in Medieval Iberia," in *Queer Iberia: Sexualities, Cultures, and Crossings from the Middle Ages to the Renaissance*, ed. Josiah Blackmore and Gregory S. Hutcheson (Durham: Duke University Press, 1999), p. 161 [157–92].

12. Jonathan Goldberg, *Sodometries: Renaissance Texts, Modern Sexualities* (Stanford: Stanford University Press, 1992), p. 22.

13. Bruce W. Holsinger, "Sodomy and Resurrection: The Homoerotic Subject of the *Divine Comedy*," in *Premodern Sexualities*, ed. Louise Fradenburg and Carla Freccero (New York: Routledge, 1996), p. 246 [243–74].

14. Holsinger, "Sodomy and Resurrection," p. 254.

15. For instance, in her fine study of the male gaze in the *Morte Darthur*, Kathleen Coyne Kelly notes how "the reader may take pleasure in traversing a number of positions (both authorized and 'perverse') from subject to object including those of victim or villain" ("Malory's Body Chivalric," *Arthuriana* 6.4 [1996]: 53 [52–71]); but she does not offer a sustained inquiry into the potential erotic dynamics between the reader and the knight/object in the text.

16. Frantzen, *Before the Closet*, p. 14.

17. Frantzen, *Before the Closet*, p. 15.

18. Carolyn Dinshaw, "A Kiss Is Just a Kiss: Heterosexuality and Its Consolations in *Sir Gawain and the Green Knight*," *Diacritics* 24.2–3 (1994): 206 [205–26]. See also, Carolyn Dinshaw, "Getting Medieval: *Pulp Fiction*, Gawain, Foucault," in *The Book and the Body*, ed. Dolores Warwick Frese and Katherine O'Brien O'Keefe (Notre Dame: University of Notre Dame Press, 1997), pp. 116–63.

19. Dinshaw, "A Kiss," 223.

20. Sheila Fisher, "Taken Men and Token Women in *Sir Gawain and the Green Knight*," in *Seeking the Woman in Late Medieval and Renaissance Writings: Essays in Feminist Contextual Criticism*, ed. Sheila Fisher and Janet E. Halley (Knoxville: University of Tennessee Press, 1989), p. 86 [71–105].

21. David L. Boyd, "Sodomy, Misogyny, and Displacement: Occluding Queer Desire in *Sir Gawain and the Green Knight*, *Arthuriana* 8.2 (1998): 88 [77–113].

22. Dinshaw actually suggests this in her conclusion: "when *we* read the lips of Gawain and Bertilak we read that text from a new perspective and contribute to a more accurate history;" our agendas differ in that I am calling for an examination of expressions of *normative* homoerotic desire in chivalric contexts, and Dinshaw is focusing on the need for "a history of the production of heterosexuality in Western Christendom via the containment

of the deviant, and the concomitant history of various strategies deployed to resist that containment" ("A Kiss" 223).

23. Alan Bray, "Homosexuality and the Signs of Male Friendship in Elizabethan England," *History Workshop* 19.1 (1990): 2 [1–19].

24. Bray is referring here to William Reynolds's account of the "unnatural intimacy" between Piers Edmonds and the Earl of Southampton and comments that "[b]ehind this account is the familiar Elizabethan stereotype that the man guilty of 'unnatural filthiness' would be also very likely a traitor" ("Homosexuality and the Signs," pp. 8–9).

25. Robert Matz, "Slander, Renaissance Discourses of Sodomy, and *Othello*," *English Literary History* 66 (1999): 262 [261–76].

26. Barbara Weissberger, "¡A tierra, puto!: Alfonso de Palencia's Discourse of Effeminacy," in *Queer Iberia*, ed. Blackmore and Hutcheson, pp. 293–94 [291–324].

27. Gregory S. Hutcheson, "Desperately Seeking Sodom: Queerness in the Chronicles of Alvaro de Luna," in *Queer Iberia*, ed. Blackmore and Hutcheson, p. 227 [222–49].

28. Edward II's relationship with Hugh Despenser, however, is the subject of an excellent recent study. See Claire Sponsler, "The King's Boyfriend: Froissart's Political Theater of 1326," in *Queering the Middle Ages*, ed. Burger and Kruger, pp. 143–67. In her examination of Jean Froissart's narrative of the events leading up to Despenser's execution in 1326, Sponsler demonstrates "how vilification of same-sex desire and homosocial relations could be enlisted in the cause of power struggles" (p. 161).

29. Richard Corum, "Henry's Desires," in *Premodern Sexualities*, ed. Fradenburg and Freccero, p. 77 [71–97].

30. Corum, "Henry's Desires," p. 77.

31. Frantzen, *Before the Closet*, p. 20.

32. John Boswell, *Christianity, Social Tolerance, and Homosexuality: Gay People in Western Europe from the Beginning of the Christian Era to the Fourteenth Century* (Chicago: University of Chicago Press, 1980), p. 44. For historians' response to Boswell's study, see *Homosexuality, Intolerance, and Christianity: A Critical Examination of John Boswell's Work* (New York: Scholarship Committee, Gay Academic Union, 1981); James A. Brundage's review in *Catholic Historical Review* 68 (1982): 62–64; Jeremy Adams's review in *Speculum* 56 (1981): 350–55.

33. Boswell, *Christianity, Social Tolerance, and Homosexuality*, p. 45.

34. John Boswell, "Revolutions, Universals, and Sexual Categories," in *Hidden from History: Reclaiming the Gay and Lesbian Past*, ed. Martin Bauml Duberman, Martha Vicinus, and George Chauncey Jr. (New York: New American Library, 1989), p. 35 [17–36]. For Boswell's further elaboration of his position, see "Categories, Experience and Sexuality," in *Forms of Desire: Sexual Orientation and the Social Constructionist Controversy*, ed. Edward Stein (New York: Routledge, 1992), pp. 133–73.

35. Dinshaw, *Getting Medieval*, p. 30.

36. Michel Foucault, *The History of Sexuality, Vol. 1: An Introduction*, trans. Robert Hurley (1978; New York: Vintage, 1990), p. 43.

37. David M. Halperin, "Forgetting Foucault: Acts, Identities, and the History of Sexuality," *Representations* 63 (Summer 1998): 99 [93–120].

38. Halperin, "Forgetting Foucault," 109.

39. Dinshaw, *Getting Medieval*, p. 194.

40. Dinshaw, *Getting Medieval*, pp. 194–95.

41. Dinshaw explores this phenomenon in great detail in her study of the Lollards; see *Getting Medieval*, pp. 55–99.

42. Robert Padgug, "Sexual Matters: Rethinking Sexuality in History," *Hidden from History*, ed. Duberman et al., p. 58 [54–64]. To Padgug's formulation, I would add individuals not necessarily born into a particular society but nevertheless desiring to be a part of it. Padgug offers an excellent list of studies written in the 1980s that take a constructionist view of homosexuality, see p. 486 n17.

43. Louis A. Montrose, "Professing the Renaissance: The Poetics and Politics of Culture," in *The New Historicism*, ed. H. Aram Veeser (New York: Routledge, 1989), p. 20 [15–36]. Other key "New Historicists" who, like Montrose, work on texts of the Renaissance include Stephen Greenblatt, Jonathan Goldberg, and Jean Howard. Brook Thomas questions the "newness" of the "New Historicists"; see his essay, "The New Historicism and other Old-fashioned Topics," in *The New Historicism*, ed. Veeser, pp. 182–203.

44. Elizabeth Fox-Genovese, "Literary Criticism and the Politics of the New Historicism," in *The New Historicism*, ed. Veeser, p. 216 [213–24].

45. Fox-Genovese, "Literary Criticism," p. 216.

46. Fox-Genovese, "Literary Criticism," p. 217.

47. Lee Patterson, *Negotiating the Past: The Historical Understanding of Medieval Literature* (Madison: University of Wisconsin Press, 1987), p. 62. For Patterson's detailed discussion and commentary on the New Historicists, see pp. 57–74.

48. Patterson, *Negotiating the Past*, p. 63.

49. Gabrielle M. Speigel, "History, Historicism, and the Social Logic of the Text In the Middle Ages," *Speculum* 65 (1990): 77 [59–86].

50. Spiegel, "History," 77.

51. Paul Strohm, *Hochon's Arrow: The Social Imagination of Fourteenth-Century Texts* (Princeton: Princeton University Press, 1992), p. 4.

52. Strohm, *Hochon's Arrow*, pp. 5–6.

53. Strohm, *Hochon's Arrow*, p. 7.

54. David Aers, *Community, Gender, and Individual Identity: English Writing 1360–1430* (London: Routledge, 1988), p. 4.

55. Louise Fradenburg and Carla Freccero, "Introduction: Caxton, Foucault, and the Pleasures of History," in *Premodern Sexualities*, ed. Fradenburg and Freccero, p. xvi [xiii–xxiv]. Fradenburg and Freccero cite William Caxton's *Policronicon* as an example of a historian's "pursuit of sameness." They maintain that "Caxton sees history as a communicative technology whose purpose is to develop the homosocial (and national) bonds made possible by sacrificial sufferings of masculinity" (p. xiv). They go on to suggest that

"[t]he first English printer announces his technological project *as* a histo-
riographical project whose purpose is to forge likenesses and relations
among men of different generations in order to produce subjects who will
sacrifice for their 'nation' " (p. xiv).

56. Fradenburg and Freccero, "Introduction," p. xvii.

57. Montrose, "Professing the Renaissance," p. 23.

58. Marilyn Butler, "Against Tradition: The Case for a Particularized Method,"
    in *Historical Studies and Literary Criticism*, ed. Jerome J. McGann (Madison:
    University of Wisconsin Press, 1985), p. 45 [25–47]. This is actually the fifth
    and final point Butler makes in outlining her proposed method. For
    points 1–4, see pp. 43–44.

59. Eve Kosofsky Sedgwick, *Between Men: English Literature and Male Homosocial
    Desire* (New York: Columbia University Press, 1985), p. 1.

60. Holsinger, "Sodomy and Resurrection," p. 245.

61. Robert Sturges neatly negotiates the essentialist/constructionist conun-
    drum, noting that "[a] theoretical analysis that is also and simultaneously
    historical…reveals not a transhistorical or essential sex, gender, or erotic
    practice, nor merely discontinuous cultural constructions, but a gradual
    accumulation of discursive constructions of all categories that cannot be
    accommodated in 'proper' language—an accumulation or sedimentation
    that only in recent years has begun to be excavated with the use of new
    theoretical languages" (*Chaucer's Pardoner*, p. xx).

62. Gregory W. Bredbeck, *Sodomy and Interpretation: Marlowe to Milton* (Ithaca:
    Cornell University Press, 1991), p. 24.

63. Karma Lochrie, Peggy McCracken, and James A. Schultz, "Introduction,"
    p. ix [ix–xviii]. They are drawing on Foucault's comments in *The Use of
    Pleasure* that "there are times in life when the question of knowing if one
    can think differently than one thinks, and perceive differently than one
    sees, is absolutely necessary if one is to go on looking and reflecting at all"
    (quoted in Lochrie, McCracken, and Schultz, "Introduction," p. ix). They
    go on to point out that "[t]he immense and immensely varied domain of
    medieval sexuality compels us to acknowledge articulations of sexuality
    that may at first seem familiar but that are actually quite different from our
    own" (p. xvi).

64. Valerie Traub, *Desire and Anxiety: Circulations of Sexuality in Shakespearean
    Drama* (London: Routledge, 1992), p. 104.

65. Two texts I examine, the French *Prose Lancelot* and Ramon Lull's *Book of
    the Ordre of Chyvalry* were actually written in the thirteenth century. I
    include them because they were both very popular in fourteenth-century
    England. William Calin maintains that the *Prose Lancelot* was "the most
    important single romance of the Middle Ages" and notes that "[w]hen
    Chaucer and Gower allude to Lancelot or Tristan, they allude to the prose
    cycles of the thirteenth century, not the verse classics of the twelfth, which
    had gone out of fashion" (*The French Tradition and the Literature of Medieval
    England* [Toronto: University of Toronto Press, 1994], p. 139). Richard W.
    Kaeuper notes that Lull's work "was undoubtedly the most popular

medieval vernacular manual for knights" (Kaeuper and Kennedy, *The Book of Chivalry of Geoffroi de Charny*, p. 25). It was translated into French in the fourteenth century and into English (by William Caxton) in the fifteenth century.

66. Frantzen, *Before the Closet*, p. 107.

Introduction to Part One

1. Richard W. Kaeuper, *War, Justice, and Public Order: England and France in the Later Middle Ages* (Oxford: Clarendon Press, 1988), p. 185.
2. Maurice Keen, "War, Peace and Chivalry," in *Nobles, Knights and Men-at-Arms in the Middle Ages* (1987; repr. London: Hambledon Press, 1996), p. 9 [1–20].
3. Quoted in Keen, "War, Peace and Chivalry," p. 13.
4. Kaeuper and Kennedy, *The Book of Chivalry of Geoffroi de Charny*, pp. 98 and 99.
5. Richard W. Kaeuper, *Chivalry and Violence in Medieval Europe* (Oxford: Oxford University Press, 2001), p. 35.
6. Ramon Lull, *The Book of the Ordre of Chyvalry*, trans. William Caxton, ed. Alfred T. P. Byles, EETS o.s. 168 (London: Oxford University Press, 1926), p. 42.
7. Maurice Keen, *Chivalry* (New Haven: Yale University Press, 1984), p. 234.
8. Lull, *The Book of the Ordre of Chyvalry*, pp. 29–30. I have emended the Middle English "yogh" to "g" in "rygtwysnes."
9. Kaeuper, *War, Justice, and Public Order*, pp. 194–95.
10. D'Arcy Jonathan Dacre Boulton, *The Knights of the Crown: The Monarchical Orders of Knighthood in Later Medieval Europe 1325–1520* (New York: St. Martin's Press, 1987), p. 107. Boulton explains that in the French prose romance, written between 1314 and 1325, the main protagonist, Perceforest "is both an ancestor and a pre-Christian prefiguration of Arthur" and "all those admitted [to the society] were to be equals" (p. 23).
11. Juliet R. V. Barker, *The Tournament in England 1100–1400* (Woodbridge, Suffolk: Boydell Press, 1986), pp. 92 and 94.
12. Boulton, *The Knights of the Crown*, pp. 108–09.
13. Juliet Vale, *Edward III and Chivalry: Chivalric Society and Its Context 1270–1350* (Woodbridge, Suffolk: Boydell Press, 1982), p. 87.
14. Vale, *Edward III and Chivalry*, p. 88.
15. Boulton, *The Knights of the Crown*, p. 164. Keen sums up Edward's enterprise similarly: "It is clear that one of the major purposes of Edward III's institution of the Order of the Garter was to glamourise the standing of the war which he was waging against the King of France—to present the war effort in the light of a great adventure pursued by a noble and valiant company of knights against an adversary who was unjustly withholding from their sovereign his rightful inheritance" (*Chivalry*, p. 184). See also Vale, *Edward III and Chivalry*, pp. 91 and 93–94.
16. Maurice Keen, "Chaucer's Knight, the English Aristocracy and the Crusade," in *Nobles, Knights and Men-at-Arms in the Middle Ages* (1983; repr. London: Hambledon Press, 1996), pp. 104–05 [101–19].

17. Keen, "Chaucer's Knight," p. 117.

18. Kaeuper, *Chivalry and Violence in Medieval Europe*, p. 47.

19. Richard W. Kaeuper, "Geoffroi de Charny and His Book," pp. 47–48 [1–64].

20. Lull, *The Book of the Ordre of Chyvalry*, pp. 32–33.

21. I assume this from the following: "Adont se doivent partir tout net de conscience de celle eaue ed de ce bain et se doivent aler gesir en un lit tout neuf et les draps blans et nez" [Then they should come out of the water in the bath with a clear conscience and should go lie in a new bed in clean white sheets] (Kaeuper and Kennedy, *The Book of Chivalry of Geoffroi de Charny*, pp. 168 and 169). It is unlikely that Charny would have omitted any information pertaining to the novice knight's resting garments in such a detailed description of the bathing and dressing ritual. Interestingly, in Charny's account of the bathing ritual, the novice knights apparently come out of the bath unassisted. In the early thirteenth-century *Ordene de Chevalerie*, a text that, according to Keen, "achieved widespread popularity and men continued to refer to its authority even in the later fifteenth century" (*Chivalry*, p. 6), the novice knight is actually taken out of the bath. Hugh, Count of Tiberias, is preparing his captor, Saladin, for knighting under Christian law: "l'a du baing osté, / Si l'a couchié en un biau lit, / Qui estoit fez par grant delit" [Hugh took him out of the bath and laid him in a fair bed, which was delightfully wrought] (*L'Ordene de Chevalerie* in *Raoul de Hodenc: Le Roman des Eles; The Anonymous Ordene de Chevalerie*, ed. and trans. Keith Busby [Amsterdam: Utrecht Publications in General and Comparative Literature, 1983], ll. 126–28; p. 171). The *Ordene* thus draws attention to a potentially erotic encounter that is not necessarily absent in Charny's account. For it is unlikely that the novice knights were unattended when they emerged from the bath.

22. Kaeuper and Kennedy, *The Book of Chivalry of Geoffroi de Charny*, pp. 168 and 169.

23. Boulton, *The Knights of the Crown*, p. 126.

24. Boulton, *The Knights of the Crown*, p. 195.

25. Keen, *Chivalry*, pp. 179–80. He names the Confraternity of the Black Swan (1352), the Order of the Tiercelet (1380), and the Order of the Golden Apple (ca. 1390).

26. Keen, *Chivalry*, p. 196.

27. Keen, *Chivalry*, p. 198.

28. Mauice Keen, "Brotherhood-in-Arms," in *Nobles, Knights and Men-at-Arms in the Middle Ages* (1964; repr. London: Hambledon Press, 1996), p. 58 [43–62].

29. Quoted in Keen, "Brotherhood-in-Arms," p. 59.

30. Keen, "Brotherhood-in-Arms," p. 61.

31. Keen, "Brotherhood-in-Arms," pp. 61–62.

32. Lull, *The Book of the Ordre of Chyvalry*, pp. 18 and 80. I have altered the spelling of "knyght" in the second quote, substituting "g" for the Middle English "yogh" and adding "h."

33. Lull suggests that society benefits when a knight joins the chivalric broth-
    erhood: "[the] newly made knyght/...is bounded to maytene & deffende
    the hyhe honour of chivalry/For so moche shal he haue more gretter
    refraynynge to do euyl" (*The Book of the Ordre of Chyvalry*, p. 75).
34. Lull, *The Book of the Ordre of Chyvalry*, p. 74.
35. Kaeuper and Kennedy, *The Book of Chivalry of Geoffroi de Charny*, pp. 88 and 89.
36. Kaeuper and Kennedy, *The Book of Chivalry of Geoffroi de Charny*, pp. 106
    and 107.
37. Kaeuper and Kennedy, *The Book of Chivalry of Geoffroi de Charny*, pp. 106
    and 107.
38. Kaeuper, *Chivalry and Violence in Medieval Europe*, p. 192.

Chapter 2   Chivalric Bonds and the Ideals of Friendship

1. Aristotle, *Nicomachean Ethics*, trans. Terence Irwin (Indianapolis: Hackett,
   1985) VIII.9.32. All subsequent quotations unless otherwise noted are from
   this edition. For a detailed discussion of Aristotle's concept of "perfect
   friendship," especially looking at the relation of an individual to another
   self, see A. W. Price, *Love and Friendship in Plato and Aristotle* (Oxford:
   Clarendon Press, 1989), pp. 103–30. See also the useful brief summaries in
   Reginald Hyatte, *The Arts of Friendship: The Idealization of Friendship in
   Medieval and Early Renaissance Literature* (Leiden: Brill, 1994), pp. 16–21, and
   Philip Culbertson, *New Adam: The Future of Male Spirituality* (Minneapolis:
   Fortress Press, 1992), pp. 92–94. For a fine study of a wide variety of classical and medieval texts on friendship, see Adele Fiske, "Paradisus Homo
   Amicus," *Speculum* 40 (1965): 436–59.
2. Aristotle, *Nicomachean Ethics* VIII.9.35.
3. Aristotle, *Nicomachean Ethics* VIII.9.35.
4. H. H. Joachim, *Aristotle: The Nicomachean Ethics* (Oxford: Clarendon Press,
   1951), p. 247. Joachim provides a detailed, nearly line-by-line commentary
   on the complete work.
5. Marcus Tullius Cicero, *Laelius de amicitia*, in *De senectute, De amicitia, De
   divinatione*, trans. William Armistead Falconer, Loeb Classical Library, vol. 20
   (1923; repr. Cambridge, MA.: Harvard University Press, 1959) V.18. For a
   brief discussion of Cicero's treatise, see Hyatte, *The Arts of Friendship*, pp. 26–33.
   For a good overview of classical theories of friendship, see Carolinne
   White, *Christian Friendship in the Fourth Century* (Cambridge: Cambridge
   University Press, 1992), pp. 13–44.
6. Cicero, *De amicitia* V.19.
7. Cicero, *De amicitia* VI.20.
8. Aristotle, *Nicomachean Ethics* VIII.9.35. Thomas Aquinas highlights the
   motivating force of love inherent in Aristotle's concept of friendship, noting
   that "et quia amicitiae actus est amatio, consequens est quod etiam sint tres
   species amicitiae aequales numero amabilibus...in singulis enim horum
   salvatur ratio amicitiae supra posita, quia secundum unumquodque horum

trium potest esse redamatio non latens" [because love is an act of friendship, there will be three kinds of friendship equal to the three objects of
love (i.e. good, useful, pleasant). ... In each of these the definition of
friendship...is fulfilled, because in each of the three a recognized return of
love by someone is possible] (*Sententia libri ethicorum, Opera omnia,*
vol. 47 [Rome, 1969] p. 1156a ll. 6.31–33, 35–38); *Commentary on the
Nicomachean Ethics,* trans. C. I. Litzinger, vol. 2 (Chicago: Henry Regency,
1964), p. 714.

9. Aristotle, *Nicomachean Ethics* IX.11.22.
10. Aristotle, *Nicomachean Ethics* VIII.9.35.
11. Aristotle, *Nicomachean Ethics* VIII.11.73.
12. White, *Christian Friendship in the Fourth Century,* p. 27.
13. Aristotle, *Nicomachean Ethics* VIII.9.46.
14. Cicero, *De amicitia* VIII.26.
15. Cicero, *De amicitia* VIII.27.
16. Cicero, *De amicitia* VIII.27.
17. Cicero, *De amicitia* VIII.28. While I am most interested here in Cicero's
    linking of love and friendship, his observation that someone could love
    a person never actually seen is relevant to my investigation of potential
    homoeroticism in visualizing images of men described in texts, which I
    take up in chapter 4. Cicero implies that emotions are stirred merely from
    listening to or reflecting on a description of a virtuous person. Thus, a
    reader of a chivalric text could feel affection for and, in a sense, love the
    image of a model knight he visualizes.
18. Aristotle, *Nicomachean Ethics* VIII.11.68.
19. Thomas Aquinas, *Sentenia libri ethicorum* in *Opera omnia,* p. 1166a, ll.
    30.170–73; *Commentary on the Nicomachean Ethics,* trans. Litzinger, p. 806.
20. Cicero, *De amicitia* VI.22.
21. Cicero, *De amicitia* VII.23.
22. Cicero, *De officiis,* trans. Walter Miller, Loeb Classical Library, vol. 21 (1913;
    repr. Cambridge, MA: Harvard University Press, 1961) I.XVII.56.
23. Aristotle, *Nicomachean Ethics* IX.11.69.
24. Aristotle, *Nicomachean Ethics,* p. 360 n1157b18.
25. Thomas Aquinas, *Commentary on the Nicomachean Ethics,* trans. Litzinger,
    p. 855; *Sententia libri ethicorum* 1171b, ll. 32.29–32: "amicitia in communi-
    catione consistit...maxime autem se ipsos sibi invicem communicant in
    convictu; unde convivere videtur esse maxime proprium et delectabile in
    amicitia."
26. Joachim, *Aristotle: The Nicomachean Ethics,* p. 247.
27. Cicero, *De amicitia* XXII.83.
28. Cicero, *De amicitia* XXII.83.
29. Cicero, *De officiis* I.XVII.55.
30. Robert Grosseteste, the Oxford scholar, translated Aristotle's *Nicomachean
    Ethics* in the mid-thirteenth century and, "[i]t became in its original or in
    a revised form the standard version in the Middle Ages," according to
    Bernard G. Dod, "Aristoteles latinus," in *The Cambridge History of Later*

Medieval Philosophy, ed. Norman Kretzmann, Anthony Kenny, and Jan Pinborg (Cambridge: Cambridge University Press, 1982), p. 61 [45–79]. Dod indicates that Grosseteste's translation survives in 33 manuscripts as well as an additional 246, which are revised versions ("Aristoteles latinus," p. 77). Nevertheless, the two medieval discourses on friendship I examine in the next section refer only to Cicero's text.

31. The title of Aelred's text often appears as *De spirituali amicitia*. Mark Williams dates Aelred's text between 1147 and 1157. *Aelred of Rievaulx's Spiritual Friendship*, trans. Mark F. Williams (Scranton: University of Scranton Press, 1994), p. 16. D. D. R. Owen notes that scholars currently date Chrétien's Arthurian romances between 1170 and 1182 ("Introduction," in *Chrétien de Troyes, Arthurian Romances* [London: Dent & Sons, 1987], p. x). For a thorough discussion of Aelred's concept of friendship, see Adele M. Fiske, *Friends and Friendship in the Monastic Tradition* (Cuernavaca, Mexico: CIDOC, 1970) 18, pp. 1–49. She provides extensive excerpts and commentary drawing on both *De spiritali amicitia* and *De speculo caritatis*. For a brief treatment of Aelred's work, see Hyatte, *The Arts of Friendship*, pp. 62–69.

32. Douglass Roby, "Introduction," *Aelred of Rievaulx: Spiritual Friendship*, trans. Mary Eugenia Laker (Kalamazoo: Cistercian Publications, 1977), p. 38.

33. Aelred of Rievaulx, *De spiritali amicitia, Aelredi Rievallensis opera omnia*, ed. A. Hoste and C. H. Talbot, *Corpus Christianorum, Continuatio Mediaevalis*, vol. 1 (Turnhout: Brepols, 1971) I.45; Aelred of Rievaulx, *Spiritual Friendship*, trans. Mary Eugenia Laker (Kalamazoo: Cistercian Publications, 1977).

34. Aelred, *De spiritali amicitia* I.46, ed. Hoste and Talbot; *Spiritual Friendship*, trans. Laker.

35. Aelred, *De spiritali amicitia* I.19; *Spiritual Friendship*, trans. Laker.

36. Aelred, *De spiritali amicitia* III.2; *Spiritual Friendship*, trans. Laker.

37. Aelred, *De spiritali amicitia* III.51; *Spiritual Friendship*, trans. Laker.

38. Aelred, *De spiritali amicitia* II.24; *Spiritual Friendship*, trans. Laker.

39. While Aelred does not explicitly state that the friends he is referring to are both male, I am making this assumption since it is unlikely he would have witnessed many instances of female friends kissing one another after being separated for a long time or male and female friends exchanging kisses on such occasions. That Aelred not only participated in male friendships, such as his loving relationship with a monk named Ivo, referred to in II.5, but also observed displays of affection between men is suggested by Roby, who, drawing on *Walter Daniel's Life of Ailred*, observes that "Aelred, unlike some other abbots, was not scandalized by demonstrations of affection, such as holding hands, by his monks" ("Introduction," pp. 21–22).

40. Aelred, *De spiritali amicitia* II.11; *Spiritual Friendship*, trans. Laker. Aelred is quoting Cicero from *De amicitia* VI.22.

41. Aelred, *De spiritali amicitia* III.69–70; *Spiritual Friendship*, trans. Laker.

42. Aelred, *De spiritali amicitia* III.6; *Spiritual Friendship*, trans. Laker. Aelred is quoting from Ambrose, *De officiis*, III.134.

43. Aelred, *De spiritali amicitia* III.48; *Spiritual Friendship*, trans. Laker. Compare Cicero, *De amicitia* XXI.81: "alterum anquirit, cuius animum ita cum suo

misceat, ut efficiat paene unum ex duobus" [(a man) seek(s) out another whose soul he may so mingle with his own as almost to make one out of two].

44. Aelred, *De spiritali amicitia* III.7; *Spiritual Friendship*, trans. Laker.

45. Brian Patrick McGuire, *Brother and Lover: Aelred of Rievaulx* (New York: Crossroad Press, 1994), pp. 114–15.

46. *The Romaunt of the Rose*, in *The Riverside Chaucer*, 5201–04. Further quotations will be cited in the text by line number.

47. Alan T. Gaylord, "Friendship in Chaucer's *Troilus*," *Chaucer Review* 3 (1968–69): 245 [239–64]. Gaylord offers a fine list, although somewhat dated, of studies examining medieval appropriations of the classical concept of ideal friendship; see "Friendship in Chaucer's *Troilus*," 247 n6. For a reference to medieval texts that draw on Cicero's idea that ideal friendship can occur only between virtuous men, see Robert G. Cook, "Chaucer's Pandarus and the Medieval Ideal of Friendship," *Journal of English and Germanic Philology* 69 (1970): 410 [407–24].

48. In his explanatory notes to the *Romaunt of the Rose*, Alfred David observes that Reason is drawing on chapters 5, 6, 13, and 17 of Cicero's *De amicitia* (*The Riverside Chaucer*, p. 1111 n5201).

49. Lull, *The Book of the Ordre of Chyvalry*, p. 18.

50. Kaeuper and Kennedy, *The Book of Chivalry of Geoffroi de Charny*, pp. 128 and 129.

51. Lull, *The Book of the Ordre of Chyvalry*, pp. 74–75. I have substituted "gh" for the Middle English "yogh."

52. Lull, *The Book of the Ordre of Chyvalry*, p. 82.

53. Kaeuper and Kennedy, *The Book of Chivalry of Geoffroi de Charny*, pp. 88 and 89.

54. Keen, "Brotherhood-in-Arms," p. 43.

55. See the introduction in *Amys and Amylion*, ed. François Le Saux (Exeter: University of Exeter Press, 1993). Le Saux also provides summaries of the Latin, French, and Anglo-Norman versions in the appendix. See also the introduction in *Amis and Amiloun*, ed. MacEdward Leech, EETS 203 (London: Oxford University Press, 1937).

56. Calin, *The French Tradition and the Literature of Medieval England*, p. 486.

57. Calin observes: "The notion of manly love—hero and companion, uncle and nephew, friend and friend—provides a sacred-oriented alternative to the more common courtly, heterosexual passion which dominates the secular books of the period" (*The French Tradition and the Literature of Medieval England*, p. 486).

58. *Amys and Amylion*, ed. François Le Saux (Exeter: University of Exeter Press, 1993) 5, 3. All quotations are taken from this edition and subsequent citations will be given in the text by stanza and line number. I follow the spelling of the protagonists' names in Le Saux's edition.

59. For a discussion of the chivalric ideal of "truth" and its expression in *Amys and Amylion*, see Dean R. Baldwin, "*Amis and Amiloun*: The Testing of *Treupe*," *Papers on Language and Literature* 16 (1980): 353–65. Baldwin does not examine the actual bond of friendship between the two protagonists, but rather is concerned with the moral world of the romance.

He concludes that it "tests treuþe on several levels. It shows the value of unswerving loyalty to a sworn oath while insisting that adherence to the spirit of the vow is more important than mere fidelity to the letter. More importantly, it tests the virtue of treuþe itself, showing it to be an imperfect substitute for faith and grace, and requiring the tempering of 'kinde'" (365).

60. In all fairness to Amylion's wife, Le Saux points out that she follows standard medieval procedure for dealing with someone afflicted with leprosy (p. 77 n129–31). It is therefore all the more remarkable that Amys would welcome a leper.

61. Compare the directions given to Moses for curing leprosy; the leper is first sprinkled with the blood of a bird, and then eight days later the priest places the blood of a sacrificed male lamb on various parts of the leper's body. See Leviticus 14.1–8, 10–15.

62. Hyatte, *The Arts of Friendship*, p. 90.

63. Hyatte, *The Arts of Friendship*, p. 106.

64. Augustine recounts how he mourned the passing of his beloved friend: "mirabar enim ceteros morales vivere, quia ille, quem quasi non moriturum dilexeram, mortuus erat, et me magis, quia ille alter eram, vivere illo mortuo mirabar" [I was astonished that other mortals lived, since he whom I loved, as if he would never die, was dead; and I wondered still more that I, who was to him a second self, could live when he was dead]. Augustine, *Confessions*, ed. James J. O'Donnell (Oxford: Clarendon Press, 1992) IV.6.11; *Confessions*, trans. Vernon J. Burke (New York: Fathers of the Church, 1953). After Basil leaves Gregory to assume his position as bishop of Caesarea, Gregory writes Basil: "Equidum ipse te magis quam aerem spiro, idque solum vivo, quod tecum sum, vel coram, vel absens per animi simulacrum" [I would rather breathe you than the air, and only live while I am with you, either actually in your presence, or virtually by your likeness in your absence]. Gregory of Nazianzus, Epistle VI, *Epistolae, Patrologiae cursus completus, series Graeca*, ed. J. P. Migne, vol. 37 (Paris, 1857); *A Selection from the Letters of Saint Gregory Nazianzen, Nicene and Post-Nicene Fathers of the Christian Church*, ed. Philip Schaff and Henry Wace, vol. 7, 2nd series (Grand Rapids: Eerdmans, 1961).

65. Gretchen Mieszkowski, "The Prose *Lancelot's* Galehot, Malory's Lavain, and the Queering of Late Medieval Literature," *Arthuriana* 5.1 (1995): 21; 28 [21–51]. Mieszkowski offers an excellent, convincing reading of Galehot and Lancelot's relationship in the non-cyclic Prose *Lancelot*—a relationship, she argues, that is decidedly unbalanced because Galehot's love for Lancelot is far more intense than Lancelot's love for Galehot. She maintains that although Lancelot loves Galehot, he always privileges his relationship with Guinevere. I am drawing on the expanded version of the story in the cyclic Prose *Lancelot* that offers evidence that the love the two knights have for each other is more equal.

66. *Le Livre de Lancelot del Lac, The Vulgate Version of the Arthurian Romances*, ed. H. Oskar Sommer, vols. 3, 4 (Washington DC: Carnegie Institution, 1910)

3:13–15, p. 247; *Sir Lancelot of the Lake: A French Prose Romance of the Thirteenth Century*, trans. Lucy Allen Paton (London: Routledge, 1929), p. 186. For a relatively recent edition of the non-cyclic *Prose Lancelot*, see *Lancelot do Lac: The Non-Cyclic Old French Prose Romance*, ed. Elspeth Kennedy, 2 vols. (Oxford: Clarendon, 1980).

67. *Le Livre de Lancelot del Lac*, 3:21–23, ed. Sommer, p. 247; *Sir Lancelot of the Lake*, trans. Paton, p. 187.

68. *Le Livre de Lancelot del Lac*, 3:6–7, p. 248; *Sir Lancelot of the Lake*, trans. Paton, p. 188.

69. *Le Livre de Lancelot del Lac*, 3:41, p. 248; *Sir Lancelot of the Lake*, trans. Paton, p. 190.

70. *Le Livre de Lancelot del Lac*, 3:7–11, p. 249, emphasis added; *Sir Lancelot of the Lake*, trans. Paton, p. 190.

71. *Le Livre de Lancelot del Lac*, 3:4–5, p. 264; *Sir Lancelot of the Lake*, trans. Paton, p. 214.

72. *Le Livre de Lancelot del Lac*, 3:34–36, p. 264; *Sir Lancelot of the Lake*, trans. Paton, p. 215.

73. *Le Livre de Lancelot del Lac*, 3:24–25, p. 427; *Sir Lancelot of the Lake*, trans. Paton, p. 220.

74. *Le Livre de Lancelot del Lac*, 3:25–26, p. 427; *Sir Lancelot of the Lake*, trans. Paton, p. 220.

75. *Le Livre de Lancelot del Lac*, 3:38–39, p. 428; *Sir Lancelot of the Lake*, trans. Paton, p. 221.

76. *Le Livre de Lancelot del Lac*, 4:14–16, p. 5; *Sir Lancelot of the Lake*, trans. Paton, p. 224.

77. *Le Livre de Lancelot del Lac*, 4:4–5, p. 155; *Sir Lancelot of the Lake*, trans. Paton, p. 249.

78. *Le Livre de Lancelot del Lac*, 4:39–42; 1–3, pp. 276 and 277; *Sir Lancelot of the Lake*, trans. Paton, pp. 297–98. Compare Achilles grieving the death of his beloved Patroclus: "and the black cloud of sorrow closed on Achilleus. / In both hands he caught up the grimy dust and poured it / over his head and face, and fouled his handsome countenance, / and the black ashes were scattered over his immortal tunic. / And he himself, mightily in his might, in the dust lay/at length, and took and tore at his hair with his hands, and defiled it" (Homer, *The Iliad*, trans. Richard Lattimore [Chicago: University of Chicago Press, 1951] XVIII, ll. 22–27).

79. Mieszkowski, "The Prose *Lancelot*'s Galehot," 42.

80. Referring only to Galehot, Mieszkowski rightly points out that "Galehot's manliness...[or his heterosexual relationship] would not have interfered with 13th-century readers' recognition of him as a man passionately in love with another man" ("The Prose *Lancelot*'s Galehot," 39). I suggest that the same would hold true for fourteenth-century readers.

81. Aelred of Rievaulx, *De speculo caritatis, Aelredi Rievallensis Opera omnia*, ed. A. Hoste and C. H. Talbot, *Corpus Christianorum, Continuatio Mediaevalis*, vol. 1 (Turnhout: Brepols, 1971) III.109; trans. Boswell, *Christianity, Social Tolerance, and Homosexuality*, p. 225.

Chapter 3   Competing Desires

1. Philip L. Culbertson, "Men and Christian Friendship," in *Men's Bodies, Men's Gods: Male Identities in a (Post-)Christian Culture*, ed. Björn Krondorfer (New York: New York University Press, 1996), pp. 161–62 [149–80].
2. Vern L. Bullough, *Sexual Variance in Society and History* (New York: John Wiley & Sons, 1976), p. 399.
3. Bullough, *Sexual Variance in Society and History*, pp. 399–400.
4. Sedgwick, *Between Men*, p. 35.
5. Geoffrey Chaucer, *Troilus and Criseyde, The Riverside Chaucer*, ed. Larry D. Benson (Boston: Houghton Mifflin, 1987) 2.330–31. All quotations unless otherwise noted are from this edition. Subsequent quotations will be cited in the text by book and line number.
6. B. A. Windeatt points to other instances in this scene where Pandarus switches to the familiar personal pronoun and suggests that they all have a persuasive effect (Geoffrey Chaucer, *Troilus and Criseyde: A New Edition of "The Book of Troilus,"* ed. B. A. Windeatt [London: Longman, 1984], p. 171 n1396). For instance, Pandarus assures Criseyde: "For me were levere thow and I and he / Were hanged, than I sholde ben his baude, / . . . / I am thyn em; the shame were to me, / As wel as the, if that I sholde assente/Thorugh myn abet that he thyn honour shente (2.352–57)." There is a difference though between using familiar address to reassure and using it to denigrate.
7. Elaine Tuttle Hansen, *Chaucer and the Fictions of Gender* (Berkeley: University of California Press, 1992), p. 154. Although I agree that the courtly words Troilus addresses to Pandarus indeed homoeroticize the moment, we should not overlook the erotic positioning of the two men.
8. Alan Bray notes that in Elizabethan England it was common for men to share a bed and because of a general lack of privacy, it was public knowledge who were "bedfellows" ("Male Friendship in Elizabethan England," 4). Likewise, Troilus's servants would most likely be aware that Pandarus is sleeping in their master's room. This normative sleeping arrangement is homoeroticzed in Chaucer's text because the two friends are alone, evidently in darkness, and make heartfelt pledges to each other.
9. I am drawing on Windeatt's gloss of "stoupen" (droop) and "Redressen hem" (stand up straight again); see *Troilus and Criseyde*, ed. Windeatt, p. 199 nn968, 969.
10. A parallel situation can be found in the *Prose Lancelot* where Galehot and Lancelot also spend an erotically charged night together after Galehot successfully serves as an intermediary between Lancelot and Guinevere.
11. It is unclear whether Troilus and Pandarus are lying on the same "paillet" or if Pandarus's bed is merely next to Troilus's. In any case, the two are evidently lying very close to each other.
12. Giovanni Boccaccio, *The Filostrato of Giovanni Boccaccio*, ed. and trans. Nathaniel Edward Griffin and Arthur Beckwith Myrick (New York: Octagon, 1978) 3.56.
13. In terms of "perfect friendship," Amys and the steward are not compatible because both partners must be virtuous. Immediately after Amys rejects the steward's offer of brotherhood, the steward plots his revenge.

14. Leah Rieber Freiwald observes that Troilus and Pandarus's relationship illustrates the type of friendship Aristotle referred to as "imperfect"—"the kind of friendship which occurs when two partners expect pleasure or utility to result from their association" ("Swych Love of Frendes: Pandarus and Troilus," *Chaucer Review* 6.2 [1971]: 122 [120–29]). While it is true that their bond is not "perfect," they demonstrate some of the key concepts of ideal friendship, such as fidelity (intended to be permanent), love, shared interests, and affection. See Gaylord, "Friendship in Chaucer's *Troilus*," and Cook, "Chaucer's Pandarus and the Medieval Ideal of Friendship."

15. René Girard, *Deceit, Desire, and the Novel: Self and Other in Literary Structure*, trans. Yvonne Freccero (Baltimore: Johns Hopkins University Press, 1965), p. 2.

16. Girard, *Deceit, Desire, and the Novel*, pp. 9 and 7.

17. Girard, *Deceit, Desire, and the Novel*, p. 10.

18. Girard, *Deceit, Desire, and the Novel*, p. 10. Freud theorizes the interrelationship between love and hate: "love so constantly manifests itself as 'ambivalent,' i.e. accompanied by feelings of hate against the same object. This admixture of hate in love is to be traced in part to those preliminary stages of love which have not been wholly outgrown, and in part is based upon reactions of aversion and repudiation on the part of the ego-instincts which, in the frequent conflicts between the interests of the ego and those of love, can claim to be supported by real and actual motives." He goes on to explain: "When a love-relationship with a given object is broken off, it is not infrequently succeeded by hate, so that we receive the impression of a transformation of love into hate. ...[W]hen this happens, the hate which is motivated by considerations of reality is reinforced by a regression of the love to the sadistic preliminary stage, so that the hate acquires an erotic character and the continuity of a love-relation is ensured" (Sigmund Freud, "Instincts and Their Vicissitudes," in *General Psychological Theory*, ed. Philip Rieff [New York: Macmillan, 1963], pp. 102–03 [83–103]).

19. Martin Blum, "Negotiating Masculinities: Erotic triangles in the *Miller's Tale*," in *Masculinities in Chaucer: Approaches to Maleness in the Canterbury Tales and Troilus and Criseyde*, ed. Peter G. Beidler (Cambridge: D. S. Brewer, 1998), p. 40 [37–52].

20. Blum, "Negotiating Masculinities," p. 40. I explore more thoroughly than Blum does sites of potential or suggested homoerotic desire and how this desire interacts or "competes" with heterosexual desire. For instance, Blum observes that in the Nicholas/Absolon/Alison triangle, Nicholas's prank on Absolon places him in a "feminine" position "that allows him virtually no control over what is going to happen to his own, male body" ("Negotiating Masculinities," p. 48). Blum rightly concludes that the narrative closes off the possibility of male–male desire here by punishing the male occupying this passive position, but he does not examine the confusion of homoerotic and heterosexual desires informing Absolon's revenge on Nicholas and Alison.

21. Mikkel Borch-Jacobsen, *The Freudian Subject*, trans. Catherine Porter (Stanford: Stanford University Press, 1988), p. 191.

22. Freud refers to cases where a younger brother is jealous of his older brother: "during early childhood feelings of jealousy derived from the mother-complex and of very great intensity arose against rivals, usually older brothers. This jealousy led to an exceedingly hostile aggressive attitude against brothers (or sisters) which might culminate in actual death-wishes, but which could not survive further development. Under the influence of training—and certainly not uninfluenced also by their own constant powerlessness—these feelings yielded to repression and to a transformation, so that the rivals of the earlier period became the first homosexual love-objects" (Sigmund Freud, "Certain Neurotic Mechanisms in Jealousy, Paranoia and Homosexuality," in *Sexuality and the Psychology of Love*, ed. Philip Rieff [New York: Macmillan, 1963], pp. 158–59 [150–60]).

23. Girard, *Deceit, Desire, and the Novel*, p. 47.

24. Sedgwick, *Between Men*, p. 23.

25. Sedgwick, *Between Men*, p. 23.

26. Since Troilus and Criseyde are in reversed positions from the earlier configuration, Troilus now represents the desired object/goal for Pandarus: namely, the consummation. As I pointed out when discussing the previous triangle, Pandarus does not necessarily desire the person occupying the position but rather the mediator's "attainment" of that person. As the endpoint in the triangular flow of desire, this person has however an eroticized valence.

27. For a very different reading of this scene, see Maud Burnett McInerney, "'Is this a mannes herte?': Unmanning Troilus through Ovidian Allusion," *Masculinities in Chaucer*, ed. Beidler, pp. 221–35. McInerney observes that Pandarus and Criseyde are here "performing a sort of sexual first aid" (p. 223). She goes on to suggest that throughout the scene Pandarus occupies the role of "sex therapist" (p. 224).

28. Because the series of actions Criseyde and Pandarus perform on Troilus are reported as a continuum, the dual actions and Criseyde's solo efforts connected by "And" (3.1116), we can assume that Pandarus is still in the direct vicinity.

29. Although at the time Criseyde makes this "threat" Pandarus has again retreated to the fireplace (3.1141), it is unlikely that he is beyond the range of sight and hearing. Earlier when Troilus swoons, he is "up as faste" at the bedside (3.1094).

30. I am assuming that Pandarus actually leaves the bedroom because there are no indications that he remains. Since there is apparently only one bed in the room and no additional chair (for Pandarus *stands* by the fireplace), it seems unlikely that we are meant to suspect that he stands all night listening and watching. In addition, the next morning he comes "Unto his nece" (3.1556), implying that he enters the room. While one could argue that he slips out sometime later during the night, the text, in effect, exits him from the scene after his final remarks to the lovers: "if ye be wise,/Swouneth nought now, lest more folk arise" (3.1189–90).

31. Gayle Rubin, "The Traffic in Women: Notes on the 'Political Economy' of Sex," in *Toward an Anthropology of Women*, ed. Rayna R. Reiter (New York:

Monthly Review, 1975), pp. 171, 173, and 174 [157–210]. See Claude Lévi-Strauss, *The Elementary Structures of Kinship* (Boston: Beacon Press, 1969).

32. Rubin, "The Traffic in Women," p. 179.

33. *Sir Gawain and the Green Knight, Sir Gawain and the Green Knight, Pearl, Cleanness, Patience*, ed. A. C. Cawley and J. J. Anderson (London: Dent & Sons, 1976), ll. 1388–89. Subsequent quotations will be cited in the text by line number.

34. Geraldine Heng, "A Woman Wants: The Lady, *Gawain*, and the Forms of Seduction," *Yale Journal of Criticism* 5 (1992): 103 [101–33]. For her discussion of the difference between speech in place of sex and speech in *the* place of sex, see 125 n7. For Foucault's theory on the discourse on sex, see *The History of Sexuality*, trans. Hurley, 1:17–35; 53–73.

35. Boyd, "Sodomy, Misogyny, and Displacement," 80.

36. Trans. Cawley and Anderson.

37. Drawing a parallel between the lady's and Bertilak's hunts, Boyd articulates the homoeroticism of these interactions as follows: "since the Lady's sexual hunt for Gawain is actually Bertilak's homosocial hunt to entrap him, and since Bertilak's homosocial hunt carries sexual traces from its relationship to the Lady's temptation, then Bertilak's masculine world of homosociality, violence, and aggression—all types of masculine exchange—discloses traces of (homo)sexual desire" ("Sodomy, Misogyny, and Displacement," 86).

38. For an excellent, provocative examination of the relationship between Gawain and Bertilak, see Dinshaw, "A Kiss."

39. Geoffrey Chaucer, *Canterbury Tales*, in *The Riverside Chaucer*, I.1132–38. Subsequent quotations will be documented in the text.

40. Patricia Clare Ingham, "Masculine Military Unions: Brotherhood and Rivalry in *The Avowing of King Arthur*," *Arthuriana* 6.4 (1996): 29 [25–44].

41. According to Ingham, "[t]he coupling of violence with pleasure in these texts [*The Avowing of King Arthur* and *Knyghthode and Bataile*] reminds us that aggression can be delightful; it reminds us, too, that militarism trades upon the pleasures of aggression to invigorate its troops" ("Masculine Military Unions," 29).

Chapter 4   Homoerotic Identifications

1. I use "listener" and "reader" interchangeably since chivalric texts were evidently both listened to and read, although in-text clues often seem to target an aural audience. This might, however, be merely a narrative devise borrowed from minstrelsy.

2. Wendy Clein notes that Lull's chivalric treatise, "in granting knighthood superior status. . .offers a picture of society that would be attractive to an aristocratic audience" (*Concepts of Chivalry in Sir Gawain and the Green Knight* [Norman, OK: Pilgrim Books, 1987], p. 35). While all male aristocrats might not have wished to engage in an active chivalric life, they might have been enthusiastic readers. Charny's treatise, according to Richard Kaeuper, had a wide audience. He maintains that it was intended "[to]

reach all layers of power, status, and wealth within the body of knights....[Charny's] thoughts could potentially go to all those who lived honorably by the profession of arms, whatever their particular social substratum." (Kaeuper and Kennedy, *The Book of Chivalry of Geoffroi de Charny*, p. 34.)

3. Thomas Aquinas, *The Commentary of St. Thomas Aquinas on Aristotle's De Anima*, trans. Kenelm Foster and Sylvester Humphries (New Haven: Yale University Press, 1951), p. 383.

4. Carolyn P. Collette, *Species, Phantasms, and Images: Vision and Medieval Psychology in The Canterbury Tales* (Ann Arbor: University of Michigan Press, 2001), p. 21.

5. Collette, *Species, Phantasms, and Images*, p. 21. Collette explains that "[i]n many ways *phantasy* in this psychology corresponds to our modern notion of imagination, the creative capacity of the mind that wills to draw upon stored material to combine, divide, and recombine it" (*Species, Phantasms, and Images*, p. 9). For additional studies of medieval faculty psychology, see E. Ruth Harvey, *The Inward Wits: Psychological Theory in the Middle Ages and the Renaissance* (London: Warburg Institute, 1975) and Murray Wright Bundy, *The Theory of Imagination in Classical and Medieval Thought* (Urbana: University of Illinois Press, 1927).

6. Aristotle, *De memoria et reminiscentia*, quoted in Richard Sorabji, *Aristotle on Memory* (Providence: Brown University Press, 1972), p. 51.

7. Augustine, *De trinitate*, ed. W. J. Mountain and Fr. Glorie, *Corpus Christianorum, series Latina*, vol. 50–50A (Turnhout: Brepols, 1968), VIII.6.9; Augustine, *The Trinity*, trans. Stephen McKenna (Washington, DC: Catholic University of America Press, 1963), pp. 257–58. For a thorough study of Augustine's theory of reading, see Brian Stock, *Augustine the Reader: Meditation, Self-Knowledge, and the Ethics of Interpretation* (Cambridge, MA: Harvard University Press, 1996). I will be drawing heavily on Augustine's theories of imagination and memory, and although he is not contemporary with the period I am concentrating on, his ideas strongly influenced later medieval writers. As David C. Lindberg points out: "because of his immense authority, Augustine came to be consulted on all sorts of matters to which he had addressed himself only incidentally; on the theory of vision in particular, later medieval writers frequently quoted Augustine when his view paralleled their own" (*Theories of Vision from Al-Kindi to Kepler* [Chicago: University of Chicago Press, 1976], p. 89.)

8. Steven F. Kruger, *Dreaming in the Middle Ages* (New York: Cambridge University Press, 1992), p. 37.

9. Augustine, *De Genesi ad litteram, Patrologiae cursus completus, series Latina*, ed. Jacques Paul Migne, vol. 34 (Paris, 1844–65), XII.12.25; Augustine, *The Literal Meaning of Genesis*, trans. John Hammond Taylor, vol. 2 (New York: Newman Press, 1982), p. 193.

10. Augustine, *De trinitate* VIII.4.7; *The Trinity*, trans. McKenna, p. 251.

11. Augustine, *Epistolae secundum ordinem temporum nunc primum dispositae, prima classis, Patrologiae cursus competus, series Latina*, ed. Jacques Paul Migne, vol. 33 (Paris: 1844–65), VII.2.4; *Saint Augustine, Letters*, trans. Sister Wilfred Parsons, vol. 1 (Washington DC: Catholic University of America Press, 1951).

12. Augustine, *Epistolae*,VII.2.4; *Saint Augustine, Letters*, trans. Parsons.

13. Richart de Fournival, *Li Bestiaires d'Amours*, quoted in Mary Carruthers, *The Book of Memory: A Study of Memory in Medieval Culture* (Cambridge: Cambridge Univesity Press, 1990), pp. 341 n10; 223.

14. Augustine, *De trinitate* XI.8.14; *The Trinity*, trans. McKenna, p. 335.

15. Augustine, *De trinitate* XI.8.13; *The Trinity*, trans. McKenna, p. 334.

16. Augustine, *De trinitate* XI.5.8; *The Trinity*, trans. McKenna, p. 326.

17. Augustine, *De trinitate* XI.4.7; *The Trinity*, trans. McKenna, p. 324. Vincent of Beauvais, writing in the thirteenth century, offers a similar description; see Collette, *Species, Phantasms, and Images*, p. 23, for the relevant passage from the *Speculum naturale*.

18. Augustine, *De trinitate* XI.4.7; *The Trinity*, trans. Edmund Hill (Brooklyn, NY: New City Press, 1991), p. 309. Hill's translation more accurately expresses the eroticism in Augustine's example than McKenna's. Compare McKenna's translation: "And I recall someone telling me that he was wont to perceive in his thoughts the form of a woman's body, so distinct and as it were solid, that even his genital organs were aroused, as though he had experienced intercourse with her" (p. 324).

19. Chandos Herald, *Life of the Black Prince*, ed. Mildred K. Pope and Eleanor C. Lodge (Oxford: Clarendon, 1910), ll. 63–66; trans. Richard Barber, *The Life and Campaigns of the Black Prince: From Contemporary Letters, Diaries and Chronicles, Including Chandos Heralds's Life of the Black Prince* (New York: St. Martin's Press, 1986), p. 86.

20. Chandos Herald, *Life of the Black Prince*, ed. Pope and Lodge, ll. 83–84; trans. Pope and Lodge, p. 135.

21. Kaeuper and Kennedy, *The Book of Chivalry of Geoffroi de Charny*, pp. 162 and 163.

22. Geoffrey Chaucer, *The Canterbury Tales, The Riverside Chaucer*, ed. Benson, IV.1580–87.

23. I am drawing on Charny's neat summary of the qualities of "true men of worth": "Et quant yteles bonnes gens d'armes sont ainsi approuvez de leur bon ouvrage de leur main et de leur corps, de leur bon travail…de leur bonnes hardiesces asseurees…de bonne contenances que l'en voit en eulx sur les durs partis que l'on peut trouver es faiz d'armes" [The quality of these good men-at-arms has been fully proved through their good works of their hand and their body, through their strenuous efforts of endurance…through their great acts of true valor…through their splendid bearing, to be seen under the very difficult conditions often to be encountered in the practice of arms] (Kaeuper and Kennedy, *The Book of Chivalry of Geoffroi de Charny*, pp. 152 and 153). I have altered one phrase in the translation so that it follows the French text more closely. Kaeuper and Kennedy render "de leur bon ouvrage de leur main et de leur corps" as "through their great physical exploits."

24. Laura Mulvey, "Visual Pleasure and Narrative Cinema," in *The Sexual Subject: A Screen Reader in Sexuality* (1975; repr. London: Routledge, 1992), p. 24 [22–34]. For Freud's early ideas on scopophilia, see *Three Essays on the*

Theory of Sexuality, trans. James Strachey (New York: Basic Books, 1962); for his later analysis, see "Instincts and Their Vicissitudes," in *General Psychological Theory*, ed. Philip Rieff (New York: Macmillan, 1963) pp. 83–103.

25. Mulvey, "Visual Pleasure and Narrative Cinema," pp. 24 and 25.

26. Mulvey, "Visual Pleasure and Narrative Cinema," p. 25.

27. Mulvey, "Visual Pleasure and Narrative Cinema," p. 33.

28. Mulvey, "Visual Pleasure and Narrative Cinema," p. 26.

29. Mulvey, "Visual Pleasure and Narrative Cinema," p. 28.

30. Paul Willemen, "Voyeurism, The Look, and Dworkin," in *Narrative, Apparatus, Ideology: A Film Theory Reader*, ed. Philip Rosen (New York: Columbia University Press, 1986), pp. 212–13 [210–18]. Willemen argues against the traditional claim made by film theorists that male spectators merely identify with the male protagonist as a mediator "in order to get at a desired woman." He offers the example of male buddy films where "the suggested homosexual gratification appears in direct proportion to the degree women are humiliated in/eliminated from the diegesis" ("Voyeurism, The Look, and Dworkin," p. 213).

31. Steve Neale, "Masculinity as Spectacle," in *The Sexual Subject*, p. 281 [277–87]. Neale is drawing on D. N. Rodowick's essay, "The Difficulty of Difference," *Wide Angle* 5 (1982): 4–15.

32. Earl Jackson Jr., *Strategies of Deviance: Studies in Gay Male Representation* (Bloomington: Indiana University Press, 1995), p. 173.

33. Teresa de Lauretis, *The Practice of Love: Lesbian Sexuality and Perverse Desire* (Bloomington: Indiana University Press, 1994), p. 98. For DeLauretis's in-depth study of female–female spectatorship, see pp. 81–148. For a collection of essays on this topic, see *How Do I Look: Queer Film and Video*, ed. Bad Object Choices (Seattle: Bay Press, 1991).

34. *Le Livre de Lancelot del Lac*, ed. Sommer, vol. 3: ll. 37–39, p. 34; ll. 5–11, p. 35; *Sir Lancelot of the Lake*, trans. Paton, pp. 76–77. "Tor" and its slightly later form, "torel" is, according to the *Dictionnaire Historique de la Langue Français*, ed. Alain Rey, 2 vols. (Paris: Le Robert, 1992), derived from the Latin form, *taurus*, thus denoting "mâle de la vache" or "bull." Could the narrator then also be admiring Lancelot's power and virility?

35. Compare the Black Knight's description of Blanche in Chaucer's *The Book of the Duchess*: "But swich a fairnesse of a nekke / Had that swete that boon nor brekke / Nas ther non sene that myssat. / Hyt was whit, smothe, streght, and pure flat, / Wythouten hole or canel-boon, / As be semynge had she noon. / Hyr throte, as I have now memoyre, / Semed a round tour of yvoyre, / Of good gretnesse, and noght to gret" (*The Riverside Chaucer*, ll. 939–47).

36. Some chivalric texts—or, at least certain moments in chivalric texts—may discourage readers from focusing on the body beneath the armor. Kathleen Coyne Kelly notes that the excessive violent acts performed on vulnerable male bodies in the *Morte Darthur* "threatens a construct of masculinity as whole and inviolate, impervious to dissolution." And thus "[t]o 'see' the male body in the *Morte Darthur*, for the masculine gaze to actually experience this body and to pull it up into consciousness, precipitates both a

psychic and social crisis: such unmediated viewing exposes the instability of the phallic body" ("Malory's Body Chivalric," *Arthuriana* 6.4 (1996): 54; 56 [52–71]). Knights wounding one another can however afford pleasure to the reader, as I will explore later in this chapter.

37. Elizabeth Cowie, *Representing the Woman: Cinema and Psychoanalysis* (Minneapolis: University of Minnesota Press, 1997), p. 5.

38. Cowie, *Representing the Woman*, p. 4.

39. Diana Fuss, "Fashion and the Homospectatorial Look," *Critical Inquiry* 18 (1992): 737 [713–37].

40. Mary F. Wack, "Imagination, Medicine, and Rhetoric in Andreas Capellanus' 'De Amore,'" in *Magister Regis: Studies in Honor of Robert Earl Kaske*, ed. Arthur Groos, Emerson Brown Jr., Giuseppe Massotta, Thomas D. Hill, and Joseph S. Wittig (New York: Fordham University Press, 1986), p. 105 [101–15].

41. Wack, "Imagination, Medicine, and Rhetoric," in *Magister* Regis, p. 106.

42. The heteronormative agenda of courtly love is clearly expressed by Andreas Capellanus: "love cannot exist except between persons of the opposite sexes. Between two men or two women love can find no place, for we see that two persons of the same sex are not at all fitted for giving each other the exchanges of love or for practicing the acts natural to it" (*The Art of Courtly Love*, trans. John Jay Parry [New York: Columbia University Press, 1960], p. 30). Among the English mystics, Margery Kempe and Richard Rolle come easily to mind regarding, respectively, heterosexual and homo-erotic encounters with Christ.

43. Rupert of Deutz, *Comm. in Math.* 12, quoted in Peter Dinzelbacher, "Über die Entdeckung der Liebe in Hochmittelalter," *Saeculum* 32 (1981): 197 n94 [185–208]. My English translation draws on both Dinzelbacher's German translation and Mary Wack's English translation (Mary Frances Wack, *Lovesickness in the Middle Ages: The Viaticum and Its Commentaries* [Philadelphia: University of Pennsylvania Press, 1990], p. 24).

44. Cowie, *Representing the Woman*, p. 128.

45. Cowie, *Representing the Woman*, pp. 127 and 140.

46. Jean Laplanche and Jean Bertrand Pontalis, "Fantasy and the Origins of Sexuality," in *Formations of Fantasy*, ed. Victor Burgin, James Donald, and Cora Kaplan (1968; repr. London: Methuen, 1986), p. 26 [5–34].

47. Judith Butler, *Bodies That Matter: On the Discursive Limits of "Sex"* (New York: Routledge, 1993), p. 268 n7.

48. Silverman, *Male Subjectivity at the Margins* (New York: Routledge, 1992), p. 173. Silverman offers a provocative reading of Henry James's "The Beast in the Jungle"; see pp. 170–74.

49. *L'Ordene de Chevalerie, Raoul de Houdenc: Le Roman des Eles; The Anonymous Ordene de Chevalerie*, ed. and trans. Keith Busby (Amsterdam: Utrecht Publications in General and Comparative Literature, 1983), ll. 126–28; 137–39. I have emended "Hue" in Busby's translation to "Hugh." Although the *Ordene* was written in the early thirteenth century, fourteenth-century readers would most likely have been familiar with it. Maurice Keen notes

that "[i]t achieved widespread popularity and men continued to refer to its authority even in the later fifteenth century. It was copied into numerous manuscripts, and appears often in company with other material interesting to knightly readers" (*Chivalry*, p. 6).

50. Terrell Scott Herring, "Frank O'Hara's Open Closet," *PMLA* 117 (2002): 422 [414–27].

51. Cowie, *Representing the Woman*, p. 140.

52. Kaeuper and Kennedy, *The Book of Chivalry of Geoffroi de Charny*, pp. 108 and 109.

53. Cowie, *Representing the Woman*, p. 140.

54. Freud, "Instincts and Their Vicissitudes," p. 91.

55. Freud, "Instincts and Their Vicissitudes," p. 92.

56. Jean Laplanche, *Life and Death in Psychoanalysis*, trans. Jeffrey Mehlman (1976; repr. Baltimore: Johns Hopkins University Press, 1985), p. 89.

57. Jean Laplanche and Jean Bertrand Pontalis, *The Language of Psycho-Analysis*, trans. Donald Nicholson-Smith (New York: Norton, 1973), p. 402.

58. Freud, "Instincts and Their Vicissitudes," p. 93.

59. Laplanche, *Life and Death in Psychoanalysis*, p. 91.

60. Freud, "Instincts and Their Vicissitudes," p. 93.

61. Sigmund Freud, "The Economic Problem in Masochism," in *General Psychological Theory*, p. 192 [190–201]. The two other expressions of masochism are "feminine" and "moral," yet, according to Freud, the "erotogenic" type "is also to be found at bottom in the other forms" ("Economic Problem in Masochism," p. 192). Kaja Silverman points out that since "[t]he adjective 'erotogenic' is one which Freud habitually links with 'zone,' and with which he designates a part of the body at which sexual excitation concentrates[,]...[i]mplicit, then , in the notion of masochism, whether feminine or moral, would seem to be the experience of corporeal pleasure, or—to be more precise—corporeal pleasure-in-pain" (*Male Subjectivity at the Margins*, p. 188). For Silverman's detailed discussion of Freud's three kinds of masochism, see *Male Subjectivity*, pp. 188–210. Laplanche expands on Freud's theory of sadism/masochism; see *Life and Death in Psychoanalysis*, pp. 85–102. For a discussion of Laplanche, see Jackson, *Strategies of Deviance*, pp. 135–39.

62. It is certainly possible that female readers could likewise form sadomasochistic identifications with male protagonists, especially when one considers the writings of female mystics focusing on the wounded body of Christ. See, for instance, Karma Lochrie, *Margery Kempe and Translations of the Flesh* (Philadelphia: University of Pennsylvania Press, 1991).

63. Quoted in Silverman, *Male Subjectivity at the Margins*, p. 201. For an in-depth discussion and commentary on the entire beating fantasy, see D. N. Rodowick, *The Difficulty of Difference: Psychoanalysis, Sexual Difference & Film Theory* (New York: Routledge, 1991), pp. 66–94. For Freud's text, see "'A Child Is Being Beaten': A Contribution to the Study of the Origin of Sexual Perversion," in *The Standard Edition of the Complete Psychological Works of Sigmund Freud*, ed. and trans. James Strachey, 24 vols. (London: Hogarth, 1953–74), 17:175–204.

64. For a different reading of masochism in a medieval romance, see Jeffrey Jerome Cohen, "Masoch/Lancelotism," *New Literary History* 28 (1997): 231–60. Drawing on Deleuze's separation of masochism and sadism, Cohen examines masochism in the realm of Lancelot's relationship with Guinevere in Chrétien's *Lancelot.* He maintains that the text "asks what it is like to embrace domination—to take the place simultaneously of servant, vassal, lover, artist with an enthusiasm that not only erodes the distinction among these roles, but also through its unwavering obedience to a hierarchized system of power threatens, at last, to topple whatever architecture it under-girds" ("Maosch/Lancelotism," 232).

65. *Stanzaic Morte Arthur,* in *King Arthur's Death: The Middle English Stanzaic Morte Arthur and Alliterative Morte Arthure,* ed. Larry D. Benson (Exeter: University of Exeter Press, 1986), ll. 269 and 272. Further quotations will be documented in the text by line number.

66. Jackson, *Strategies of Deviance,* p. 118.

67. Jackson, *Strategies of Deviance,* p. 118.

68. Quoted in Teresa de Lauretis, *Alice Doesn't: Feminism, Semiotics, Cinema* (Bloomington: Indiana University Press, 1984), p. 108.

Chapter 5   Male–Male Gazing

1. Kaeuper and Kennedy, *The Book of Chivalry of Geoffroi de Charny,* pp. 104 and 105; 154 and 155. Although he does not focus on the visual act as clearly as Charny does, Lull also recommends that a novice knight (a squire) pay close attention to an accomplished knight: "it behoueth that a noble man that loueth the ordre of chyualrye/and wyl be a knyght/haue first a mayster that is a knyght / . . . / and that he goo with hym to tornoyes and batuylles. . . / . . . / & that the arte were shewed and redde/in suche maner as other sciences" (*The Book of the Ordre of Chyvalry,* p. 22).

2. Christian Metz, *The Imaginary Signifier: Psychoanalysis and the Cinema,* trans. Celia Britton, Annwyl Williams, Ben Brewster, and Alfred Guzzetti (Bloomington: Indiana University Press, 1977), p. 48.

3. Mulvey, "Visual Pleasure and Narrative Cinema," p. 27.

4. Mulvey, "Visual Pleasure and Narrative Cinema," p. 27. In all fairness, Mulvey is focusing on mainstream cinema. However, her concept leaves little room for a "transgressive" positioning of spectator and object.

5. Cowie, *Representing the Woman,* pp. 169–70. A number of recent studies by film theorists examine the objectified male figure in films, some I have already drawn on; see Jackson, *Strategies of Deviance*; D. N. Rodowick, *The Difficulty of Difference*; Silverman, *Male Subjectivity at the Margins*; and the collection of essays in *Screening the Male: Exploring Masculinities in Hollywood Cinema,* ed. Steven Cohan and Ina Rae Hark (London: Routledge, 1993) and *Masculinity: Bodies, Movies, Culture,* ed. Peter Lehman (New York: Routledge, 2001). In drawing attention to potential homoeroticism in chival-ric spectatorship, I am engaging in a project that parallels that of film theorists

who problematize the heteronormative assumptions in classical film theory; for heteronormative readings of chivalric texts fail to recognize that observed knights could be erotic objects of a male gaze.

6. Sarah Stanbury, "Regimes of the Visual in Premodern England: Gaze, Body, and Chaucer's *Clerk's Tale*," *New Literary History* 28 (1997): 266 [261–89].

7. Stanbury, "Regimes of the Visual," 278.

8. Stanbury, "Regimes of the Visual," 278.

9. Stanbury, "Regimes of the Visual," 279.

10. For an in-depth study of ancient and medieval theories of vision, see David C. Lindberg, *Theories of Vision from Al-Kindi to Kepler* (Chicago: University of Chicago Press, 1976). See also Katherine H. Tachau, *Vision and Certitude in the Age of Ockham: Optics, Epistemology, and the Foundation of Semantics 1250–1345* (Leiden: Brill, 1988). For brief discussions, see N. Klassen, "Optical Allusions and Chaucerian Realism: Aspects of Sight in Late Medieval Thought and *Troilus and Criseyde*," *Stanford Humanities Review* 2.2–3 (1992): 130–37 [129–46]; and Collette, *Species, Phantasms, and Images*, pp. 13–20.

11. Augustine, *De trinitate* XI.2.3; *The Trinity*, trans. McKenna, p. 318. For a discussion of Augustine's theory of vision, see Margaret Miles, "Vision: The Eye of the Body and the Eye of the Mind in Saint Augustine's *De trinitate* and *Confessions*," *Journal of Religion* 63 (1983): 125–42.

12. Collette, *Species, Phantasms, and Images*, p. 14.

13. Lindberg, *Theories of Vision*, p. 109. For a lucid discussion of Bacon's concept of vision in the context of earlier theories, see Lindberg, *Theories of Vision*, pp. 107–16.

14. Lindberg, *Theories of Vision*, p. 113.

15. Roger Bacon, *The "Opus Majus" of Roger Bacon*, ed. John Henry Bridges (Frankfurt/Main: Minerva, 1964) 2: pt. 5.1, dist. 7, chap. 4, p. 52; trans. Lindberg, *Theories of Vision*, p. 115.

16. Bacon, *Opus maius*, 2: pt. 5.1, dist. 7, chap. 4, p. 52; trans. Lindberg, *Theories of Vision*, p. 115.

17. Bacon, *Opus maius*, 2: pt. 5.1, dist. 7, chap. 3, p. 52; trans. Robert Belle Burke, *The Opus Majus of Roger Bacon* (New York: Russell & Russell, 1962) 2:470.

18. David C. Lindberg, ed. and trans., *John Pecham and the Science of Optics: Perspectiva communis* (Madison: University of Wisconsin Press, 1970), pp. 30–31. Lindberg notes that "the *Perspectiva communis* served as more than an elementary textbook or source for university lectures. It was the basis, in the late fourteenth century, for several long technical commentaries—the *Questiones super perspectivam* of Henry of Langenstein (d. 1397) and a similar work by Blasius of Parma (written about 1390)" (*John Pecham and the Science of Optics*, p. 31). For a thorough examination of theories of vision and epistemology in the early fourteenth century, see Tachau, *Vision and Certitude in the Age of Ockham*.

19. *Perspectiva communis* 38, ll. 748–50, in Lindberg, *John Pecham and the Science of Optics*, p. 120; trans. Lindberg, p. 121.

20. Sarah Stanbury, "The Lover's Gaze in *Troilus and Criseyde*," in *Chaucer's Troilus and Criseyde, "Subgit to alle Poesy": Essays in Criticism*, ed. R. A. Shoaf (Binghamton: Medieval & Renaissance Text & Studies, 1992), p. 229 [224–38].

21. Miriam Moore rightly notes: "Criseyde is clearly the object of others' gazes, as they 'hir beholden in hir blake wede' " ("Troilus's Mirror: Vision and Desire in *Troilus and Criseyde*," *Medieval Perspectives* 14.1 (1999): 155 [152–65]).

22. Stanbury, "The Lover's Gaze," p. 230. Likewise, Moore observes that "his look affects him, not her" ("Troilus's Mirror," 157). Elaine Tuttle Hansen elaborates on the difficulties of articulating agency here; see *Chaucer and the Fictions of Gender*, pp. 143–48.

23. Stanbury draws a different conclusion: "Troilus, possessed by Criseyde's gaze, is created in it. This constructed self, Troilus as lover, shaped by the imagined gaze of the other, is what the rest of the poem (at least in part) is about" ("The Lover's Gaze," p. 232).

24. I am not denying that there are female spectators in addition to Criseyde, as the neutral term "peple" implies (2.643, 646), but "men" are highlighted in the scene.

25. Stanbury, "The Lover's Gaze," p. 237.

26. Stanbury, "The Lover's Gaze," pp. 237–38.

27. Cowie, *Representing the Woman*, p. 170. Drawing on Lacan, Jackson neatly summarizes this poststruturalist view of the gazing subject: "The supposed subject *of* the gaze is…actually always subject to the gaze that exceeds the subject's control. If the gaze is always outside the body, the subject's access to visual perception (thus to mastery) also situates the subject as exterior to itself, placing the body in the field of visibility (and the potential mastery of the 'annihilating' other)" (*Strategies of Deviance*, p. 127). My discussion focuses not on the spectator's anxiety—and defense mechanisms put in place to assuage that anxiety—but rather the heightened pleasure such a role reversal may afford the spectator.

28. *Sir Gawain and the Green Knight*, ed. Cawley and Anderson, ll. 842–47. Trans. Cawley and Anderson. Subsequent quotations will be documented in the text by line number.

29. The text does not explicitly state that women enter the scene until the lady and her maids enter (l. 941).

30. Sarah Stanbury, *Seeing the Gawain-Poet: Description and the Act of Perception* (Philadelphia: University of Pennsylvania Press, 1991), p. 103. Stanbury notes the qualifiers "hit semed," and "hem thoght," and adds that in the case of the latter, its "placement…in the two-word 'bob' intensifies the qualifier, further pointing to the court's subjective judgment" (*Seeing the Gawain-Poet*, pp. 103–04).

31. The narrator's attentive "touching" of the Green Knight's "swange" has a homoerotic valence if we look at different meanings of the word. In her verse translation, Marie Borroff renders "swange" as buttocks (*Sir Gawain and the Green Knight: A New Verse Translation by Marie Borroff* [New York: Norton, 1967]). The *Middle English Dictionary* defines "swange" (n) as "the middle of the body; the lower abdomen"; the second definition thus situates "swange" near the sexual organ.

32. Trans. Cawley and Anderson.
33. Greg Walker, "The Green Knight's Challenge: Heroism and Courtliness in Fitt I of *Sir Gawain and the Green Knight*," *Chaucer Review* 32 (1997): 112 [111–28].
34. Stanbury, *Seeing the Gawain-Poet*, p. 96.
35. All of his observers are not of course male. Guinevere is watching him and undoubtedly so are other unidentified women. But the Green Knight does not address Guinevere (or any other woman) and in his searching gaze and assessment he is focusing on the knights who are present in the hall.
36. Heng, "A Woman Wants," 109.
37. He does not reveal his "private" purposes until later: "Ho [Morgan] wayned me upon this wyse to your wynne halle / For to assay the surquidré, yif hit soth were / That rennes of the grete renoun of the Rounde Table. / Ho wayned me this wonder your wyttes to reve" (2456–59). Morgan's agency in constructing his imposing form notwithstanding, in Arthur's hall *he* is mesmerizing them with *his* body. For a study of Morgan's agency, see Sheila Fisher, "Taken Men and Token Women in *Sir Gawain and the Green Knight*," in *Seeking the Woman in Late Medieval and Renaissance Writings*, pp. 71–105.
38. I am drawing on Mulvey's claim that in classical cinema, "[t]he image of woman [is]…(passive) raw material for the (active) gaze of man" ("Visual Pleasure and Narrative Cinema," p. 32).
39. Jackson, *Strategies of Deviance*, p. 142.
40. Jackson, *Strategies of Deviance*, p. 143. Jackson elaborates on this transgressive action: "Embracing the specular mode of annihilation to assert one's 'identity' as object of the other's gaze suggests a subject type inconceivable within anaclitic subject politics: the narcissistic exhibitionist, expressed as a subject spectacle or *intentional* [i.e. deliberate] spectacle" (*Strategies of Deviance*, p. 142). Rather than readily submitting to an exhibitionist role, the male protagonist in a heteronormative film may construct it; see Steven Cohan, "Masquerading as the American Male in the Fifties: *Picnic*, William Holden and the Spectacle of Masculinity in Hollywood Film," in *Male Trouble*, ed. Constance Penley and Sharon Willis (Minneapolis: University of Minnesota Press, 1993), pp. 203–32. See also the collection of essays in *Screening the Male*, ed. Cohan and Hark. For an explanation of the Freudian term, "anaclisis," see Laplanche, *Life and Death in Psychoanalysis*, pp. 15–18; and Cowie, *Representing the Woman*, pp. 79–80.
41. I am drawing on the two opposite meanings of "bearer of the look" that, according to Jackson, the gay male exhibitionist illustrates: "his right as male to 'bear' or wield the desiring look, and his transgressive desire as deviant to 'bear' or sustain the desiring look of the other" (*Strategies of Deviance*, p. 143). Jackson is problematizing Mulvey's contention that the male figure regularly engages in the former but not the latter; see Mulvey, "Visual Pleasure and Narrative Cinema," p. 28.
42. He seems to be staring at Guinevere ("the derrest on the dece" [445]) while addressing Gawain, but he could also have turned from her to Gawain when he begins to speak to him.

43. Heng, "A Woman Wants," 109–10.

44. Steven Shaviro, *The Cinematic Body* (Minneapolis: University of Minnesota Press, 1993), p. 170.

45. Shaviro, *The Cinematic Body*, p. 173.

46. Kaeuper and Kennedy, *The Book of Chivalry of Geoffroi de Charny*, pp. 100 and 102; 101 and 103.

47. That this is a French text addressing French novice knights does not mean that its political agenda is not applicable to English chivalric society. As I demonstrated earlier, chivalric orders were being established during the fourteenth century in both England and France, and Edward III was keenly aware of the political advantages of forming brotherhoods of exemplary men-at-arms.

Introduction to Part Two

1. Derrick Sherwin Bailey, *Homosexuality and the Western Christian Tradition* (1955; repr. Hamden, CT: Archon, 1975), p. 8. For Bailey's examination of references to Sodom in canonical and apocryphal texts, see pp. 9–28.

2. Boswell, *Christianity, Social Tolerance, and Homosexuality*, p. 94. Boswell is referring to Matt. 10:14–15: "Whosoever shall not receive you, nor hear your words, when ye depart out of that house or city, shake off the dust of your feet. Verily I say unto you, it shall be more tolerable for the land of Sodom and Gomorrah in the day of judgment, than for that city" (quoted in Boswell, *Christianity, Social Tolerance, and Homosexuality*, p. 94).

3. Mark D. Jordan, *The Invention of Sodomy in Christian Theology* (Chicago: University of Chicago Press, 1997), p. 30. Jordan goes on to trace the use of the Sodom story in both the Old and the New Testament as well as in writings of the early Church fathers; see pp. 30–44. For a brief survey of the concept of sodomy/homosexuality across the centuries, see Arthur N. Gilbert, "Conceptions of Homosexuality and Sodomy in Western History," *Journal of Homosexuality* 6 (1980/81): 57–68.

4. Jordan, *The Invention of Sodomy in Christian Theology*, p. 1.

5. Boswell, *Christianity, Social Tolerance, and Homosexuality*, p. 270.

6. James A. Brundage, *Law, Sex, and Christian Society in Medieval Europe* (Chicago: University of Chicago Press, 1987), p. 313.

7. Boswell, *Christianity, Social Tolerance, and Homosexuality*, p. 284. For a discussion of how the term "bougre" came to denote "heretic" and eventually "sodomite," see Bailey, *Homosexuality and the Western Christian Tradition*, pp. 137–41.

8. Guibert de Nogent, *Autobiographie*, ed. Edmond-René Labande (Paris: Société D'Éditions "Les Belles Lettres," 1981), p. 430; *Self and Society in Medieval France: The Memoirs of Abbot Guibert of Nogent (1064?–c.1125)*, ed. John F. Benton (New York: Harper and Row, 1970), p. 212.

9. Vern L. Bullough, "Heresy, Witchcraft, and Sexuality," *Journal of Homosexuality* 1 (1974): 187 [183–201]. Bullough does not rule out the possibility

that some members of heretic sects actually engaged in deviant sexual acts, just as some orthodox (Roman) Christians undoubtedly did ("Heresy, Witchcraft, and Sexuality," 184). My purpose here, however, is not to uncover evidence of same-sex acts but rather to survey instances where accusations of sodomy are hurled at a despised group.

10. Boswell, *Christianity, Social Tolerance, and Homosexuality*, p. 279.

11. Quoted in Boswell, *Christianity, Social Tolerance, and Homosexuality*, p. 280. Guibert de Nogent offers another version of this letter that is less sweeping in its list of Christian victims but nevertheless condemns Muslims for their beast-like lust: "in masculinum, pecualitate transgressa, solutis humanitatum legibus itur. Unde, ut unius execranda et penitus intolerabili auribus maiestate flagitii illa, quae in mediocres et infimos defurebat, petulantia panderetur, dicit quendam eos abusione sodomitica interemisse episcopum" [they became worse than animals, breaking all human laws by turning on men. Their lust overflowed to the point that the execrable and profoundly intolerable crime of sodomy, which they committed against men of middle or low station, they also committed against a certain bishop, killing him] (*Dei gesta per Francos*, ed. R. B. C. Huygens, *Corpus Christianorum, Continuatio Mediaevalis*, vol. 127A (Turnhout: Brepols, 1996), p. 102; *The Deeds of God through the Franks: A Translation of Guibert de Nogent's Gesta Dei per Francos*, trans. Robert Levine (Woodbridge: Boydell, 1997), p. 37. For an excellent discussion of Guibert's text, see Steven F. Kruger, "Medieval Christian (Dis)identifications: Muslims and Jews in Guibert of Nogent," *New Literary History* 28 (1997): 185–203.

12. Quoted in Boswell, *Christianity, Social Tolerance, and Homosexuality*, p. 281.

13. Boswell, *Christianity, Social Tolerance, and Homosexuality*, p. 279. Brundage notes that during the second half of the thirteenth century there was an increase in legislation prescribing extremely harsh penalties for homosexual activity. He suggests that "[t]he new hostility toward homosexuals may have stemmed in part from fear that their presence might trigger a salvo of divine wrath against the whole community" (*Law, Sex, and Christian Society in Medieval Europe*, p. 472).

14. Joseph R. Strayer, *The Reign of Philip the Fair* (Princeton: Princeton University Press, 1980), pp. 275–76. On the longstanding conflict between Philip IV and Boniface VIII, see Strayer, *The Reign of Philip the Fair*, pp. 237–85. The entire act of accusation is printed in Georges Picot, *Documents Relatifs aux États Généraux et Assemblées Réunis sous Philippe Le Bel* (Paris, 1901), pp. 36–45.

15. Strayer, *The Reign of Philip the Fair*, p. 276.

16. Brundage, *Law, Sex, and Christian Society*, p. 472. Brundage notes that deviant sexual practices apparently remained relatively common despite the harsh legislation of the later Middle Ages. He supports this, in part, by drawing attention to Pierre de La Palude, who "found it necessary to explain at length why the Church did not allow homosexuals to marry one another" (*Law, Sex, and Christian Society*, pp. 473–74).

17. Quoted in James A. Brundage, "The Politics of Sodomy: Rex V. Pons Hugh De Ampurias (1311)," in *Sex in the Middle Ages: A Book of Essays*, ed. Joyce E. Salisbury (New York: Garland, 1991), pp. 239 and 244 n2 [239–46].

18. Brundage, "The Politics of Sodomy," pp. 241–42.

19. Quoted in Brundage, "The Politics of Sodomy," p. 244 n2: "quibus ciuitates cum hominibus periculum perisse leguntur et terre motus fames et pestilencie multiplicare increspescant et aere pestilens redditur et turbatur ne, quod absit, predicta a nostris manibus requirantur sed ea conuiuentibus ecclesiis transiremus."

20. Brundage, "The Politics of Sodomy," p. 240.

21. Brundage, "The Politics of Sodomy," p. 243.

22. Weissberger, " '¡A tierra, puto!'," p. 296.

23. Weissberger, " '¡A tierra, puto!'," p. 296.

Chapter 6   Sodomy, Politics, and Male–Male Desire

1. There is a good deal of literature on the Templars. For a general history of the order, see Malcolm Barber, *The New Knighthood: A History of the Order of the Temple* (Cambridge: Cambridge University Press, 1994), and Edith Simon, *The Piebald Standard: A Biography of the Knights Templars* (London: Cassell, 1959). The most recent full-length study of the Knights Templar in England is Thomas M. Parker, *The Knights Templar in England* (Tucson: University of Arizona Press, 1963). For a study of the trial in England, see Clarence Perkins, "The Trial of the Knights Templars in England," *English Historical Review* 24 (1909): 432–47. Henry Charles Lea offers a full account of the persecution of the Templars in Europe in *A History of the Inquisition of the Middle Ages*, vol. 3 (New York: Harper, 1887), pp. 238–334. For a more recent, detailed study of the events leading up to the trials as well as facts regarding the trials themselves, primarily in France, see Malcolm Barber, *The Trial of the Templars* (Cambridge: Cambridge University Press, 1978). Anne Gilmour-Bryson offers an engaging discussion of the charges of sodomy leveled against the Templars in "Sodomy and the Knights Templar," *Journal of the History of Sexuality* 7 (1996): 151–83. Her article is also useful for its wealth of references to primary sources of the various trials.

2. Boswell, *Christianity, Social Tolerance, and Homosexuality*, p. 296.

3. Barber, *The Trial of the Templars*, p. 246.

4. Barber, *The Trial of the Templars*, p. 44.

5. Boswell, *Christianity, Social Tolerance, and Homosexuality*, p. 297.

6. James B. Given, *Inquisition and Medieval Society: Power, Discipline, and Resistance in Languedoc* (Ithaca: Cornell University Press, 1997), p. 165.

7. John H. Arnold, *Inquisition and Power: Catharism and the Confessing Subject in Medieval Languedoc* (Philadelphia: University of Pennsylvania Press, 2001), p. 79.

8. Anne Gilmour-Bryson, *The Trial of the Templars in the Papal State and the Abruzzi* (Vatican City: Biblioteca Apostolica Vaticana, 1982), p. 17. For a complete list of the charges in English, see Barber, *The Trial of the Templars*, pp. 248–52.

9. Gilmour-Bryson, "Sodomy and the Knights Templar," 165.

10. Vern Bullough, *Sexual Variance in Society and History* (New York: John Wiley & Sons, 1976), p. 395.

11. Quoted in Gilmour-Bryson, *The Trial of the Templars*, pp. 76–77; Barber, *The Trial of the Templars*, p. 249. The two groups of charges are numbered 30–33 and 40–45 respectively.

12. Gilmour-Bryson, "Sodomy and the Knights Templar," 153.

13. Gilmour-Bryson, "Sodomy and the Knights Templar," 175. "Witness" is generally the term used to describe the person, either Templar or non-Templar, giving testimony at the trial. Gilmour-Bryson explains that testimony was generally given in the vernacular, which the notary took down in note form. Then, some time later it was written up in Latin using "standard formal notarial language." She also points out that the manuscripts of the trials were generally quite lengthy, which demonstrates the care the notaries took in writing up the proceedings ("Sodomy and the Knights Templar," 166–67).

14. Gilmour-Bryson, "Sodomy and the Knights Templar," 172; 175.

15. I am referring here only to statements concerning charges of indecent kisses. I am basing my observation on a sample of depositions I consulted from trials in France, the Papal States, and England.

16. "Item de osculis dixit, quod recipiens dixit ei, quod punctus ordinis erat, quod dictus receptus oscularetur recipientem in ore, et in umbilico et in fine spine dorsi" (quoted in Konrad Schottmüller, *Der Untergang des Templer-Ordens*, vol. 2 [Berlin: Mittler, 1887], p. 43). James Noel Adams, *The Latin Sexual Vocabulary* (Baltimore: Johns Hopkins University Press, 1982), notes that the "back or it lower part could...be used...for anus" (quoted in Gilmour-Bryson, "Sodomy and the Knights Templar," 157 n22).

17. Quoted in Schottmüller, *Der Untergang des Templer-Ordens*, 2 : 20.

18. Iohannes de Villaribus: "Gonterius et Ymbricus fratres dicti ordinis... duxerunt eum ad partem camere, ubi fuit receptus et fecerunt eum spoliari et ambo unus post alium osculati sunt ipsum in ore, in umbilico et in fine spine dorsi et duxerunt ipsum ad preceptorem." Iacobus de Castilhione: "De oculus dixit, quod recipiens osculatus fuit eum in fine spine dorsi, secundo in umbilico, tercio in ore." Both quotations are taken from Heinrich Finke, *Papsttum und Untergang des Templerordens*, vol. 2 (Münster: Aschendorf, 1907), pp. 329 and 331.

19. Quoted in Finke, *Papsttum und Untergang des Templerordens*, 2 : 331.

20. "Item dixit, quod dictus magister in presentia dictorum fratrum injunxit ei, quod ipse non recusaret aliquem de fratribus ipsius ordinis, si vellet cum eo carnaliter commisceri, et quod ipse finaliter commisceatur cum fratribus, quando vellet" (quoted in Schottmüller, *Der Untergang des Templer-Ordens*, 2:20).

21. "dixit quod ipse cohabitavit cum quatuor fratribus ejusdem ordinis, videlicet, cum fratre Stephano de Bosco...et cum tribus aliis fratribus jam defunctis de quorum nominibus non recolit, dicens quod quando jacebat et cognoscebat eos, ipsi cogniti ponebant os versus terram et cum pedibus et manibus sustinebant se, et ipse qui loquitur ascendebat supra illum quem carnaliter volebat cognoscere et intromitebat virgam suam virilem per anum ipsius sic prostrati, dicens etiam quod quinquagesies et pluribus vicibus cognovit predictos" (quoted in Roger Sève and Anne-Marie Chagny-Sève, *Le Procès des Templiers d'Auvergne (1309–1311)* [Paris: Comité des Travaux Historiques et Scientifiques, 1986], p. 148).

22. Like at the Poitiers trial, the overwhelming majority of witnesses admit that permission was given to engage in sexual acts with other knights but they themselves neither required anyone to do this not did anyone require it of them.

23. Most of the testimony at the English trials conforms closely to that given by Radulphus de Barton: "Item super 30. articulo, qui sic incipit: 'Item, quod in receptione fratrum,' etc. respondit, quod osculantur in ore, et caetera contenta in articulo negavit...Item interrogatus super 40. articulo, qui sic incipit: 'Item, quod fratribus,' etc. dicit, quod nec audivit, nec scivit, nec intellexit, quod contentum in articulo fuit praeceptum, vel super hoc licentia data" (quoted in David Wilkins, *Concilia magnae Britanniae et Hiberniae*, vol. 2 [London, 1737], p. 336).

24. Perkins, "The Trial of the Knights Templars in England," 440.

25. Schottmüller, *Der Untergang des Templer-Ordens*, 2:77: "Mit besonderer Breite aber wird das Gerede alter Weiber und einzelner Minoritenmönche berichtet, welche nicht aus eigener Kenntnissnahme, sondern aus dem Gerede Anderer, die wiederum berichten, dasselbe von Anderen gehört zu haben."

26. "Robertus le Dorturer notarius London, qui dicit, quod frater Guido de Foresta, magnus preceptor Anglie voluit ipsum opprimere per sodomiam, ipse tamen aufugit" (quoted in Schottmüller, *Der Untergang des Templer-Ordens*, 2:89).

27. "frater Johannes de Presbur ordinis Carmelit., qui dixit, quod audivit a quodam consanguineo suo, vocato Wilhelmo de Winchub, quod quidam Templarius de Templo Guite Gaynggls dioc. Wignorniensis predictum consanguineum suum opprimere voluit vicio sodomie" (quoted in Schottmüller, *Der Untergang des Templer-Ordens*, 2:89).

28. One should not underestimate the role the charges of heresy, sacrilegious acts, and idol worshipping had in bringing about the dissolution of the order. Nevertheless, considering the significant space the sodomy charges occupy in the testimonies, it is fair to assume that these accusations intensified the case against the Templars.

29. For a good survey of the important events during the reign of Edward II, see May McKisack, *The Fourteenth Century 1307–1399* (Oxford: Clarendon, 1959), pp. 1–96; Anthony Tuck, *Crown and Nobility 1272–1461: Political Conflict in Late Medieval England* (Totowa, NJ: Barnes and Noble, 1985),

pp. 50–83. For a detailed study of political and administrative affairs in Edward II's reign, see T. F. Tout, *The Place of the Reign of Edward II in English History* (Manchester: Manchester University Press, 1914). There are also several biographies of Edward II. Hilda Johnstone, *Edward of Carnarvon 1284–1307* (Manchester: Manchester University Press, 1946), offers a study of Edward's early years. A well-illustrated but undocumented study of Edward's life is Caroline Bingham, *The Life and Times of Edward II* (London: Weidenfeld and Nicolson, 1973). For a recent biography, see Mary Saaler, *Edward II 1307–1327* (London: Rubicon, 1997). For a very readable but undocumented account of the events leading up to the death of Edward II, see R. Perry, *Edward the Second: Suddenly at Berkeley* (Wotton-under-Edge, Gloucestershire: Ivy House, 1988). There are also two fairly recent studies of Gaveston: Pierre Chaplais, *Piers Gaveston: Edward II's Adoptive Brother* (Oxford: Clarendon, 1994); and J. S. Hamilton, *Piers Gaveston, Earl of Cornwall 1307–1312: Politics and Patronage in the Reign of Edward II* (Detroit: Wayne State University Press, 1988). The two authors have opposing views on the relationship between Edward and Gaveston: Chaplais is not convinced that it was sexual while Hamilton maintains that it was.

30. Tuck, *Crown and Nobility*, p. 53.
31. Bingham, *The Life and Times of Edward II*, p. 54.
32. Saaler, *Edward II*, p. 35.
33. Alan K. Smith, "Fraudomy: Reading Sexuality and Politics in Burchiello," *Queering the Renaissance*, ed. Jonathan Goldberg (Durham: Duke University Press, 1994), p. 85 [84–106].
34. For a thorough discussion of all the major chronicles of the reign of Edward II, see Antonia Gransden, *Historical Writing in England II: c. 1307 to the Early Seventeenth Century* (Ithaca: Cornell University Press, 1982), pp. 1–42.
35. Charles T. Wood, "Personality, Politcs, and Constitutional Progress: The Lessons of Edward II," *Studia Gratiana* 15 (1972): 524 [521–36].
36. British Museum, MS. Cotton Cleopatra D. IX, fols. 83–85, quoted in George L. Haskins, "A Chronicle of the Civil Wars of Edward II," *Speculum* 14 (1939): 75 [73–81]. Except for the first phrase, the English translation is taken from Chaplais, *Piers Gaveston: Edward II's Adoptive Brother*, pp. 12–13. Chaplais suggests that *firmitatis* should be emended to *fraternitatis* (p. 13 n42).
37. *Annales Paulini*, in *Chronicles of the Reign of Edward I and Edward II*, ed. William Stubbs, vol. 1 (1882–83; repr. Wiesbaden: Kraus, 1965), p. 257: "Hic statim Petrum de Gavastone ab exilio in Angliam revocavit"; *Annales Londonienses*, in *Chronicles of the Reign of Edward I and Edward II*, ed. Stubbs, vol. 1, p. 151: "quem revertentem rex retinuit secum unice dilexit."
38. Quoted in Haskins, "A Chronicle of the Civil Wars of Edward II," 75: "Petrum reuocauit ab exilio et in/statum pristinum restituit solitique flaminam amoris in frunita mente renouauit." I am reading *flaminam* as *flammam*.

39. *Annales Paulini*, ed. Stubbs, 1:257: "statim spreto consilio senum, sicut Roboam, adhaesit consilio juvenum qui secum ab adolescentia fuerant conversati, et praesipue et super omnia consilio Petri de Gavastone."

40. *Vita Edwardi secundi monachi cuiusdam Malmesberiensis*, ed. and trans. N. Denholm-Young (London: Thomas Nelson and Sons, 1957), p. 1; trans. Denholm-Young, p. 1.

41. Johannis de Trokelowe, *Annales Edwardi II, Angliae Regis*, ed. Thomas Hearne (London, 1729), p. 4. I am using Saaler's translation of *ultra modum* (*Edward II 1307–1327*, p. 35).

42. Johannis de Trokelowe, *Annales*, ed. Hearne, p. 5. I have drawn on Hamilton's translation of this passage (*Piers Gaveston, Earl of Cornwall*, p. 47).

43. Alan Bray and Michel Rey, "The Body of the Friend: Continuity and Change in Masculine Friendship in the Seventeenth Century," *English Masculinities: 1660–1800*, ed. Tim Hitchcock and Michèle Cohen (London: Longman, 1999), p. 68 [65–84].

44. *Annales Paulini*, ed. Stubbs, 1:258: "Rex Franciae dedit regi Angliae genero suo annulum regni sui, cubile suum quam pulcrum oculis non videt aliud, destrarios electos et alia donaria multa nimis. Quae omnia rex Angliae concito Petro misit."

45. *Vita Edwardi secundi*, ed. Denholm-Young, p. 9; trans. Denholm-Young, p. 9.

46. *Annales Paulini*, ed. Stubbs, 1:262: "Karolus et Ludowicus patrui reginae, cernentes quod rex plus exerceret Petri triclinium quam reginae, cum indignatione ad Franciam remigarunt." I conclude that the classical Latin meaning of *triclinium* is still current in the Middle Ages since this word is not included in either J. F. Niermeyer, *Mediae Latinitatis Lexicon Minus* (Leiden: Brill, 1976) or R. E. Latham, *Revised Medieval Word-List from British and Irish Sources* (London: Oxford University Press, 1965).

47. *Annales Paulini*, ed. Stubbs, 1:262: "In omnem igitur terram exiit rumor iste, quod rex plus amaret hominem magum et maleficum quam sponsam suam elegantissimam dominam et pulcherrimam mulierem."

48. *Annales Paulini*, ed. Stubbs, 1:261: "coronam Sancti Edwardi tradidit Petro ad portandum manibus inquinatis."

49. Robert of Reading, *Flores historiarum*, ed. Henry Richards Luard, vol. 3 (1890; repr. Wiesbaden: Kraus, 1965), p. 331.

50. Leviticus 18:22, *Biblia sacra Latina ex biblia sacra vulgatae editionis* (London: Samuel Bagster & Sons, 1970): "Cum masculo non commiscearis coitu foemineo, quia abominatio est" [You shall not lie with a male as with a woman because it is an abomination].

51. *Vita Edwardi secundi*, ed. Denholm-Young, p. 19; trans. Denholm-Young, p. 19.

52. *Annales Londonienses*, ed. Stubbs, 1:204: "Emericus de Valencia comes Penbrochiae et Johannes comes Warenniae adiret versus, ut seductorem Petrum caperent et regem informarent." R. E. Latham, *Revised Medieval Latin Word-List*, defines *seductor* as being used in a biblical sense, meaning "seducer, deceiver, traitor." I suggest that the chronicler is using the first two meanings that are in effect complementary and carry a sexual connotation.

53. Years later, similar charges were made against the Despensers, particularly Hugh the younger, who became an intimate friend of the king and was accused of giving him evil counsel. The nobles reportedly condemned both father and son as "seducers" (as well as "conspirators" or "disinheritors") of Edward. *Vita Edwardi secundi*, ed. Denholm-Young, p. 114: "prolatum est iudicium in Hugonem Despenser patrem et filium. Nam uterque tanquam malus et falsus domini regis consiliarius, tanquam seductor et conspirator uel exheredator corone et destructor populi, et inimicus regis et regni, condempnatur, proscribitur et exheredatur" [judgment was given against the Despensers father and son. Each was found guilty, proscribed, and disinherited, as an evil and false counsellor of the lord king, as a seducer and conspirator or disinheritor of the crown and a destroyer of the people, and an enemy of the king and kingdom]; trans. Denholm-Young, p. 114. For an examination of the repercussions of Edward's relationship with Hugh Despenser, the younger, see Claire Sponsler, "The King's Boyfriend: Queer Politics and Edward II," in *Queering the Middle Ages*, ed. Burger and Kruger, pp. 143–67. In her excellent study of Froissart's narrative concerning the persecution and execution of Hugh, the younger, Sponsler points to the negative politicization of this same-sex relationship. Referring specifically to Froissart's account of Despenser's execution, which was orchestrated by Isabella, Sponsler observes that "Froissart shows not just how effectively scapegoating could work as a form of public spectacle, but also how vilification of same-sex desire could be enlisted in the cause of political power struggles" ("The King's Boyfriend," p. 161).

54. Robert of Reading, *Flores historiarum*, ed. Luard, 3:229; trans. Gransden, *Historical Writing in England*, p. 21. I have substituted "copulations" for "bed" in her translation and emended "should not love." While in classical Latin, *concubitus* could mean lying together (for sleeping or dining) or copulation, it is apparently the latter sense that had currency in the Middle Ages. R. E. Latham, *Dictionary of Medieval Latin from British Sources* (London: Oxford University Press, 1975), defines it as "lying together (sexual)."

55. *Gesta Edwardi de Carnarvan auctore canonico Bridlingtoniensi*, in *Chronicles of the Reigns of Edward I and Edward II*, ed. Stubbs, vol. 2, p. 34: "comites praefatum Petrum, tanquam ligii domini sui et regni seductorem, convictum et dampnatum pronuntiarent." For Stubbs's discussion of the date of composition, see 1:xxvi.

56. Thomas de Burton, *Chronica monasterii de Melsa*, ed. Edward A. Bond, vol. 2 (London, 1867), p. 355. This comment occurs following his report of Edward's death and thus he apparently draws this conclusion as he looks back over Edward's life. For a discussion of the possible date of Thomas's chronicle, see Bond's introduction, *Chronica monasterii de* Melsa, 1: lxi–lxix.

57. Thomas Walsingham, *Historia Anglicana*, ed. Henry Thomas Riley, vol. 1 (London, 1863–64), p. 120.

58. Walsingham, *Historia Anglicana*, ed. Riley, 1:128. Compare, *Annales Londonienses*: "De hoc genere, quod est Sodomia, deponunt plures" (ed. Stubbs, 1:192). The original articles of accusation do not actually use the word

"sodomy," but rather refer to sexual relations among brothers of the order. It is possible that *Annales Londonienses* was a source for Walsingham because of all the major chronicles for this period it is the only one that provides extensive information on the affair, listing the specific charges made against the Templars. There is, however, one curious point. In describing the initiation ceremony, Walsingham states: "adduxerunt illum ad locum privatum, et totaliter denudaverunt; et tunc unus accederet ad eundem, et eum oscularetur in posteriori parte" [they led him (i.e. the initiate) to a private place and completely undressed him, and then one approached him and kissed him on his rear end] (*Historia Anglicana*, ed. Riley, 1:127). Neither the *Annales Londonienses* nor the original articles of accusation (#30–33) state that the initiate was naked at the time of the illicit kisses. While some of the witnesses do confess that this was the case, this is generally found in testimony from trials in France. Thus, either Walsingham actually read these foreign trial records or, more likely, he is repeating what was circulating in his day.

59. The most recent major study of Richard II, is Nigel Saul, *Richard II* (New Haven: Yale University Press, 1997). Other major studies are Anthony Tuck, *Richard II and the English Nobility* (New York: St. Martin's Press, 1974), and Anthony Steel, *Richard II* (Cambridge: Cambridge University Press, 1941); see also Gervase Mathew, *The Court of Richard II* (New York: Norton, 1968). The Lords Appellant were Thomas, duke of Gloucester, Henry, earl of Derby, Richard, earl of Arundel, Thomas, earl of Warwick, and Thomas, earl of Nottingham (later duke of Norfolk). For a detailed examination of each of the Lords Appellant, see Anthony Goodman, *The Loyal Conspiracy: The Lords Appellant under Richard II* (Coral Gables: University of Miami Press, 1971). Richard's relations with the nobles throughout his reign is studied in Richard H. Jones, *The Royal Policy of Richard II: Absolutism in the Later Middle Ages* (Oxford: Basil Blackwell, 1968). For a wider historical view of the Lancastrian affinity that centered on John of Gaunt, see Simon Walker, *The Lancastrian Affinity, 1361–1399* (Oxford: Clarendon, 1990).

60. Tuck, *Richard II*, p. 58.

61. Tuck, *Richard II*, p. 71.

62. Henry Knighton, *Knighton's Chronicle 1337–1396*, ed. and trans. G. H. Martin (Oxford: Oxford University Press, 1995), p. 360; trans. Martin, p. 361. Historians agree that this is unmistakably a reference to the deposition of Edward II; see Saul, *Richard II*, p. 158; Tuck, *Richard II*, p. 102; Martin, ed., *Knighton's Chronicle*, p. 360 n1.

63. For a discussion of each of the court favorites, see Saul, *Richard II*, pp. 112–34; Tuck, *Richard II*, pp. 73–86.

64. Tuck, *Richard II*, p. 77.

65. Saul, *Richard II*, p. 182.

66. Saul, *Richard II*, p. 182.

67. For a detailed discussion of the major chronicles of the reign of Richard II, see Gransden, *Historical Writing in England II*, who devotes a chapter to Thomas Walsingham and his chronicles (pp. 118–56) and studies all the other chronicles in the following chapter (pp. 157–93). Louisa D. Duls,

Richard II in the Early Chronicles (The Hague: Mouton, 1975), concentrates on how the events that occurred between 1386 and 1388 are reported in the major chronicles. Her most thorough discussion is of Knighton's chronicle; see pp. 35–51. Two other valuable studies are provided by George B. Stow; see his article, "Richard II in Thomas Walsingham's Chronicles," *Speculum* 59 (1984): 68–102, and his essay, "Chronicles Versus Records: The Character of Richard II," in *Documenting the Past: Essays in Medieval History Presented to G. P. Cuttino*, ed. J. S. Hamilton and P. Bradley (Woodbridge: Boydell, 1989), pp. 155–76. Walsingham's chronicles are also briefly discussed in John Taylor, *English Historical Literature in the Fourteenth Century* (Oxford: Clarendon, 1987), pp. 64–70.

68. Although V. H. Galbraith proposed a rather late date of composition for the *Chronicon Angliae*, ca. 1394–97, historians have recently argued for a date closer to the events recorded, namely, ca. 1388; see Stow, "Richard II," 77–79. The *Historia* was completed ca. 1402, but in his introduction to his edition of the text, Stow suggests that the first half of the work was written ca. 1390–92; see *Historia vitae et regni Ricardi secundi*, ed. George B. Stow, Jr. (Philadelphia: University of Pennsylvania Press, 1977), p. 14.

69. *Westminster Chronicle, 1381–1394*, ed. and trans. L. C. Hector and Barbara Harvey (1966; repr. Oxford: Clarendon, 1982), p. 42: "Contigit ipso die quod quidam miles regis, nomine Jacobus Beernes, regi summe familiaris, ictu fulminis cecus efficeretur in presencia regis. . . .Ob hoc rex jussit clerum processionaliter ad tumbam Sancte Ethelthrethe Virginis devotissime pergere quatinus interveniente populi devota oracione excecatus visum recuperaret"; trans. Hector and Harvey, p. 43.

70. *Westminster Chronicle*, ed. Hector and Harvey, p. 122; trans. Hector and Harvey, p. 123.

71. One can argue that the Westminster chronicler is generally sympathetic to Richard and thus if no observer criticized Richard's behavior, the chronicler would hardly take it upon himself to do so. However, Knighton, who is clearly unsympathetic to Richard, merely reports in regard to the second incident that the king exiled the offender, Sir John Holland, and confiscated his property; see *Knighton's Chronicle*, ed. Martin, pp. 338–39.

72. *Historia vitae et regni Ricardi secundi*, ed. Stow, p. 92.

73. Thomas Walsingham, *Chronicon Angliae 1328–1388*, ed. Edward Maunde Thompson (London: Longman, 1874), p. 372: "submurmurantibus ceteris nobilibus et baronibus ac indigne ferentibus tantae promotionis appetitum in viro dudum tam mediocri, quem non plus ceteris commendabant vel generis sui sublimitas vel reliquarum virtutum dotes." Tuck notes that the nobles were especially furious at this appointment because de Vere "had received. . .an honour which had hitherto been bestowed upon only one man who was not of royal blood, and he was the greatest of magnates at Edward III's court" (*Richard II*, p. 85). De Vere was however an aristocrat. Gervase Mathew points out that de Vere "was a magnate in his own right, ninth Earl of Oxford and Chamberlain of England and husband of the King's first cousin, Philippa de Coucy" and thus not technically a "mignon" or "favourite" (*The Court of Richard II*, p. 19).

74. *Westminster Chronicle*, ed. Hector and Harvey, p. 54; trans. Hector and Harvey, p. 55.

75. *Westminster Chronicle*, ed. Hector and Harvey, p. 54: "predecessores sui reges nobilissimi temporibus retroactis dominorum consilio regebantur, et quamdiu illorum gubernacio fuerat accepta regnum Anglie magnificis prosperitatibus affluebat"; trans. Hector and Harvey, p. 55.

76. *Westminster Chronicle*, ed. Hector and Harvey, p. 54; trans. Hector and Harvey, p. 55.

77. Knighton, *Knighton's Chronicle*, ed. Martin, p. 392. Martin oddly omits "abominable" from his translation. The *Oxford Latin Dictionary*, ed. P. G. W. Glare (Oxford: Clarendon, 1982), defines *nefandus, a, um* as "wicked, impious, heinous" when referring to persons, and "abominable" for "other things involved in wicked conduct." I am reading *nephandi* here as "abominable" since Knighton is referring not merely to the men's character but also the actions they perform on the king. Furthermore, "abominable" situates Knighton's condemnatory label in a biblical/religious context, which is perhaps the meaning Knighton had in mind given that he was an Augustinian canon who devotes many pages to the Lollard controversy. Dinshaw notes that "the adjective 'nephandum,' [is] traditionally (after Saint Paul…) used for same-sex sodomy" (*Getting Medieval*, p. 105). On the association between the Lollards and sodomy, see Dinshaw, *Getting Medieval*, pp. 55–99.

78. *Historia*, ed. Stow, p. 98. For a discussion of Michael de la Pole's policy of appeasement in the years 1383–85 and in 1386, see Saul, *Richard II*, pp. 135–47 and 151–58.

79. Walsingham, *Chronicon Angliae*, ed. Thompson, p. 374.

80. Walsingham, *Chronicon Angliae*, ed. Thompson, p. 374. Compare the Westminster chronicler's report of the same situation: "Rex…permisit dominum Michaelem de Poole comitem Southfolchie libertate gaudere et penes eum retinuit, et ad quemcumque locum se divertere contingebat deinceps fuit ipse cum eo" [The king…not only allowed Michael de la Pole, earl of Suffolk, to enjoy his freedom but kept him in his own society, so that wherever circumstances took the king he was henceforward joined by the earl] (*Westminster Chronicle*, ed. Hector and Harvey, p. 178; trans. Hector and Harvey, p. 179). In the discussion that follows I examine how Walsingham's language creates an eroticized picture of Richard's relations with his favorites at this time. For the actual articles of impeachment brought against Michael de la Pole, see Knighton, *Knighton's Chronicle*, ed. Martin, pp. 362–69. For an in-depth study of the affair, see J. S. Roskell, *The Impeachment of Michael de la Pole, Earl of Suffolk, in 1386 in the Context of the Reign of Richard II* (Manchester: Manchester University Press, 1984).

81. Walsingham, *Chronicon Angliae*, ed. Thompson, p. 374. Additional meanings of *susurrare*, "to murmur or mutter," do not contradict the substance of my argument.

82. Walsingham, *Chronicon Angliae*, ed. Thompson, p. 374.

83. Thomas Favent, *Historia sive narracio de modo et forma mirabilis parliamenti apud Westmonasterium*, ed. M. McKisack, Camden Miscellany 14

(London: Offices of the Society, 1926), p. 3. I am reading *obcecarunt* as a variant spelling of *occaecarunt*.

84. *Westminster Chronicle*, ed. Hector and Harvey, p. 240: "veiantz le tendresce del age nostre seignur le roi et la innocence de sa roial persone luy firent entendre com pur verite tantz de faux choses par eux countre loialte et bone foy ymaginez et controvez qe entierement eux luy firent de tout a eux doner son amour et ferme foy et credence." The thirty-nine articles of appeal are printed in their entirety in this edition of the *Westminster Chronicle* that the editors have collated with the text of the *Rotuli Parliamentorum*.

85. *Westminster Chronicle*, ed. Hector and Harvey, p. 240; trans. Hector and Harvey, p. 241.

86. Quoted in Hutcheson, "Desperately Seeking Sodom," pp. 234–35.

87. Hutcheson, "Desperately Seeking Sodom," p. 235.

88. *Westminster Chronicle*, ed. Hector and Harvey, p. 240: "ses loialx seignurs et lieges par queux il duist de droit pluis avoir este governe"; trans. Hector and Harvey, p. 241.

89. *Westminster Chronicle*, ed. Hector and Harvey, p. 242; trans. Hector and Harvey, p. 243.

90. *Westminster Chronicle*, ed. Hector and Harvey, p. 242; trans. Hector and Harvey, p. 243.

91. I am drawing on both "covin" (Br.), defined in *The Concise Oxford Dictionary*, ed. R. E. Allen, 8th ed. (Oxford: Clarendon, 1990), as "a conspiracy to commit a crime etc. against a third party," and "coven" (Br; Am), an agreement or assembly.

92. Hutcheson, "Desperately Seeking Sodom," p. 234.

93. Walsingham, *Chronicon Angliae*, ed. Thompson, p. 375.

94. Favent, *Historia sive narracio*, p. 1: "viciose viuentes, dictum regem deludentes."

95. I am drawing on Jonathan Dollimore, who defines "perversion" as "a concept involving: (1) an erring, straying, deviation, or being diverted from (2) a path, destiny, or objective which is (3) understood as natural or right—usually right because natural (with the natural possibly having a yet higher legitimation in divine law)" (*Sexual Dissidence: Augustine to Wilde, Freud to Foucault* [Oxford: Clarendon, 1991], p. 104).

96. John Gower, *Chronicon tripertita*, *The Complete Works of John Gower*, ed. G. C. Macaulay, vol. 4 (Oxford: Clarendon, 1902), p. 220; *The Major Works of John Gower*, trans. Eric W. Stockton (Seattle: University of Washington Press, 1962), p. 297.

97. Thomas Walsingham, *Historia Anglicana*, ed. Henry Thomas Riley, vol. 2 (London, 1863), p. 148; emphasis added.

98. Stow dates the manuscript, Royal 13.E.ix, at 1397 ("Richard II," 83).

99. In July 1397, Richard called for the arrest of the earl of Arundel, earl of Warwick, and duke of Gloucester. For a discussion of Richard's tyrannical rule in the late 1390s, see Saul, *Richard II*, pp. 366–404.

100. *Historia*, ed. Stow, p. 166; emphasis added. With the exception of the first phrase, English translation is taken from Ordelle G. Hill and Gardiner

Stillwell, "A Conduct Book for Richard II," *Philological Quarterly* 73 (1994): 322 [317–28].

101. Adam of Usk, *Chronicle of Adam Usk 1377–1421*, ed. and trans. Chris Given-Wilson (Oxford: Clarendon, 1997), p. 62: "per sertos doctores, episcopos et alios, quorum presencium notator unus extiterat, deponendi regem Ricardum...committebatur disputanda." Given-Wilson accepts Usk's claim that he was present at the meeting because elsewhere in the chronicle "Usk refers to himself as *compilator presencium*—'the compiler of the present work.'" Given-Wilson goes on to explain that "'Notator' had more of the meaning of a notary or scribe, a person publicly authorized to draw up memoranda and so forth" (*Chronicle of Adam Usk*, p. lxxxiv).

102. Adam of Usk, *Chronicle of Adam Usk*, ed. Given-Wilson, p. 62; trans. Given-Wilson, p. 63; emphasis added.

103. *Chronicle of Adam Usk*, ed. Given-Wilson, p. 63 n4.

104. See *Annales Ricardi secundi, regis Angliae*, in *Johannis de Trokelowe et Henrici de Blaneforde, monachorum S. Albani, chronica et annales*, ed. Henry Thomas Riley (London: Longman, 1866), pp. 252–87. An English translation of the thirty-three articles of the deposition is printed in Chris Given-Wilson, ed. and trans., *Chronicles of the Revolution 1397–1400: The Reign of Richard II* (Manchester: Manchester University Press, 1993), pp. 172–84.

105. Walsingham, *Chronicon Angliae*, p. 385: "rex cor apponeret ad vivendum et moriendum cum eo." The letter from Richard urging de Vere to come to London with a large force was found in a pack-saddle de Vere left behind when he was fleeing the nobles' forces at Radcot Bridge in 1387.

106. Lee Patterson, *Chaucer and the Subject of History* (Madison: University of Wisconsin Press, 1991), p. 187.

107. Sponsler, "The King's Boyfriend," p. 161.

108. Gaveston was executed in 1312, Hugh Despenser, the younger, in 1326; de Vere, de la Pole, Tresilian, and Brembre were executed in 1388. For an account of Gaveston's capture and execution, see *Vita Edwardi secundi*, ed. Denholm-Young, pp. 23–27; for a thorough examination of the events leading up to Despenser's execution, see Sponsler, "The King's Boyfriend," pp. 143–67. Saul summarizes the capture and execution of Richard's favorites, see *Richard II*, pp. 192–94; the *Westiminster Chroncle*, ed. Hector and Harvey, reports on Brembre and Tresilian; see pp. 309–15.

Chapter 7   Dramatized Sodomitical Discourse: The case of Troilus and Pandarus

1. Regarding the date of composition of *Troilus and Criseyde*, see Lee Patterson, *Chaucer and the Subject of History*, p. 156 n149; and Paul Strohm, *Social Chaucer* (Cambridge, MA: Harvard University Press, 1989), p. 207 n41. Donald R. Howard notes that on October 12, 1385, Chaucer was appointed one of the justices of the peace for Kent, and served under Simon Burley (*Chaucer: His Life, His Works, His World* [New York: Dutton, 1987], pp. 383–84). Burley, who fell victim to the purge of Richard's

favorites by the Lords Appellant, had earlier been Richard's tutor and allegedly first brought Robert de Vere into the young king's company; see the *Westminster Chronicle*, ed. Hector and Harvey, pp. 276–77. Given his proximity to Burley, Chaucer would have been well positioned to hear of criticism directed at Robert de Vere. Strohm maintains that Chaucer would have known the other favorites as well, particularly Nicholas Brembre, who was "Chaucer's immediate superior throughout most of…[his] term as controller [i.e. 1382–86]" (*Social Chaucer*, p. 28). For a thorough discussion of Chaucer's circle of acquaintances, see Strohm, *Social Chaucer*, pp. 24–46.

2. Derek Pearsall, *The Life of Geoffrey Chaucer: A Critical Biography* (Oxford: Basil Blackwell, 1992), p. 203. It was at this parliament that Richard's chancellor, Michael de la Pole, was impeached.

3. Patterson recognizes that "[t]he 1380s were a time of disputed sovereignty, conspiratorial factionalism, and disastrous militarism—all issues upon which *Troilus and Criseyde* reflects….[Yet] [d]eriving from and speaking to the unhappy world of the 1380s, the *Troilus* refuses to offer any clear message" (*Chaucer and the Subject of History*, pp. 162 and 163). For a general survey of Chaucer's political position during the last fifteen years of his life, see S. Sanderlin, "Chaucer and Ricardian Politics," *Chaucer Review* 22 (1988): 171–84.

4. John Clark observes that the association between England and Troy goes back at least as far as Geoffrey of Monmouth who established the connection between London and Trinovantum, the legendary Trojan settlement on the banks of the Thames ("Trinovantum—Evolution of a Legend," *Journal of Medieval History* 7 [1981]: 143 [135–51]). This connection also surfaces in literature of the fourteenth century such as *St. Erkenwald*, Gower's *Vox Clamantis*, and *Sir Gawain and the Green Knight*. In addition, the fact that England was faced with invasion by the French, particularly in 1385 and 1386, also adds to the topicality of the Trojan story. For a discussion of the invasion panic during these years, see John Barnie, *War in Medieval Society: Social Values and the Hundred Years War 1337–99* (London: Weidenfeld and Nicolson, 1974), pp. 43–48. On the connections between Troy and London/England in the 1380s, see also Craig A. Berry, "The King's Business: Negotiating Chivalry in *Troilus and Criseyde*," *Chaucer Review* 26 (1992): 240–41 [236–65]. On the political context of *Troilus and Criseyde* and Chaucer's possible message, see D. W. Robertson Jr., "The Probable Date and Purpose of Chaucer's *Troilus*," *Medievalia et Humanistica* 13 (1985): 143–71.

5. Patterson, *Chaucer and the Subject of History*, p. 94.

6. About the same time that Chaucer was composing *Troilus and Criseyde* John Trevisa was translating Ranulf Higden's mid-fourteenth-century *Polychronicon* into English. Higden/Trevisa's observation of Edward's relationship with Gaveston, like comments found in the earlier chronicles, highlights the negatively viewed excessive love between them: "[Edward] loved strongliche oon of his queresters, and dede him grete reverence, and worschipped and made hym greete and riche. Of þis doynge fel vilenye to þe lovyer, yvel speche and bacbitynge to þe love" (Ranulf Higden, *Polychronicon Ranulphi Higden monachi*

Cestrensis, ed. Joseph Rawson Lumby, vol. 8 [1857; repr. Wiesbaden: Kraus, 1964], p. 298). Trevisa's English translation is printed alongside Higden's Latin text. Although I am not suggesting that Chaucer was aware of Trevisa's project or that he had read Higden's original text—which he might well have, given its enormous popularity—it does indicate that Edward and Gaveston's relationship was still "in the air" in the 1380s.

7. It is also possible to read Pandarus's actions as illustrating his concern for his "ailing" friend, which is in keeping with the text's affirmation of homosocial intimacy. The contradictory discourses generated in Chaucer's text do not cancel each other out. For studies of Pandarus's role as healer, see Martin Camargo, "The Consolation of Pandarus," *Chaucer Review* 25 (1991): 214–28; and Mary Wack, "Pandarus, Poetry, and Healing," *Studies in the Age of Chaucer, Proceedings* 2 (1986): 127–33.

8. Windeatt provides the relevant passage from Chaucer's translation of Boethius's *De consolatione philosophiae*: "Why wepistow, why spillestow teeris? Yif thou abidest after help of thi leche, the byhoveth discovre thy wownde" (I, pr. 4, 3–6; quoted in *Troilus and Criseyde*, ed. Windeatt, p. 137 n857–58). Drawing a parallel between Pandarus and Lady Philosophy, Camargo observes that "Both advisers explicitly cast themselves in the role of physician, and both recognize that their first task is diagnosis." Camargo goes on to point out that both "physicians" then "attack the symptoms," and next "try to inspire trust" ("The Consolation of Pandarus," 220).

9. "For my love, telle me this [i.e. the lady's name]" can be read as "if you love me, tell me her name." While Chaucer follows Boccaccio here, there are two important differences. In Boccaccio's text, rather than having Troilus look at him, Pandarus tells him to "get up" and does not offer his love as an incentive. See *The Filostrato*, ed. Griffin and Myrick, 2.17.

10. Foucault, *The History of Sexuality*, 1:59.

11. Foucault, *The History of Sexuality*, 1:45.

12. Foucault, *The History of Sexuality*, 1:61. Karma Lochrie questions Foucault's view of confession in the Middle Ages. For her examination of how the practice of confession developed in the Middle Ages, see her book, *Covert Operations: The Medieval Uses of Secrecy* (Philadelphia: University of Pennsylvania Press, 1999), pp. 24–42.

13. The idea that Troilus is submitting to both the god of love and Pandarus is underscored by the fact that he later addresses Pandarus as "lord" (2.975; 981). I will discuss shortly how this negatively politicizes Pandarus's relation to Troilus. I am drawing on the translation of "consente" (refl.) as "to submit" listed in Norman Davis, Douglas Gray, Patricia Ingham, and Anne Wallace-Hadrill, comp., *A Chaucer Glossary* (Oxford: Clarendon, 1979).

14. *Troilus and Criseyde*, ed. Windeatt, p. 211 n1087. Troilus displays more of a royal bureaucratic manner here than in Boccaccio's text: "E sulle guance tutte lagrimose/Bagnò la gemma, e quindi suggellolla" [(he) wetted the seal against his tearful cheeks. Then he sealed it] (*The Filostrato*, ed. and trans. Griffin and Myrick, 2.107).

15. Pandarus's social status is not actually revealed. However, given the fact that he enjoys close relations not only with Troilus but also with other members of the royal family suggests that he belongs in the upper class.

16. *Filostrato*, ed. and trans. Griffin and Myrick, 2.79; emphasis added.

17. *Filostrato*, ed. and trans. Griffin and Myrick, 2.81: "Poi Pandaro abbracciò ben mille fiate,/E baciollo altrettante" [Then he embraced Pandarus fully a thousand times, and kissed him as much again].

18. I am drawing on Bray and Rey's discussion of the relationship between a king and his favorites; see "The Body of the Friend," pp. 68–69.

19. Commenting on the above exchange between Troilus and Pandarus, Strohm distinguishes between Pandarus, who "lives in a time-bound world in which commitments are subject to renegotiation as new facts emerge," and Troilus, whose "commitments are indivisible and eternal, aspiring to transcend time and circumstance" (*Social Chaucer*, p. 104). Strohm goes on to note that "Chaucer and the members of his circle were beneficiaries of the redefinition of sworn vassalage into a variety of more supple forms" (*Social Chaucer*, p. 108). Strohm thus implies that Chaucer would be more inclined to support Pandarus's position. Although Troilus's unswerving fidelity had become somewhat old-fashioned, chivalric texts current in the fourteenth century still affirmed long-lasting intimate bonds between knights, and likewise chroniclers use a language informed by chivalric values in suggesting that a king should be tied to responsible noblemen. For a fine reading of Chaucer's poem in chivalric contexts, see Berry, "The King's Business." For a brief examination of *Troilus and Criseyde* against the social changes of late fourteenth-century England, see Arlyn Diamond, "*Troilus and Criseyde*: The Politics of Love," in *Chaucer in the Eighties*, ed. Julian N. Wasserman and Robert J. Branch (Syracuse: Syracuse University Press, 1986), pp. 93–103.

20. Although Hector does not approve of the exchange agreement, he (and by implication the other members of the royal family) accepts the parliament's decision because it reflects the view of the majority of Trojans. And the royal family would logically expect Troilus to uphold it as well. Of course, in the end, it is not in Troy's best interests to trade Criseyde for Antenor. However, since Antenor's future betrayal of Troy is not included in the narrative world of the poem, I am taking the parliament decision at face value.

21. Richard's privileging his intimate friends over the nobles, while not necessarily representing a conscious decision does indicate a failure to recognize and learn from the misguided actions of his great-grandfather, Edward II. One can speculate whether Chaucer might not be hiding his political views behind Troilus here. In his reading of the parliament scene, John M. Ganim remarks that "[w]e do need to consider the possibility that Chaucer is engaging current political controversies surrounding the questions of advice and the prerogatives of rule, perhaps even criticizing impulsive tendencies on the part of his superiors" ("Chaucer and the Noise of the People," *Exemplaria* 2 [1990]: 75 [71–88].)

22. If Troilus were to follow through with Pandarus's scheme, they both would be in a sense outlaws. Although the circumstances are indeed different, there is a striking parallel between Pandarus's imagined scene and the chroniclers' reports that Robert de Vere and other favorites instigated conflicts that set Richard against the nobles and, ostensibly, the interests of the realm. One of the "outlaws" Richard was harboring was Michael de la Pole, who was impeached at the parliament of 1386. This analogy enables us to observe how Chaucer's text, like the chronicles, paints a negative picture of an influential adviser/friend in order to justify the actions taken against him. My reading of Pandarus's counsel in a political context parallels that of Josephine Bloomfield, who observes: "Since Pandarus is closely aligned (as Chaucer was in his own time) with the royal family and would be expected to have their military and social goals at heart, Troilus is receiving this subversive advice from a counselor who is apparently ambivalent about goals he is deeply involved in forwarding" ("Chaucer and the Polis: Piety and Desire in *Troilus and Criseyde*," *Modern Philology* 94 [1997]: 296 [291–304]). Bloomfield does not, however, offer an in-depth study of Pandarus's role as Troilus's counselor.

23. It is not at all certain that Chaucer or his readers would condemn Pandarus's proposed action purely on sexual grounds. In her examination of rape in the Middle Ages, Shulamith Shahar notes that even when there was no doubt that rape had occurred, "there was a suspicion that the woman had enjoyed the act" (*The Fourth Estate: A History of Women in the Middle Ages*, trans. Chaya Galai [London: Methuen, 1983], p. 16). See also Christopher Cannon, "Chaucer and Rape: Uncertainty's Certainties," in *Representing Rape in Medieval and Early Modern Literature*, ed. Elizabeth Robertson and Christine M. Rose (New York: Palgrave, 2001), pp. 255–79; and "*Raptus* in the Chaumpaigne Release and a Newly Discovered Document Concerning the Life of Geoffrey Chaucer," *Speculum* 68 (1993): 74–94. For a study of rape as it appears in fourteenth-century French pastourelles and court cases, see Kathryn Gravdal, "The Poetics of Rape Law in Medieval France," in *Rape and Representation*, ed. Lynn A. Higgins and Brenda R. Silver (New York: Columbia University Press, 1991), pp. 207–26; see also Gravdal's more extensive study, *Ravishing Maidens: Writing Rape in Medieval French Literature* (Philadelphia: University of Pennsylvania Press, 1991).

24. We find one indication of the times they formerly shared at the end of book 3, when "by the hond ful ofte he [Troilus] wolde take/This Pandarus, and into gardyn lede,/And swich a feste and swich a proces make/Hym of Criseyde, and of hire wommanhede,/And of hire beaute, that withouten drede/It was an hevene his wordes for to here" (3.1737–42). The "hevene" that Pandarus (and the narrator) experiences is vicariously realized erotic pleasure.

25. Kruger, "Claiming the Pardoner," 130 n43. Kruger cites this connotation in "The Miller's Tale" (I.3237) and "The Merchant's Tale" (IV.1839–41).

He also cites "pleye" in a homosocial context. In "The Pardoner's Tale," one reveler tells his accomplice how to distract the third companion whom they plan to rob and murder: "Arys as though thow woldest with hym pleye,/And I shal ryve hym thurgh the sydes tweye/Whil that thou strogelest with hym as in game" (VI.827–29; quoted in Kruger, "Claiming the Pardoner," 130).

26. *Filostrato*, ed. and trans. Griffin and Myrick, 5.71: "E con lui Pandaro era sempre mai/Che a ciò far sovente il confortava" [And with him was ever Pandarus, who often comforted him in his lamenting].

27. Again the text allows one to draw a parallel between Pandarus and Edward and Richard's personal companions. Edward's Gaveston and Richard's de la Pole were distrusted by the nobles: Gaveston because he was French; de la Pole because he advocated a pacifist policy in the war with France.

28. The related term, "traitor," is often used in the chronicles to describe Richard's favorites. For instance, the first article of appeal at the Merciless Parliament refers to these men as "faux traitours du roy et du roiaume" [false traitors of the king and of the realm] (*Westminster Chronicle*, ed. Hector and Harvey, p. 240; trans. Hector and Harvey, p. 241). Knighton's version of this phrase varies slightly: "faux traytours et enmys au roy et a realme" [false traitors and enemies of the king and of the realm] (*Knighton's Chronicle*, ed. Martin, p. 458; trans. Martin, p. 459). On this topic, see Michael Hanrahan, "Seduction and Betrayal: Treason in the *Prologue* to the *Legend of Good Women*," *Chaucer Review* 30 (1996): 229–40.

29. For an examination of Troilus's end in a political context, see Bloomfield, "Chaucer and the Polis."

Afterword

1. Donald E. Hall, "Introduction: Queer Works," *College Literature* 24.1 (1997): 3 [2–10].

2. Sturges, *Chaucer's Pardoner and Gender Theory*, p. xx.

3. Diana Fuss, "Inside/Out," in *Inside/Out: Lesbian Theories, Gay Theories*, ed. Diana Fuss (New York: Routledge, 1991), p. 3 [1–10].

4. I explore this and offer some possible class assignments in my essay, "Befriending the Medieval Queer: A Pedagogy for Literature Classes," *College English* 65.1 (2002): 67–80.

5. Dinshaw, "Chaucer's Queer Touches," 76.

BIBLIOGRAPHY

Primary Sources

Adam of Usk, *Chronicle of Adam Usk 1377–1421*. Ed. and trans. Chris Given-Wilson. Oxford: Oxford University Press, 1997.

Aelred of Rievaulx. *Aelred of Rievaulx's Spiritual Friendship*. Trans. Mark F. Williams. Scranton: University of Scranton Press, 1994.

——. *De speculo caritatis*. In *Aelredi Rievallensis opera omnia*. Ed. A. Hoste and C. H. Talbot. *Corpus Christianorum, Continuatio Mediaevalis*. Vol. 1. Turnhout: Brepols, 1971.

——. *De spiritali amicitia*. In *Aelredi Rievallensis opera omnia*. Ed. A. Hoste and C. H. Talbot. *Corpus Christianorum, Continuatio Mediaevalis*. Vol. 1. Turnhout: Brepols, 1971.

——. *Spiritual Friendship*. Trans. Mary Eugenia Laker. Kalamazoo: Cistercian Publications, 1977.

Amys and Amylion. Ed. François Le Saux. Exeter: University of Exeter Press, 1993.

Annales Londonienses. In Stubbs. Vol. 1. 1–251.

Annales Paulini. In Stubbs. Vol. 1. 255–370.

Annales Ricardi secundi, Regis Angliae. In *Johannis de Trokelowe et Henrici de Blaneforde, monachorum S. Albani, chronica et annales*. Ed. Henry Thomas Riley. London: Longman, 1866. 252–87.

Aristotle. *Nicomachean Ethics*. Trans. Terence Irwin. Indianapolis: Hackett, 1985.

Augustine. *Confessions*. Ed. James J. O'Donnell. 3 vols. Oxford: Clarendon, 1992.

——. *Confessions*. Trans. Vernon J. Bourke. New York: Fathers of the Church, 1953.

——. *De Genesi ad litteram*. *Patrologiae cursus completus. Series Latina*. Ed. Jacques Paul Migne. Vol. 34. Paris, 1844–65.

——. *De trinitate*. Ed. W. J. Mountain and Fr. Glorie. *Corpus Christianorum. series Latina*. Vol. 50–50A. Turnhout: Brepols, 1968.

——. *Epistolae secundum ordinem temporum nunc primum dispositae, prima classis. Patrologiae cursus completus. Series Latina*. Vol. 33.

——. *Saint Augustine: Letters*. Trans. Sister Wilfrid Parsons. Vol. 1. Washington, DC: Catholic University of America Press, 1951.

——. *Saint Augustine: The Literal Meaning of Genesis*. Trans. John Hammond Taylor. Vol. 2. New York: Newman, 1982.

Augustine. *The Trinity*. Trans. Edmund Hill. Brooklyn, NY: New City Press, 1991.

——. *The Trinity*. Trans. Stephen McKenna. Washington, DC: Catholic University of America Press, 1963.

Bacon, Roger. *The "Opus Majus" of Roger Bacon*. Ed. John Henry Bridges. Vol. 2. Frankfurt/Main: Minerva, 1964.

——. *The Opus Majus of Roger Bacon*. Trans. Robert Belle Burke. Vol. 2. 1928. Repr. New York: Russell & Russell, 1962.

Biblia sacra latina ex biblia sacra vulgatae editionis. London: Samuel Bagster & Sons, 1970.

Boccaccio, Giovanni. *The Filostrato of Giovanni Boccaccio*. Ed. and trans. Nathaniel Edward Griffin and Arthur Beckwith Myrick. New York: Octagon, 1978.

Capellanus, Andreas. *The Art of Courtly Love*. Trans. John Jay Parry. New York: Columbia University Press, 1960.

Chandos Herald. *The Life of the Black Prince*. Ed. Mildred K. Pope and Eleanor C. Lodge. Oxford: Clarendon, 1910.

——. *The Life of the Black Prince*. In *The Life and Campaigns of the Black Prince: From Contemporary Letters, Diaries and Chronicles, Including Chandos Herald's Life of the Black Prince*. Trans. Richard Barber. New York: St. Martin's Press, 1986.

Chaucer, Geoffrey. *The Riverside Chaucer*. Ed. Larry D. Benson. 3rd ed. Boston: Houghton Mifflin, 1987.

——. *Troilus and Criseyde: A New Edition of "The Book of Troilus."* Ed. Barry A. Windeatt. London: Longman, 1984.

Cicero, Marcus Tullius. *De officiis*. Trans. Walter Miller. Loeb Classical Library. Vol. 21. 1913. Repr. Cambridge, MA: Harvard University Press, 1961.

——. *Laelius de amicitia*. In *De senectute, de amicitia, de divinatione*. Trans. William Armistead Falconer. Loeb Classical Library. Vol. 20. 1923. Repr. Cambridge, MA: Harvard University Press, 1959.

Favent, Thomas. *Historia sive narracio de modo et forma mirabilis parliamenti apud Westmonasterium*. Ed. M. McKisack. Camden Miscellany 14. London: Offices of the Society. 1926.

Finke, Heinrich. *Papsttum und Untergang des Templerordens*. Vol. 2. Münster: Aschendorf, 1907.

Gesta Edwardi de Carnarvan auctore canonico Bridlingtoniensi. In Stubbs. Vol. 2. 25–92.

Gilmour-Bryson, Anne, ed. *The Trial of the Templars in the Papal State and the Abruzzi*. Vatican City: Biblioteca Apostolica Vaticana, 1982.

Given-Wilson, Chris. *Chronicles of the Revolution 1397–1400: The Reign of Richard II*. Manchester: Manchester University Press, 1993.

Gower, John. *Cronica tripertita*. In *The Complete Works of John Gower*. Ed. G. C. Macaulay. Vol. 4. Oxford: Clarendon, 1902.

——. *The Major Latin Works of John Gower*. Trans. Eric W. Stockton. Seattle: University of Washington Press, 1962.

Gregory of Nazianzus. *Epistolae. Patrologiae cursus completus. Series Graeca*. Ed. Jacques Paul Migne. Vol. 37. Paris, 1857.

——. *A Selection from the Letters of Gregory Nazianzen*. In *Nicene and Post-Nicene Fathers of the Christian Church*. Ed. Philip Schaff and Henry Wace. 2nd series. Vol. 7. Grand Rapids: Eerdmans, 1961.

Guibert de Nogent. *Autobiographie.* Ed. and trans. Edmond-René Labande. Paris: Société d'Éditions "Les Belles Lettres," 1981.

——. *The Deeds of God through the Franks: A Translation of Guibert de Nogent's Gesta Dei per Francos.* Trans. Robert Levine. Woodbridge, Suffolk: Boydell, 1997.

——. *Dei gesta per Francos.* Ed. R. B. C. Huygens. *Corpus Christianorum, Continuatio Mediaevalis.* Vol. 127A. Turnholt: Brepols, 1996.

——. *Self and Society in Medieval France: The Memoirs of Abbot Guibert of Nogent (1064?–c. 1125).* Ed. John F. Benton. New York: Harper and Row, 1970.

Haskins, George L. "A Chronicle of the Civil Wars of Edward II." *Speculum* 14 (1939): 73–81.

Higden, Ranulph. *Polychronicon Ranulphi Higden monachi Cestrensis.* Ed. Joseph Rawson Lumby. Vol. 8. 1857. Repr. Wiesbaden: Kraus, 1964.

Historia vitae et regni Ricardi secundi. Ed. George B. Stow Jr. Philadelphia: University of Pennsylvania Press, 1977.

Homer. *The Illiad.* Trans. Richard Lattimore. Chicago: University of Chicago Press, 1951.

Johannis de Trokelowe. *Annales Edwardi II, Angliae regis.* Ed. Thomas Hearne. London, 1729.

Kaeuper, Richard W. and Elspeth Kennedy. *The Book of Chivalry of Geoffroi de Charny: Text, Context, and Translation.* Philadelphia: University of Pennsylvania Press, 1996.

Knighton, Henry. *Knighton's Chronicle 1337–1396.* Ed. and trans. G. H. Martin. Oxford: Oxford University Press, 1995.

Lancelot do Lac: The Non-Cyclic Old French Prose Romance. Ed. Elspeth Kennedy. 2 vols. Oxford: Clarendon, 1980.

Le Livre de Lancelot del Lac. In *The Vulgate Version of the Arthurian Romances.* Ed. H. Oskar Sommer. Vols. 3, 4. Washington, DC: Carnegie Institution, 1910.

Lindberg, David C., ed. and trans. *John Pecham and the Science of Optics: Perspectiva communis.* Madison: University of Wisconsin Press, 1970.

L'Ordene de Chevalerie. In *Raoul de Hodenc: Le Roman des Eles: The Anonymous Ordene de Chevalerie.* Ed. and trans. Keith Busby. Amsterdam: Utrecht Publications in General and Comparative Literature, 1983.

Lull, Ramon. *The Book of the Ordre of Chyvalry.* Trans. William Caxton. Ed. A. T. P. Byles. EETS o.s. 168. London: Oxford University Press, 1926.

Picot, Georges. *Documents Relatifs aux États Généraux et Assemblées Réunis sous Philippe Le Bel.* Paris: Imprimerie Nationale, 1901.

Robert of Reading. *Flores historiarum* (Continuation). Ed. Henry Richards Luard. Vol. 3. 1890. Repr. Wiesbaden: Kraus, 1965.

The Romaunt of the Rose. In Geoffrey Chaucer, *The Riverside Chaucer.*

Schottmüller, Konrad. *Der Untergang des Templer-Ordens.* Vol. 2. Berlin: Mittler, 1887.

Sève, Roger and Anne-Marie Chagny-Sève. *Le Procès des Templiers d'Auvergne (1309–1311).* Paris: Comité des Travaux Historiques et Scientifiques, 1986.

Sir Gawain and the Green Knight. Ed. A. C. Cawley and J. J. Anderson. London: Dent, 1976.

Sir Gawain and the Green Knight: A New Verse Translation. Trans. Marie Borroff. New York: Norton, 1967.

Stanzaic Morte Arthur. In *King Arthur's Death: The Middle English Stanzaic Morte Arthur and Alliterative Morte Arthure.* Ed. Larry D. Benson. Exeter: University of Exeter Press, 1986.

Stubbs, William, ed. *Chronicles of the Reigns of Edward I and Edward II.* 2 vols. 1882–83. Repr. Wiesbaden: Kraus, 1965.

Thomas Aquinas. *The Commentary of St. Thomas Aquinas on Aristotle's De anima.* Trans. Kenelm Foster and Silvester Humphries. New Haven: Yale University Press, 1951.

———. *Commentary on the Nicomachean Ethics.* Trans. C. I. Litzinger. Vol. 2. Chicago: Henry Regnery, 1964.

———. *Sententia libri ethicorum. Opera omnia.* Vol. 47. Rome, 1969.

Thomas de Burton. *Chronica monasterii de Melsa.* Ed. Edward A. Bond. Vol. 2. London, 1867.

Vita Edwardi secundi monachi cuiusdam Malmesberiensis. Ed. and trans. N. Denholm-Young. London: Thomas Nelson and Sons, 1957.

Walsingham, Thomas. *Chronicon Angliae 1328–1388.* Ed. Edward Maunde Thompson. London: Longman, 1874.

———. *Historia Anglicana.* Ed. Henry Thomas Riley. 2 vols. London, 1863–64.

Westminster Chronicle, 1381–1394. Ed. and trans. L. C. Hector and Barbara Harvey. 1966. Repr. Oxford: Clarendon, 1982.

Wilkins, David. *Concilia magnae Britanniae et Hiberniae.* Vol. 2. London, 1737.

Secondary Sources

Adams, James Noel. *The Latin Sexual Vocabulary.* Baltimore: Johns Hopkins University Press, 1982.

Adams, Jeremy. Rev. of *Christianity, Social Tolerance, and Homosexuality: Gay People in Western Europe from the Beginning of the Christian Era to the Fourteenth Century,* by John Boswell. *Speculum* 56 (1981): 350–55.

Aers, David. *Community, Gender, and Individual Identity: English Writing 1360–1430.* London: Routledge, 1988.

Arnold, John H. *Inquisition and Power: Catharism and the Confessing Subject in Medieval Languedoc.* Philadelphia: University of Pennsylvania Press, 2001.

Bailey, Derrick Sherwin. *Homosexuality and the Western Christian Tradition.* 1955. Repr. Hamden, CT: Archon, 1975.

Baldwin, Dean R. "*Amis and Amiloun:* The Testing of 'Treupe.'" *Papers on Language and Literature* 16 (1980): 353–63.

Barber, Malcolm. *The New Knighthood: A History of the Order of the Temple.* Cambridge: Cambridge University Press, 1994.

———. *The Trial of the Templars.* Cambridge: Cambridge University Press, 1978.

Barker, Juliet R. V. *The Tournament in England 1100–1400.* Woodbridge, Suffolk: Boydell, 1986.

Barnie, John. *War in Medieval Society: Social Values and the Hundred Years War 1337–99.* London: Weidenfeld and Nicolson, 1974.

Beidler, Peter G., ed. *Masculinities in Chaucer: Approaches to Maleness in the Canterbury Tales and Troilus and Criseyde.* Cambridge: Brewer, 1998.

Berry, Craig A. "The King's Business: Negotiating Chivalry in *Troilus and Criseyde*." *Chaucer Review* 26 (1992): 236–65.

Bingham, Caroline. *The Life and Times of Edward II*. London: Weidenfeld and Nicolson, 1973.

Blackmore, Josiah and Gregory S. Hutcheson, eds. *Queer Iberia: Sexualities, Cultures, and Crossings from the Middle Ages to the Renaissance*. Durham: Duke University Press, 1999.

Bloomfield, Josephine. "Chaucer and the Polis: Piety and Desire in *Troilus and Criseyde*." *Modern Philology* 94 (1997): 291–304.

Blum, Martin. "Negotiating Masculinities: Erotic Triangles in the *Miller's Tale*." In Beidler. 37–52.

Borch-Jacobsen, Mikkel. *The Freudian Subject*. Trans. Catherine Porter. Stanford: Stanford University Press, 1988.

Boswell, John. *Christianity, Social Tolerance, and Homosexuality: Gay People in Western Europe from the Beginning of the Christian Era to the Fourteenth Century*. Chicago: University of Chicago Press, 1980.

———. "Concepts, Experiences, and Sexuality." In *Forms of Desire: Sexual Orientation and the Social Constructionist Controversy*. Ed. Edward Stein. New York: Routledge, 1992. 133–73.

———. "Revolutions, Universals, and Sexual Categories." In Duberman, Vicinus, and Chauncey. 17–36.

Boulton, D'Arcy Jonathan Dacre. *The Knights of the Crown: The Monarchical Orders of Knighthood in Later Medieval Europe 1325–1520*. New York: St. Martin's Press, 1987.

Boyd, David L. "Sodomy, Misogyny, and Displacement: Occluding Queer Desire in *Sir Gawain and the Green Knight*." *Arthuriana* 8.2 (1998): 77–113.

Bray, Alan. "Homosexuality and the Signs of Male Friendship in Elizabethan England." *History Workshop* 19 (1990): 1–19.

Bray, Alan and Michel Rey. "The Body of the Friend: Continuity and Change in Masculine Friendship in the Seventeenth Century." In *English Masculinties: 1660–1800*. Ed. Tim Hitchcock and Michèle Cohen. London: Longman, 1999. 65–84.

Bredbeck, Gregory W. *Sodomy and Interpretation: Marlowe to Milton*. Ithaca: Cornell University Press, 1991.

Brundage, James A. *Law, Sex, and Christian Society in Medieval Europe*. Chicago: University of Chicago Press, 1987.

———. "The Politics of Sodomy: Rex V. Pons Hugh de Ampurias (1311)." In *Sex in the Middle Ages: A Book of Essays*. Ed. Joyce E. Salisbury. New York: Garland, 1991. 239–46.

———. Rev. of *Christianity, Social Tolerance, and Homosexuality: Gay People in Western Europe from the Beginning of the Christian Era to the Fourteenth Century*, by John Boswell. *Catholic Historical Review* 68 (1982): 62–64.

Bullough, Vern L. "Heresy, Witchcraft, and Sexuality." *Journal of Homosexuality* 1 (1974): 183–201.

———. *Sexual Variance in Society and History*. New York: John Wiley & Sons, 1976.

Bundy, Murray Wright. *The Theory of the Imagination in Classical and Medieval Thought*. Urbana: University of Illinois Press, 1927.

Burger, Glenn. "Kissing the Pardoner." *PMLA* 107 (1992): 1143–56.

——. "Queer Chaucer." *English Studies in Canada* 20.2 (1994): 153–70.

Burger, Glenn and Steven F. Kruger. "Introduction." In Burger and Kruger. xi–xxiii.

Burger, Glenn and Steven F. Kruger, eds. *Queering the Middle Ages*. Minneapolis: University of Minnesota Press, 2001.

Butler, Judith. *Bodies that Matter: On the Discursive Limits of "Sex."* New York: Routledge, 1993.

Butler, Marilyn. "Against Tradition: The Case for a Particularized Method." In *Historical Studies and Literary Criticism*. Ed. Jerome J. McCann. Madison: University of Wisconsin Press, 1985. 25–47.

Calin, William. *The French Tradition and the Literature of Medieval England*. Toronto: University of Toronto Press, 1994.

Camargo, Martin. "The Consolation of Pandarus." *Chaucer Review* 25 (1991): 214–28.

Cannon, Christopher. "Chaucer and Rape: Uncertainty's Certainties." In *Representing Rape in Medieval and Early Modern Literature*. Ed. Elizabeth Robertson and Christine M. Rose. New York: Palgrave, 2001. 255–79.

——. "*Raptus* in the Chaumpaigne Release and a Newly Discovered Document Concerning the Life of Geoffrey Chaucer." *Speculum* 68 (1993): 74–94.

Carruthers, Mary. *The Book of Memory: A Study of Memory in Medieval Culture*. Cambridge: Cambridge University Press, 1990.

Chaplais, Pierre. *Piers Gaveston: Edward II's Adoptive Brother*. Oxford: Clarendon, 1994.

Clark, John. "Trinovantum—The Evolution of a Legend." *Journal of Medieval History* 7 (1981): 135–51.

Clein, Wendy. *Concepts of Chivalry in Sir Gawain and the Green Knight*. Norman, OK: Pilgrim Books, 1987.

Cohan, Steven. "Masquerading As the American Male in the Fifties: *Picnic*, William Holden and the Spectacle of Masculinity in Hollywood Film." In *Male Trouble*. Ed. Constance Penley and Sharon Willis. Minneapolis: University of Minnesota Press, 1993. 203–22.

Cohan, Steven and Ina Rae Hark, eds. *Screening the Male: Exploring Masculinities in Hollywood Cinema*. New York: Routledge, 1993.

Cohen, Jeffrey Jerome. "Masoch/Lancelotism." *New Literary History* 28 (1997): 231–60.

Collette, Carolyn P. *Species, Phantasms, and Images: Vision and Medieval Psychology in the Canterbury Tales*. Ann Arbor: University of Michigan Press, 2001.

Cook, Robert G. "Chaucer's Pandarus and the Medieval Ideal of Friendship." *Journal of English and Germanic Philology* 69 (1970): 407–24.

Corum, Richard. "Henry's Desires." In Fradenburg and Freccero. 71–97.

Cowie, Elizabeth. *Representing the Woman: Cinema and Psychoanalysis*. Minneapolis: University of Minnesota Press, 1997.

Culbertson, Philip L. "Men and Christian Friendship." In *Men's Bodies, Men's Gods: Male Identities in a (Post-)Christian Culture*. Ed. Björn Krondorfer. New York: New York University Press, 1996. 149–80.

——. *New Adam: The Future of Male Spirituality*. Minneapolis: Fortress Press, 1992.

Davis, Norman, Douglas Gray, Patricia Ingham, and Anne Wallace-Hadrill, comps. *A Chaucer Glossary*. Oxford: Clarendon, 1979.

De Lauretis, Teresa. *Alice Doesn't: Feminism, Semiotics, Cinema*. Bloomington: Indiana University Press, 1984.

——. *The Practice of Love: Lesbian Sexuality and Perverse Desire*. Bloomington: Indiana University Press, 1994.

——. "Queer Theory: Lesbian and Gay Sexualities—an Introduction." *Differences* 3.2 (Summer 1991): iii–xviii.

Diamond, Arlyn. "*Troilus and Criseyde*: The Politics of Love." In *Chaucer in the Eighties*. Ed. Julian N. Wasserman and Robert J. Blanch. Syracuse: Syracuse University Press, 1986. 93–103.

Dictionnaire Historique de la Langue Française. Ed. Alain Rey. 2 vols. Paris: Le Robert, 1992.

Dinshaw, Carolyn. "Chaucer's Queer Touches/A Queer Touches Chaucer." *Exemplaria* 7.1 (1995): 75–92.

——. "A Kiss Is Just a Kiss: Heterosexuality and Its Consolations in *Sir Gawain and the Green Knight*." *Diacritics* 24 (1994): 205–26.

——. "Getting Medieval: *Pulp Fiction*, Gawain, Foucault." In *The Book and the Body*. Ed. Dolores Warwick Frese and Katherine O'Brien O'Keefe. Notre Dame: University of Notre Dame Press, 1997. 116–63.

——. *Getting Medieval: Sexualities and Communities, Pre- and Postmodern*. Durham: Duke University Press, 1999.

Dinzelbacher, Peter. "Über die Entdeckung der Liebe im Hochmittelalter." *Saeculum* 32 (1981): 185–208.

Dod, Bernard G. "Aristotles latinus." In *The Cambridge History of Later Medieval Philosophy from the Rediscovery of Aristotle to the Disintegration of Scholasticism 1100–1600*. Ed. Norman Kretzmann, Anthony Kenny, and Jan Pinborg. Cambridge: Cambridge University Press, 1982. 45–79.

Dollimore, Jonathan. *Sexual Dissidence: Augustine to Wilde, Freud to Foucault*. Oxford: Clarendon, 1991.

Duberman, Martin Bauml, Martha Vicinus, and George Chauncey Jr., eds. *Hidden from History: Reclaiming the Gay and Lesbian Past*. New York: New American Library, 1989.

Duls, Louisa D. *Richard II in the Early Chronicles*. The Hague: Mouton, 1975.

Fisher, Sheila. "Taken Men and Token Women in *Sir Gawain and the Green Knight*." In *Seeking the Woman in Late Medieval and Renaissance Writings: Essays in Feminist Contextual Criticism*. Ed. Sheila Fisher and Janet E. Halley. Knoxville: University of Tennessee Press, 1989. 71–105.

Fiske, Adele M. *Friends and Friendship in the Monastic Tradition*. Cuernavaca, Mexico: CIDOC, 1970.

——. "Paradisus Homo Amicus." *Speculum* 40 (1965): 436–59.

Foucault, Michel. *The History of Sexuality, Vol. 1: An Introduction*. Trans. Robert Hurley, 1978. Repr. New York: Vintage, 1990.

Fradenburg, Louise and Carla Freccero. "Introduction: Caxton, Foucault, and the Pleasures of History." In Fradenburg and Freccero. xiii–xxiv.

Fradenburg, Louise and Carla Freccero, eds. *Premodern Sexualities*. New York: Routledge, 1996.

Frantzen, Allen J. *Before the Closet: Same-Sex Love from Beowulf to Angels in America*. Chicago: University of Chicago Press, 1998.

Freiwald, Leah Rieber. "Swych Love of Frendes: Pandarus and Troilus." *Chaucer Review* 6.2 (1971): 120–29.

Freud, Sigmund. "Certain Neurotic Mechanisms in Jealousy, Paranoia, and Homosexuality." In *Sexuality and the Psychology of Love*. Ed. Philip Rieff. New York: Macmillan, 1963. 150–60.

——. "'A Child Is Being Beaten': A Contribution to the Study of the Origin of Sexual Perversion." In *The Standard Edition*. Vol. 17. 175–204.

——. "The Economic Problem in Masochism." In *General Psychological Theory*. Ed. Philip Rieff. New York: Macmillan, 1963. 190–201.

——. "Instincts and Their Vicissitudes." In *General Psychological Theory*. Ed. Philip Rieff. New York: Macmillan, 1963. 83–103.

——. *The Standard Edition of the Complete Psychological Works of Sigmund Freud*. Ed. and trans. James Strachey. 24 vols. London: Hogarth, 1953–74.

——. *Three Essays on the Theory of Sexuality*. Ed. and trans. James Strachey. New York: Basic Books, 1962.

Fuss, Diana. "Fashion and the Homospectatorial Look." *Critical Inquiry* 18 (Summer 1992): 713–37.

——. "Inside/Out." In *Inside/Out: Lesbian Theories, Gay Theories*. Ed. Diana Fuss. New York: Routledge, 1991. 1–10.

Ganim, John M. "Chaucer and the Noise of the People." *Exemplaria* 2 (1990): 71–88.

Gaylord, Alan T. "Friendship in Chaucer's *Troilus*." *Chaucer Review* 3 (1968–69): 239–64.

Gilbert, Arthur N. "Conceptions of Homosexuality and Sodomy in Western History." *Journal of Homosexuality* 6 (1980–81): 57–68.

Gilmour-Bryson, Anne. "Sodomy and the Knights Templar." *Journal of the History of Sexuality* 7 (1996): 151–83.

Girard, René. *Deceit, Desire, and the Novel: Self and Other in Literary Structure*. Trans. Yvonne Freccero. Baltimore: Johns Hopkins University Press, 1965.

Given, James B. *Inquisition and Medieval Society: Power, Discipline, and Resistance in Languedoc*. Ithaca: Cornell University Press, 1997.

Goldberg, Jonathan. *Sodometries: Renaissance Texts, Modern Sexualities*. Stanford: Stanford University Press, 1992.

González-Casanovas, Roberto J. "Male Bonding as Cultural Construction in Alfonso X, Ramon Llull, and Juan Manuel: Homosocial Friendship in Medieval Iberia." In Blackmore and Hutcheson. 157–92.

Goodman, Anthony. *The Loyal Conspiracy: The Lords Appellant under Richard II*. Coral Gables: University of Miami Press, 1971.

Gransden, Antonia. *Historical Writing in England II: c. 1307 to the Early Seventeenth Century*. Ithaca: Cornell University Press, 1982.

Gravdal, Kathryn. "The Poetics of Rape Law in Medieval France." In *Rape and Representation*. Ed. Lynn A. Higgins and Brenda R. Silver. New York: Columbia University Press, 1991. 207–26.

——. *Ravishing Maidens: Writing Rape in Medieval French Literature*. Philadelphia: University of Pennsylvania Press, 1991.

Hall, Donald E. "Introduction: Queer Works." *College Literature* 24.1 (1997): 1–10.

Halperin, David M. "Forgetting Foucault: Acts, Identities, and the History of Sexuality." *Representations* 63 (Summer 1998): 93–120.

Hamilton, J. S. *Piers Gaveston, Earl of Cornwall 1307–1312: Politics and Patronage in the Reign of Edward II*. Detroit: Wayne State University Press, 1988.

Hanrahan, Michael. "Seduction and Betrayal: Treason in the *Prologue* to the *Legend of Good Women*." *Chaucer Review* 30 (1996): 229–40.

Hansen, Elaine Tuttle. *Chaucer and the Fictions of Gender*. Berkeley: University of California Press, 1992.

Harvey, E. Ruth. *The Inward Wits: Psychological Theory in the Middle Ages and the Renaissance*. London: Warburg Institute, 1975.

Heng, Geraldine. "A Woman Wants: The Lady, *Gawain*, and the Forms of Seduction." *Yale Journal of Criticism* 5 (1992): 101–33.

Herring, Terrell Scott. "Frank O'Hara's Open Closet." *PMLA* 117 (2002): 414–27.

Hill, Ordelle G. and Gardiner Stillwell. "A Conduct Book for Richard II." *Philological Quarterly* 73 (1994): 317–28.

Holsinger, Bruce W. "Sodomy and Resurrection: The Homoerotic Subject of the *Divine Comedy*." In Fradenburg and Freccero. 243–74.

Homosexuality, Intolerance, and Christianity: A Critical Examination of John Boswell's Work. New York: Gay Academic Union, 1981.

Howard, Donald R. *Chaucer: His Life, His Works, His World*. New York: Dutton, 1987.

How Do I Look: Queer Film and Video. Ed. Bad Object Choices. Seattle: Bay Press, 1991.

Hutcheson, Gregory S. "Desperately Seeking Sodom: Queerness in the Chronicles of Alvaro de Luna." In Blackmore and Hutcheson. 222–49.

Hyatte, Reginald. *The Arts of Friendship: The Idealization of Friendship in Medieval and Early Renaissance Literature*. Leiden: Brill, 1994.

Ingham, Patricia Clare. "Masculine Military Unions: Brotherhood and Rivalry in *The Avowing of King Arthur*." *Arthuriana* 6.4 (1996): 25–44.

Jackson, Earl Jr. *Strategies of Deviance: Studies in Gay Male Representation*. Bloomington: Indiana University Press, 1995.

Jagose, Annamarie. *Queer Theory: An Introduction*. New York: New York University Press, 1996.

Joachim, H. H. *Aristotle: The Nicomachean Ethics*. Oxford: Clarendon, 1951.

Johnstone, Hilda. *Edward of Carnarvon 1284–1307*. Manchester: Manchester University Press, 1946.

Jones, Richard H. *The Royal Policy of Richard II: Absolutism in the Later Middle Ages*. Oxford: Basil Blackwell, 1968.

Jordan, Mark D. *The Invention of Sodomy in Christian Theology*. Chicago: University of Chicago Press, 1997.

Kaeuper, Richard W. *Chivalry and Violence in Medieval Europe*. Oxford: Oxford University Press, 2001.

——. "Geoffroi de Charny and His Book." In Kaeuper and Kennedy. 1–64.

——. *War, Justice, and Public Order: England and France in the Later Middle Ages*. Oxford: Clarendon, 1988.

Keen, Maurice. "Brotherhood-in-Arms." 1964. Repr. in Keen, *Nobles, Knights and Men-at-Arms in the Middle Ages*. 43–62.

———. "Chaucer's Knight, the English Aristocracy and the Crusade." 1983. Repr. in Keen, *Nobles, Knights and Men-at-Arms in the Middle Ages*. 101–19.

———. *Chivalry*. New Haven: Yale University Press, 1984.

———. *Nobles, Knights and Men-at-Arms in the Middle Ages*. London: Hambledon Press, 1996.

———. "War, Peace and Chivalry." 1987. Repr. in Keen, *Nobles, Knights and Men-at-Arms in the Middle Ages*. 1–20.

Kelly, Kathleen Coyne. "Malory's Body Chivalric." *Arthuriana* 6.4 (1996): 52–71.

Klassen, N. "Optical Allusions and Chaucerian Realism: Aspects of Sight in Late Medieval Thought and *Troilus and Criseyde*." *Stanford Humanities Review* 2.2–3 (1992): 129–46.

Kruger, Steven F. "Claiming the Pardoner: Toward a Gay Reading of Chaucer's *Pardoner's Tale*." *Exemplaria* 6.1 (1994): 115–39.

———. *Dreaming in the Middle Ages*. New York: Cambridge University Press, 1992.

———. "Medieval Christian (Dis)identifications: Muslims and Jews in Guibert of Nogent." *New Literary History* 28 (1997): 185–203.

Laplanche, Jean. *Life and Death in Psychoanalysis*. Trans. Jeffrey Mehlman. 1976 Repr. Baltimore: Johns Hopkins University Press, 1985.

Laplanche, Jean and J.-B. Pontalis. "Fantasy and the Origins of Sexuality." 1968. Repr. in *Formations of Fantasy*. Ed. Victor Burgin, James Donald, and Cora Kaplan. London: Methuen, 1986. 5–34.

———. *The Language of Psycho-Analysis*. Trans. Donald Nicolson-Smith. New York: Norton, 1973.

Latham, R. E. *Dictionary of Medieval Latin from British Sources*. London: Oxford University Press, 1975.

———. *Revised Medieval Latin Word-List from British and Irish Sources*. London: Oxford University Press, 1965.

Lea, Henry Charles. *A History of the Inquisition of the Middle Ages*. 3 vols. New York: Harper, 1887.

Lehman, Peter, ed. *Masculinity: Bodies, Movies, Culture*. New York: Routledge, 2001.

Lévi-Strauss, Claude. *The Elementary Structures of Kinship*. Boston: Beacon Press, 1969.

Lindberg, David C. *Theories of Vision from Al-Kindi to Kepler*. Chicago: University of Chicago Press, 1976.

Lochrie, Karma. *Covert Operations: The Medieval Uses of Secrecy*. Philadelphia: University of Pennsylvania Press, 1999.

———. *Margery Kempe and Translations of the Flesh*. Philadelphia: University of Pennsylvania Press, 1991.

———. "Mystical Acts, Queer Tendencies." In Lochrie, McCracken, and Schultz. 180–200.

Lochrie, Karma, Peggy McCracken, and James A. Schultz. "Introduction." In Lochrie, McCracken, and Schultz. ix–xviii.

Lochrie, Karma, Peggy McCracken, and James A. Schultz, eds. *Constructing Medieval Sexuality*. Minneapolis: University of Minnesota Press, 1997.

Mathew, Gervase. *The Court of Richard II*. London: John Murray, 1968.

Matz, Robert. "Slander, Renaissance Discourses of Sodomy, and *Othello*." *English Literary History* 66 (1999): 261–76.

McGuire, Brian Patrick. *Brother and Lover: Aelred of Rievaulx*. New York: Crossroad Press, 1994.

———. *Friendship and Community: The Monastic Experience 350–1250*. Kalamazoo: Cistercian Publications, 1988.

McInerney, Maud Burnett. " 'Is this a mannes herte?': Unmanning Troilus through Ovidian Allusion." In Beidler. 221–35.

McKisack, May. *The Fourteenth Century 1307–1399*. Oxford: Clarendon, 1959.

Metz, Christian. *The Imaginary Signifier: Psychoanalysis and the Cinema*. Trans. Celia Britton, Annwyl Williams, Ben Brewster, and Alfred Guzzetti. Bloomington: Indiana University Press, 1977.

Mieszkowski, Gretchen. "The Prose *Lancelot*'s Galehot, Malory's Lavain, and the Queering of Late Medieval Literature." *Arthuriana* 5.1 (1995): 21–51.

Miles, Margaret. "Vision: The Eye of the Body and the Eye of the Mind in Saint Augustine's *De trinitate* and *Confessions*." *Journal of Religion* 63 (1983): 125–42.

Montrose, Louis A. "Professing the Renaissance: The Poetics and Politics of Culture." In Veeser. 15–36.

Moore, Miriam. "Troilus's Mirror: Vision and Desire in *Troilus and Criseyde*." *Medieval Perspectives* 14.1 (1999): 152–65.

Mulvey, Laura. "Visual Pleasure and Narrative Cinema." 1975. Repr. in *The Sexual Subject*. 22–34.

Neale, Steve. "Masculinity as Spectacle." In *The Sexual Subject*. 277–87.

Niermeyer, J. F. *Mediae Latinitatis lexicon minus*. Leiden: Brill, 1976.

The Oxford Latin Dictionary. Ed. P. G. W. Glare. Oxford: Clarendon, 1982.

Owen, D. D. R. "Introduction." *Chrétien de Troyes, Arthurian Romances*. London: Dent & Sons, 1987. ix–xviii.

Padgug, Robert. "Sexual Matters: Rethinking Sexuality in History." In Duberman, Vicinus, and Chauncey. 54–64.

Parker, Thomas M. *The Knights Templars in England*. Tucson: University of Arizona Press, 1963.

Patterson, Lee. *Chaucer and the Subject of History*. Madison: University of Wisconsin Press, 1991.

———. *Negotiating the Past: The Historical Understanding of Medieval Literature*. Madison: University of Wisconsin Press, 1987.

Pearsall, Derek. *The Life of Geoffrey Chaucer: A Critical Biography*. Oxford: Blackwell, 1992.

Perkins, Clarence. "The Trial of the Knights Templars in England." *English Historical Review* 24 (1909): 432–47.

Perry, R. *Edward the Second: Suddenly at Berkeley*. Wotton-under-Edge, Gloucestershire: Ivy House, 1988.

Price, A. W. *Love and Friendship in Plato and Aristotle*. Oxford: Clarendon, 1989.

Robertson, D. W. Jr. "The Probable Date and Purpose of Chaucer's *Troilus*." *Medievalia et Humanistica* 13 (1985): 143–71.

Roby, Douglass. "Introduction." In *Aelred of Rievaulx: Spiritual Friendship*. Trans. Laker. 3–40.

Rodowick, D. N. "The Difficulty of Difference." *Wide Angle* 5 (1982): 4–15.

Rodowick, D. N. *The Difficulty of Difference: Psychoanalysis, Sexual Difference, and Film Theory*. New York: Routledge, 1991.

Roskell, J. S. *The Impeachment of Michael de la Pole, Earl of Suffolk, in 1386 in the Context of the Reign of Richard II*. Manchester: Manchester University Press, 1984.

Rubin, Gayle. "The Traffic in Women: Notes on the 'Political Economy' of Sex." In *Toward an Anthropology of Women*. Ed. Rayna R. Reiter. New York: Monthly Review, 1975. 157–210.

Saaler, Mary. *Edward II 1307–1327*. London: Rubicon, 1997.

Sanderlin, S. "Chaucer and Ricardian Politics." *Chaucer Review* 22 (1988): 171–84.

Saul, Nigel. *Richard II*. New Haven: Yale University Press, 1997.

Sedgwick, Eve Kosofsky. *Between Men: English Literature and Male Homosocial Desire*. New York: Columbia University Press, 1985.

The Sexual Subject: A Screen Reader in Sexuality. London: Routledge, 1992.

Shahar, Shulamith. *The Fourth Estate: A History of Women in the Middle Ages*. Trans. Chaya Galai. London: Methuen, 1983.

Shaviro, Steven. *The Cinematic Body*. Minneapolis: University of Minnesota Press, 1993.

Silverman, Kaja. *Male Subjectivity at the Margins*. New York: Routledge, 1992.

Simon, Edith. *The Piebald Standard: A Biography of the Knights Templars*. London: Cassell, 1959.

Smith, Alan K. "Fraudomy: Reading Sexuality and Politics in Burchiello." In *Queering the Renaissance*. Ed. Jonathan Goldberg. Durham: Duke University Press, 1994. 84–106.

Smith, Bruce R. *Homosexual Desire in Shakespeare's England: A Cultural Poetics*. 1991. Repr. Chicago: University of Chicago Press, 1994.

Sorabji, Richard. *Aristotle on Memory*. Providence: Brown University Press, 1972.

Spiegel, Gabrielle M. "History, Historicism, and the Social Logic of the Text in the Middle Ages." *Speculum* 65 (1990): 59–86.

Sponsler, Claire. "The King's Boyfriend: Queer Politics and Edward II." In Burger and Kruger. 143–67.

Stanbury, Sarah. "The Lover's Gaze in *Troilus and Criseyde*." In *Chaucer's Troilus and Criseyde, "Subgit to alle Poesy": Essays in Criticism*. Ed. R. A. Shoaf. Binghamton: Medieval and Renaissance Texts and Studies, 1992. 224–38.

———. "Regimes of the Visual in Premodern England: Gaze, Body, and Chaucer's *Clerk's Tale*." *New Literary History* 28 (1997): 261–89.

———. *Seeing the Gawain-Poet: Description and the Act of Perception*. Philadelphia: University of Pennsylvania Press, 1991.

Steel, Anthony. *Richard II*. Cambridge: Cambridge University Press, 1941.

Stock, Brian. *Augustine the Reader: Meditation, Self-Knowledge, and the Ethics of Interpretation*. Cambridge, MA: Harvard University Press, 1996.

Stow, George B. "Chronicle Versus Records: The Character of Richard II." In *Documenting the Past: Essays in Medieval History Presented to G. P. Cuttino*. Ed. J. S. Hamilton and P. Bradley. Woodbridge, Suffolk: Boydell, 1989. 155–76.

———. "Richard II in Thomas Walsingham's Chronicles." *Speculum* 59 (1984): 68–102.

Strayer, Joseph R. *The Reign of Philip the Fair*. Princeton: Princeton University Press, 1980.

Strohm, Paul. *Hochon's Arrow: The Social Imagination of Fourteenth-Century Texts.* Princeton: Princeton University Press, 1992.

——. *Social Chaucer.* Cambridge. MA: Harvard University Press, 1989.

Sturges, Robert S. *Chaucer's Pardoner and Gender Theory: Bodies of Discourse.* New York: St. Martin's Press, 2000.

Tachau, Katherine H. *Vision and Certitude in the Age of Ockham: Optics, Epistemology and the Foundations of Semantics 1250–1345.* Leiden: Brill, 1988.

Taylor, John. *English Historical Literature in the Fourteenth Century.* Oxford: Clarendon, 1987.

Tout, T. F. *The Place of the Reign of Edward II in English History.* Manchester: Manchester University Press, 1914.

Traub, Valerie. *Desire and Anxiety: Circulations of Sexuality in Shakespearean Drama.* London: Routledge, 1992.

Tuck, Anthony. *Crown and Nobility 1272–1461: Political Conflict in Late Medieval England.* Totowa, NJ: Barnes and Noble, 1985.

——. *Richard II and the English Nobility.* New York: St. Martin's Press, 1974.

Vale, Juliet. *Edward III and Chivalry: Chivalric Society and Its Context 1270–1350.* Woodbridge, Suffolk: Boydell, 1982.

Veeser, H. Aram, ed. *The New Historicism.* New York: Routledge, 1989.

Wack, Mary F. "Imagination, Medicine, and Rhetoric in Andreas Capellanus' 'De Amore'." In *Magister Regis: Studies in Honor of Robert Earl Kaske.* Ed. Arthur Groos, Emerson Brown Jr., Giuseppe Massotta, Thomas D. Hill, and Joseph S. Wittig. New York: Fordham University Press, 1986. 101–15.

——. *Lovesickness in the Middle Ages: The Viaticum and Its Commentaries.* Philadelphia: University of Pennsylvania Press, 1990.

——. "Pandarus, Poetry, and Healing." *Studies in the Age of Chaucer. Proceedings* 2 (1986): 127–33.

Walker, Greg. "The Green Knight's Challenge: Heroism and Courtliness in Fitt I of *Sir Gawain and the Green Knight*." *Chaucer Review* 32 (1997): 111–28.

Walker, Simon. *The Lancastrian Affinity, 1361–1399.* Oxford: Clarendon, 1990.

Weissberger, Barbara. " '¡A tierra, puto!: Alfonso de Palencia's Discourse of Effeminacy." In Blackmore and Hutcheson. 291–324.

White, Carolinne. *Christian Friendship in the Fourth Century.* Cambridge: Cambridge University Press, 1992.

Willemen, Paul. "Voyeurism, the Look, and Dworkin." In *Narrative, Apparatus, Ideology: A Film Theory Reader.* Ed. Philip Rosen. New York: Columbia University Press, 1986. 210–18.

Wood, Charles T. "Personality, Politics, and Constitutional Progress: The Lessons of Edward II." *Studia Gratiana* 15 (1972): 521–36.

Zeikowitz, Richard E. "Befriending the Medieval Queer: A Pedagogy for Literature Classes." *College English* 65.1 (2002): 67–80.

INDEX